RED REI

With all best wishes

John Gray

RED REPORTER
COVERT
CORRESPONDENT
FOR EAST GERMANY
JOHN GREEN

ARTERY PUBLICATIONS

First published in Germany by Dietz Verlag, under the title *Anonym Unterwegs* (1991),
English first edition by Artery Publications under the title *Taking the Pulse* (1994)

Artery Publications, 11 Dorset Road, London W5 4HU

Copyright © John Green 2008

Photographs property of the author

Book and cover designed by Michal Boñcza, www.artloud.com

Printed by Cambrian Printers Ltd, www.cambrian-printers.co.uk

ACIP catalogue record for this book is available from the British Library

ISBN 978-0-9558228-1-0

Cover photographs: *front:* filming during the Munich Olympics with the old, heavy but much loved Arriflex BL 16mm; *back top:* filming in Portugal during the Revolution of 1974; *back bottom:* an array of official press credentials.

Other books by the author:
- *Engels – A Revolutionary Life*
- *Ken Sprague – People's Artist*
- *Afon Ystwyth – the story of a river*
- *Wings over the Valley – a bird watcher's Wales diary*

Contents

	INTRODUCTION	7
1.	A BRITISH STUDENT BEHIND THE 'WALL'	12
2.	RETURN TO THE OTHER WORLD	30
3.	BEHIND ENEMY LINES	
	GREECE – VISIT TO THE COLONELS	41
	SPAIN – AUTUMN OF THE PATRIARCH	50
	IRELAND – WAR WITHOUT END	56
	WEST GERMANY – GATHERING OF THE VETERANS	65
4.	NEW APPROACHES TO FOREIGN REPORTING	
	THE SERIES ALLTAG IM WESTEN (EVERYDAY LIFE IN THE WEST)	69
	THE SHADOW SIDE	77
	BRITAIN ON THE PICKET LINES.	83
5.	VICTORIES OF THE LIBERATION MOVEMENTS	
	NAMIBIA/SOUTH AFRICA – THE LAST OUTPOSTS	87
	MOZAMBIQUE – FROM LIBERATION TO NEW SUFFERING	104
	PORTUGAL – THE CARNATION REVOLUTION	110
	GRENADA – REVOLUTION IN PARADISE	120
6.	THE OPEN VEINS OF LATIN AMERICA	
	EL SALVADOR – WITHOUT A SAVIOUR	125
	GUATEMALA – BLOOD AND VOLCANOES	138
	CHILE – GHOSTS AND FEARS	148

7. **THE USA – LAND OF POSSIBLE IMPOSSIBILITIES**
    FASCINATION AND IRRITATION 156
    WELCOME TO CALIFORNIA 167
    APPALACHIAN INTERLUDE 172
    BEN CHAVIS – MAN OF CHRIST AND REVOLUTION 179
    MISSILES IN THE PRAIRIES 184
    AN FBI MAN OPTS OUT 189

8. **BEHIND OUR OWN LINES**
    AFGHANISTAN – FALCONS AND MINARETS 193
    SOLIDARNOSC AND THE PROBLEM OF TRUTH 196

9. **A NEW NAME BUT OLD POLITICS** 202
10. **AND THE WALL CAME TUMBLING DOWN** 214
12. CHRONOLOGY OF IMPORTANT EVENTS 224

Introduction

This book came about as a direct result of the demise of the German Democratic Republic in 1989. Although I had kept a lot of material – interview texts, diary notes, treatments and photos collected as background to the films I and my colleagues made, I had no inkling that these would one day end up as raw material for a book of reminiscences.

With the fall of The Wall and the rapid collapse of 'real existing socialism' I felt that my experience, as a foreign correspondent, working closely with colleagues in GDR television, participating in an attempt to create a socialist approach to journalism and documentary film-making, would be of interest to a wider audience. I was also concerned that a significant personal, historical experience in the battle between the two competing systems, socialism and capitalism – would be lost if I maintained a silence.

In writing this book, I was primarily motivated by the knowledge that history is invariably written by the victorious generals or their scribes, and narratives that don't fit the new hegemony are invariably suppressed; much valuable experience gained by, what are often only, the foot soldiers is erased from the collective memory. I am more than ever convinced that witnessing at first hand both the attempt at building socialism in the GDR as well as the realities of capitalism throughout the rest of the world can provide a miniscule contribution to complementing the 'official' narratives of this period.

Many of the events and experiences described here may surprise and even disconcert some readers, looking back with today's perspective. We are experiencing now, in the new Millennium, a period of apathy, cynicism, of internecine struggles and bloody, seemingly senseless civil wars. When I was filming, almost all the struggles seemed to us to be clear battles between socialist aspirations and imperialist oppression, or put simplistically: between the good and the bad; they had an altruistic quality, they were about freedom, liberation, dignity, they were taking place everywhere and victories were being won. Many, if not all those victories have turned sour, but I believe they were not in vain. If struggle and sacrifice for a better world are in vain, then what hope is there for humanity?

I feel convinced that my experience, working for more than two decades, during one of the most revolutionary periods of the twentieth century, reporting on liberation struggles in the developing world, social problems in the capitalist countries as well as on some of the momentous labour struggles, will be of historical interest to those who sympathised or identified with those struggles, as well as to those who may still draw inspiration from them today.

The world has undergone a veritable counter-revolution in the few short years since I finished working for television. The hopes for a more humane and democratised socialist system associated with Gorbachov's accession were soon dispelled. In the years I covered the liberation struggles in Latin America, I and my colleagues entertained hopes that it was there that a new socialist impetus would emerge. Those hopes were rapidly crushed by the brutal repression instigated by the para-military regimes put in place and supported by the United States. The liberation forces were suppressed at enormous cost in terms of the numbers of dead and tortured, as well as increased poverty and the sense of hopelessness. Little did we then realise that those sparks would reignite hope in Venezuela and other Latin American countries during the first years of the new Millennium.

Media coverage of the former socialist countries since their collapse has only served to confirm my worst fears about the distortion of history. There has been no attempt to constructively evaluate the attempts to build socialism or to differentiate between the different countries and their governments, no admission that there might have been positive aspects or ideas of value, no attempt to investigate what went wrong – merely a demonising of the very concept of socialism by suppressing all and every positive memory.

The GDR itself has been stigmatised as 'Stasi Land' and compared directly with the nazi era, as if it were a comparable totalitarian dictatorship and its people oppressed by a cynical and brutal security service. Films like *The Lives of Others* (made by the West German scion of aristocracy, Florian von Donnersmarck) only serve to perpetuate this travesty. The fact that a large proportion of East Germans still, 20 years after the GDR ceased to exist, vote for socialist parties and still look back on life in the GDR as a differentiated one with many positive aspects, alongside the negative ones, is a reality the present political rulers don't wish to acknowledge.

As we can see from recent developments in the former socialist countries, capitalism has triumphed with a vengeance – and not in the way many imagined it would. In East Germany the 'Change', as everyone calls it, has been materially cushioned; shops have a full range of consumer goods, but what hit one most was the ludicrous proliferation of car showrooms – even the smallest village had several, and cars now clog the formerly quiet roads. Banks occupy former public buildings while numerous book shops have closed – those that still remain, sell the usual, bland international fare of the big publishers plus porno magazines. The Federal Republic has pumped millions into the country – made necessary, largely, by the shut-down of virtually the whole of GDR industry, its academic and research institutions and co-operative agricultural enterprises – eastern Germany now has the dubious record for the highest unemployment level for academics and intellectuals in the world.

There are few people in East Germany who would welcome a return to the old regime, but there is a widespread awareness that there were social institutions, values and attitudes in the past which were worth preserving, but which have been abolished. People miss the sense of community, the stability afforded by job security and the right to a home, cheap childcare available to all, a rich, subsidised culture as well as an assured future. Most people are overjoyed by the freedom to travel to the West, and glad to be released from the oppressive omniscience of the ruling SED, but are perturbed by the concomitant downside of a new, aggressive individualism, mushrooming crime and job losses.

Almost the whole academic and intellectual workforce in East Germany made unemployed; there was a vendetta against anyone who was 'close to the state', as it is termed – progressive teachers, doctors, lecturers etc have been blacklisted. With the socialist block gone, big business had a free run. It no longer had to look over its shoulder at what the socialist countries were doing. In Germany too, we have seen a whittling away of conditions and standards won over decades of struggle by the labour movement and grassroots organisations.

The demise of 'real existing socialism' had repercussions far beyond its former borders. Despite the real shortcomings of GDR socialism, the working conditions, social welfare structures enjoyed by workers in the socialist countries were a vital bargaining factor (even if only implicitly) when workers in the West, and to some extent in the developing world, negotiated their own pay and conditions. And simply the idea of a 'workers' state', of a real existing socialist alternative, whatever its failings, was a continuous thorn in the side of capitalism and a strong restraining factor on its rapaciousness; it was also a beacon of hope for the poor and oppressed everywhere.

Once the GDR joined the Federal Republic, virtually all its industry and public assets were privatised at knock-down prices and with unparalleled haste with the result that now East Germans own only 6% of their own country, the remaining 87% being owned by West Germans and 7% foreign-owned. The population plummeted catastrophically with over 3 million (out of a pre-unification population of around 16 million) leaving the country to find jobs; immediately following unification the birth-rate fell to an unprecedented 0.77 children per woman, before rising later to the West German level of 1.4 per woman, the lowest in Europe. In the territory of the former GDR, 43% of the population is now made up of pensioners; many villages are virtually devoid of anyone under 60. And the situation is not improving, with 10%, as a percentage of births, still leaving the territory of the former GDR each year.

These are just a few of the devastating statistics that expose the blemished side of the shiny unification coin.

In my work as a documentary film maker I was able to see at first hand how capitalism and imperialism, in terms of the big transnationals, IMF and World Bank tore nations and communities apart. It was this which consolidated my opposition to the injustice and inhumanity of aggressive capitalism and fuelled my conviction that a socialist form of society, albeit of a truly democratic nature, is human kind's only solution if we and our planet are to survive.

My film making was dedicated to that end. This book is a selection of those reminiscences which I feel are of particular relevance and interest to those who wish to know more about those decades of struggle before the socialist world collapsed.

My film work and indeed these reminiscences would have been impossible without the many comrades, socialists and progressive Christians in many countries who helped and assisted us, often at great risk. I would like to think that, for them too, our films were useful.

CHAPTER 1
A British student behind the Wall

Everyone alights from the train at Bahnhof Zoo in West Berlin. I am the only passenger staying on to Friedrichstrasse, the frontier station for entering East Berlin. It is early evening and the bomb-damaged, shrapnel-scarred blocks of flats stand dark and gaunt like war-weary sentries alongside the railway tracks. The train chugs at a snail's pace the last few hundred metres. The recently erected wall dividing the city runs alongside the track, obscuring the view. It is January and bitterly cold. Friedrichstrasse station is virtually deserted. I open the carriage door, clamber out through the clouds of steam into its drab greyness. At one end two guards, well-wrapped in khaki padded coats and grey fur hats stand with their Kalashnikovs, observing the train just arrived. Friedrichstrasse itself is enough to deter anyone entering the GDR, it confirms all one's worst dreams: the yellowy-green tiled walls, faded hoardings and peeling paint, illuminated by a few anaemic neon tubes, and the only people about are armed guards.

It is 1964 and the Cold War is still tangible. For me, though, this icy welcome is not off-putting, but the beginning of an adventure, the entrance hall to another world. I fasten the horn toggles on my duffle coat, pick up my small bag and walk towards the exit marked 'Berlin-Hauptstadt der DDR'. I feel like a pioneer entering unexplored territory; I have a certain apprehension but at the same time feel exhilarated that I am now going to live in the Communist world. Most people are too frightened even to travel through the country. It is widely accepted that you will be kidnapped by the KGB, brain-washed or sent to the Siberian salt- mines. Many think it is a Russian colony where only Russian is spoken. For me to want to go and live there is, in their eyes, an act of madness. The British Passport Office even issued printed leaflets warning its citizens that if they went to the 'Soviet Zone' they were doing so at their own risk and could expect no protection from Her Majesty's government.

East Germany was still widely referred to as 'The Zone' and was viewed universally as the incarnation of all the evils of Communism: a people walled in by concrete and barbed wire, nazi- style border guards who shot those trying to escape, an oppressive regime that dealt brutally with anyone opposed to it, a place no one in their right mind would visit. For me, brought up in a communist household, it represented the aspirations of a people freed from nazism attempting to build a new society in face of hatred and animosity. Even so I can't shake off the feeling that I am somehow some sort of spy defecting to the other side. At immigration more soldiers, in black boots and with pistols strapped to their belts, take my passport, give me forms to fill out in quadruplicate, stamp my passport and wave me through to the other side. As I emerge through the metal door, a short, haggard-looking man with white hair and a black beret comes up to me and asks me if I am John Green. He is Rudi, my 'Betreuer', the person responsible for looking after me during my stay.

After finishing a zoology degree at Bristol University, I had decided that I wasn't cut out for a life dissecting animal corpses, acrid with the stench of formaldehyde or meticulously calculating the growth rates of microscopic bacterial cultures. I was interested in people and in social processes; I wanted to be out on the streets, not incarcerated in some cramped laboratory doing obscure research for the weapons industry or multi-national pesticide company.

In my teens, growing up in Coventry – a cultural desert at the Time – I had been fascinated by the many foreign films I was taken to see by my mother. There was a tiny, grubby little cinema aptly named The Continental which specialised in showing these films. It was there that I fell in love with the cinema. Such classics as de Sica's *Bicycle Thieves* or *Miracle of Milan*, Visconti's *Rocco and his Brothers*, Kalatasov's *The Cranes are Flying*, moved me to tears, transported me to worlds I'd never even dreamt of, providing me with a tiny window in the thick wall of Coventry provincialism. Then there were the films of Vigo, Renoir, Kurosawa, Rossellini and the many others, who ignited in me a life-long fascination for film. There was no national film school in Britain at the time and my application to the French film school in Paris, the only other western one I knew of, remained without a reply. The idea of studying in a socialist country was attractive, because I was interested in combining the creative potential of film with a social commitment. Being pragmatically inclined I decided not to apply to Moscow or Lodz, the Polish school because, although they had excellent reputations, I would have to learn Russian or Polish before I could begin picking up the craft of film making. I had already been a student for longer than I cared for, and was keen to begin actually doing something other than just studying. In East Germany or the GDR, as we knew it, there was a flourishing documentary film studio where I thought I could perhaps work as a trainee and pick up the language as I went along. I did have some contacts there and so tried to find out whether such an arrangement would be possible.

At the height of the Cold War, when East Germany was trying to establish its claim to be the only truly de-nazified part of Germany it made a number of films about former nazis then prominent in the West German military hierarchy. One of these was about General Speidel, then a prominent officer in NATO. The film was distributed by Stanley Forman of ETV Films. He was also someone with strong links to the GDR, and gave me valuable advice about the situation in the film industry there.

Of course such films never had a proper commercial distribution, no cinema would touch them, but small groups of Communists and peace people organised showings in various halls up and down the country, and small companies like ETV helped promote them at no small risk to themselves (General Speidel actually took out a libel action against Stanley Forman's company. When the Speidel film was shown an official from the GDR Ministry of Culture, Frau Irene Gysi was present (she was the mother of Gregor Gysi, the former charismatic chairman of the PDS, the successor party of the East German SED). My mother looked after her during her stay in Coventry, and it was Frau Gysi I wrote to after graduating from Bristol, asking if there was a possibility of my working in a film studio in the GDR. To my surprise she wrote back within a very short time, saying that the DEFA Documentary Film Studio in Berlin was willing to offer me a place as 'Praktikant' or trainee, under a scheme of solidarity with fraternal parties. Of course I had to have the recommendation and sanction of the British Communist Party.

Because I had been active in building up a party branch at my university and been involved in party work in the city, I had no problem on that score.

For the first weeks of my stay in the GDR I lived with a family who knew my mother from England. The man had been a German Jewish exile and married a former student friend of my mother's. This was until the DEFA could find me a room to rent; accommodation was at a premium in East Berlin, which was still in the same war-ravaged state it had been at the end of the war.

I travel into the centre of Berlin every morning with the S-Bahn or city railway. In winter East Berlin lives up to its cliché image: as the train rattles through the suburbs the views through the frost-obscured panes give the impression of an enormous cemetery. Black skeletal trees stand bleak against the leaden skies, the small allotment houses are all shuttered-up and empty, the remaining blocks of pre-war flats stand like enormous tombstones between the empty spaces created by the bombing and artillery, dirty-grey snow, hardened to ice lies in a permanent sheet over the ground and the only lights are the sparsely scattered and dim electric street lamps.

To reach the studios in the Otto Nuschke Strasse I have to walk from the S-Bahn station past some of Berlin's most prestigious buildings, now eerie ruins. The streets resemble the mouths of old crones, dark and cavernous, the cobblestones wet like tongues and the few grey blocks of undamaged houses the remaining molars clinging to the gums of the pavements. The wispy trees and weeds sprout from the cracks, like whiskers in the wrinkles around the mouth. The rib-cage of the neo-classical national theatre and the decapitated French Cathedral (now, since 1990, fully restored to their original splendour) stand opposite each other, separated by weed-covered waste ground, close to the studios. In winter it is grey and oppressive everywhere. The greenery has vanished and the grass takes on the uniform dirty brown-grey colour of everything else. Only the snow, when it is first fresh, softens the harshness of the cityscape. Colour just doesn't exist in the GDR at this time. There are virtually no neon lights, and no advertising. Even the people look grey: clothing is of poor quality and uniform-like, many are still wearing items from the pre-war period.

Despite all this, though, I feel it is a new country, a new society desperately trying to emerge from the ruins of war. The tinselly prostitution of West Berlin only confirms this idea. The West had

Marshall Aid dollars, and the big companies like Krupp, BASF and Siemens which had flourished under Hitler simply continued where they'd left off at the end of the war. The GDR had been obliged to pay enormous reparations to the Soviet Union itself devastated by the war, and had now to pull itself up by its own frayed boot straps.

I am together with a small group of Latin American comrades who have been delegated by their respective parties to learn the techniques of film making. In our group are two Guatemalans, only in their twenties but already veterans of the guerrilla struggle, a Venezuelan and a Costa Rican. These two Guatemalans, one of them the poet Otto René Castillo, were later killed in the mountains of Guatemala after returning home and rejoining the guerrilla struggle. (A short documentary of his life was made in 1979 by the GDR director Karlheinz Mund: *Erinnerungen an Otto René Castillo*). I soon pal up with the Costa Rican and with our pidgin German we manage an adequate communication.

To begin with it is a bit of a weird situation: we would turn up to the studio in the morning, go up to Rudi's office, sit around and chat for a while, have lunch and then go off on our own into town. Rudi, like all Germans, is in his office punctually by 7.00 a.m., so that by the time we arrive he has already been behind his desk for two hours – but he never seems to do anything. I rarely see him do more than sit and stare vacantly out of the window or at the wall. When we chat and try to involve him he offers the odd comment or smiles slightly but can rarely be drawn properly into the conversation or become animated. He is almost like a ghost, a body without a being inside it. His face has an expression of long suffering, of some traumatic experience which is incommunicable. My German at that time is still very primitive so that I can't really converse or understand complex ideas and it is probable that this, too, intimidates him from really trying to talk much with us. It is only a long time afterwards that I hear he had been in a concentration camp under the nazis and the experience has left him physically and mentally wrecked. He had probably been given the job of looking after the foreign trainees in order to give him some sense of use or purpose. At that time there were many people like Rudi, not able to do really responsible jobs, but given employment as caretakers or minor clerks so that they felt socially useful.

The 'Doc Studio', as we call it, occupies an old building in the Otto Nuschke Strasse, only a rifle shot away from Friedrichstrasse and Checkpoint Charlie and also within a stone's throw of the headquarters of the SED. Most of the buildings in the streets and squares around about are still in ruins or are pock-marked with shrapnel and shallow craters from machine-gun bullets. In winter the French cathedral and the old museum buildings on the river Spree look obstinately beautiful with a delicate filigree adornment of snow over their classical sculptures and architraves. Birch saplings sprout from fissures in the ruined walls of the French Cathedral and National Concert House on the Gendarmenmarkt. There isn't much life in the city – a few cafes, the odd corner pub, a couple of cinemas and, of course, the theatres which were the first cultural establishments to re-open after the war. Something the Soviet people could never comprehend was how a nation of such culture, one that had given us Beethoven, Schumann, Heine and Schiller, not to mention Marx and Engels, could behave like a maddened beast. One of the first things they did when they took over the defeated country was to encourage the re-opening of theatres and cinemas; culture was a high priority. One of the directors I worked with in the Doc Studios, Hans Müller, was one of those promoted by the Russians after the war, put in charge of a theatre and given the go-ahead to start producing plays.

In those first weeks with little actual filming work to do, I concentrate on improving the rudimentary German I have. I watch TV avidly, note down every new word I hear, look it up in the dictionary when I get home in the evening and memorise my list at the end of each day. In this way I soon have a commendable vocabulary, can speak quite fluently but have an atrocious command of grammar. With Manuel, my Costa Rican friend, I also improve my understanding of the language by regular visits to the theatre (we get 90% of the seat price refunded by the Doc-Studio). For me, coming from a provincial city like Coventry, which was still a cultural backwater when I left it, Berlin with its many theatres and its opera houses, offering seats at prices everyone can afford, is a cultural pot of honey.

During that period Berlin's theatrical life reached its zenith and many of the performances we saw are treasured memories still. Helene Weigel, Brecht's widow, was still running the Berliner Ensemble and Brecht's original productions of *Mother Courage*, *The Threepenny Opera* and *Caucasian Chalk Circle* were some of those I saw several times; Walter Felsenstein was creating his fabulously

17

imaginative and vibrant opera productions at the Komische Oper, at the Maxim Gorki Theater there were experimental productions of modern Soviet plays and in the Deutsches Theater I was able to see many of the German classics. Eventually Rudi manages to find me a room in the suburb of Weissensee. My landlady is having to take in lodgers because her husband has been imprisoned for embezzling funds from the state factory where he was manager. She is very kind to me and at weekends she sometimes takes me to her sister's family, which adopts me as a member, giving me, for the first time since I arrived, a feeling of home. I very soon become tired of going into the studio everyday, chatting to Rudi and slowly realise that he is unable to organise assignments for us. I had imagined he was preparing a plan of work but this doesn't seem to be the case, so we take the initiative ourselves and make our own arrangements to work with different teams in the studio. I am often sent out on location with the lighting crew and, to begin with, think I am learning the wrong language because their Berlin brogue is so strong and full of slang that I can't understand a word. In the end I manage to pick it up and find that it makes my vocabulary much more colourful and colloquial, if somewhat strong.

One of the chief lighting technicians who often comes along with us is nicknamed the 'death's head' because he looks like a skeleton. His eyes are sunk in their sockets and his yellowing skin is pulled taut over the bones. I never see him eat a thing but he always orders a vodka and beer whenever we stop for a break. His hands shake as he raises his vodka glass to his lips. Everyone says he had been a supreme lighting technician and his knowledge is still respected but he is now kept on out of human pity rather than because he is useful. I suppose he is one of what would be called the 'hidden unemployed'. On these location trips, mostly shooting items for the *Wochenschau*, the weekly cinema newsreel, I am able to pick up many useful tips about film-making. The older directors are particularly good to work with because they all have strong anti-fascist sentiments and a deep sense of humanity which infuses their film-making.

After several weeks of travelling around the GDR with various film crews and only being allowed to watch others working, I am offered the opportunity of actually doing something, of working as an assistant director with Hans Müller. The studio is to make a documentary about the Berliner Ensemble's production of *Coriolanus*, Brecht's adaptation of the Shakespearean tragedy of the same name. I am never quite able to overcome the feeling of contradiction when I sit in the Berliner Ensemble: it is a tiny baroque theatre, with gilt stucco proscenium arch, red velvet seats, replete with royal box, and seems an incongruous place for Brecht's iconoclastic, socialist plays. On the other hand, that is perhaps his desired intention – a conscious alienation. Brecht's sense of humour was legendry. Guenther Naumann, one of the actors, tells me that Brecht, after a tournee in France, laid out a large table with a selection of French cheeses in the foyer, with a notice saying, 'This is Culture!' On another occasion Brecht had notices hung around the auditorium with comments such as, 'Don't gawp so romantically! Eckehard Schall, Helene Weigel's son-in-law, plays the lead as Coriolanus, the popular hero turned tyrant.

Helene Weigel often sits in on rehearsals and chats to me about England, in her strong southern German accent, telling me how much she loves the London theatres. Although no longer young, she still has a tremendous vitality and sharp sense of humour. She feels herself to be Brecht's only true heir and rules the B.E., as the Ensemble was known, with an authoritarian school ma'am efficiency. She hardly ever allowed productions of his plays outside the B.E. and was no doubt largely responsible for it eventually becoming a museum rather than, as Brecht wished, a centre for theatrical experimentation. For this production all the actors are dressed in black or dark brown leather to underline the fascist nature of the army, but Coriolanus is swathed in a large, flowing, red cloak. I remember being amazed that the crimson kid's leather for this cloak has to be imported especially from Austria at tremendous cost because only such expensive leather would fall and fold in the manner desired. Although the GDR is still a relatively poor country, no money is spared on its theatres. For this production Paul Dessau wrote the music and Ruth Berghaus did the choreography, and both succeeded in creating a dramatic and awesome synthesis of movement and sound, conveying the tragic dimensions of the play.

On the afternoon of 30 April that year the studio comes to a standstill early, as it does every year, for the traditional May Day celebration . We have little money as students but are readily plied with free drinks by everyone we'd worked with. Not being familiar with German drinks, I mix everything: Kirsch, schnapps, bock- beer, weinbrand, vodka and I am then so drunk that I want to climb over the fence of the neighbouring zoo to join the lions. The following morning the sky is a limpid blue and the sun shines strongly on the flag-bedecked streets. We walk to Karl Marx Allee (formerly Stalin Allee) to watch the march-past. My head is still reeling and every stamping foot and drum roll shatters my cranium. Ulbricht and the party leaders are up on the platform with their uniforms of grey overcoats, trilbies and ties, giving their royal waves. On the street column after column of well practised groups march by: the blue-shirted Free German Youth (FDJ), led by their Prussian-style band (despite the fact that it is a Communist youth organisation I find the visual similarity to the Hitler Youth even at this time disturbing), then the 'Kampfgruppen', the blue- uniformed workers' militia, the police and army, followed by ordinary citizens. I see and feel no sign of compulsion or have the feeling that the sense of fun and enjoyment is forced. Fathers shouldering small children are laughing, bunches of flowers are waved and everyone seems determined to have a good day out. Of course the glorious sunshine – it always seemed to shine on May Day – helps relax people too.

My tiny room in the flat where I am staying is gradually becoming oppressive as the spring arrives. My landlady seems to wallow in her 'widowhood' and keeps the flat shuttered and draped with dark curtains almost all the time so that it feels like a dungeon. She spends most of the time sitting in the kitchen commiserating with herself and pampering her little dachshund. After a few months I am relieved to be told that the studio has rented and renovated a large flat for the trainees and we can move in immediately. It is not far from Alexanderplatz, in Heinrich Roller Strasse, overlooking the cemetery. Prenzlauer Berg is one of those typical old Berlin inner-city boroughs captured so lovingly by Heinrich Zille in his cheeky, finely observed sketches of working class life in the twenties.

The houses look semi-derelict and slum- like from the outside with their chipped stucco, peeling paint and falling plaster. Inside, however, they offer a very different picture: generous staircases kept polished by the house-proud inhabitants; majestic wooden French doors opening into spacious, high-ceilinged and stucco-decorated rooms, with large French windows facing out onto the road and flooding the rooms with light. Myself, Manuel and the two Guatemalans, who are seldom there, occupy the four rooms plus kitchen and bathroom. The only real drawback with the flat is the heating: each room has one of those typically German, large tiled stoves which has to be filled with lignite briquettes each morning and lit; not an easy task if you don't understand the peculiar physical properties of lignite fuel, which are not dissimilar to those of dried cow dung but dustier and heavier. The coals have to be carried up from the cellar bucket by bucket each day. Luckily the cold weather is almost gone and we won't need to heat for much longer.

Quite soon after we've moved in we are joined by a fifth trainee, a very special person. We had read the book and seen the film, *Naked Among Wolves*, a true story about the Buchenwald concentration camp, where the inmates had successfully hidden and kept alive a small Jewish boy throughout the war without the guards finding him. This boy had disappeared after the end of the war but was then rediscovered in France and the GDR government offered him the opportunity of studying in their country. We are determined to make his stay with us an enjoyable one, prepare a welcoming meal and offer to show him around the city and help him settle in. Unfortunately it doesn't turn out as we had planned. It appears that his new-found fame and the accolades he receives have gone to his head and he feels that he is too special to live simply with other students who have to look after themselves. He soon shows his disdain for us and moves out after a week. We learn that he is not staying to join us in the documentary studios but going to the national film school – so we decide to apply to go there too. The Doc-studio has its filming schedules to fulfil and as trainees we were able to tag along and pick up things but were given no formal training as such. After a time it becomes repetitive and we feel we aren't learning very much anymore. We are accepted at the film school and are told we can begin in September. We can hardly contain our excitement. Despite the obvious lack of resources and limited availability of technical equipment in the country as a whole, the film school offers surprisingly wide opportunities for actually shooting films and places an emphasis on practical film-making. This will be no dry theoretical course.

The film school is based in Babelsberg, the 'Hollywood' of pre-war Germany where all the old UFA films were made. It is in the 'Grenzgebiet' or border zone, between West Berlin and Potsdam, which means that we all have to have special passes to enter and can take in no guests. Babelsberg is situated in a picturesque area, surrounded by parks, woodland and lakes, close to Potsdam and Friedrich the Great's palace of Sanssouci. Many film stars and directors lived here and the place is littered with neglected old villas and mansions, some of which now provide accommodation for the students. Potsdam itself – Babelsberg is really only a suburb – is the epitome of Prussia. It was the seat of the Prussian king and the baroque splendour of the town is still tangible even though many of the buildings are at this time still only ruined shells. The picturesque and incongruous little enclave he built in Dutch architectural style for his Dutch mercenaries adds an odd quaintness. Friedrich apparently only felt safe from attack by his rebellious subjects when protected by bodyguards who were over six feet tall. He had them specially selected in Holland and brought back to Potsdam. They didn't fit comfortably into the normal sized barracks, so he had these quarters specially built to house them. The streets with their cobblestones provided an ideal backdrop for a film I later made together with a Venezuelan student about a corpse being robbed on the way to the cemetery. Potsdam symbolised so much of GDR thinking: its Prussian rigour, order and siege mentality but also its provinciality.

The former West German Consul, Guenther Gauss comments on the causes for this in his excellent book on his experiences as consul in the GDR. We are living in the former residence of the famous tenor, Richard Tauber. The wrought iron gateway, now rusted and a sad reminder of its former elegance, leads to the big house where 10 students now live. We are a relatively small number of students at the college, comprising in total no more than 100. We all live close to each other and within a short walk from the college itself so that an intimate atmosphere is readily created. Manuel and I are in a class of foreign students, studying directing or camera. There are two Cubans, a Venezuelan, a Sudanese, two Iraqis, an Indian, a Mongolian, two Bulgarian girls, an Ethiopian, Jerzy Zweig, the Buchenwald boy, Manuel and me. Later we are joined by a Brazilian, a Bolivian and students from Ghana and Mali.

Most of us have been delegated by our respective communist parties or governments and are solely reliant on our small grants (400 Marks a month) to live on, but one or two are delegated by their governments or even come privately. Our Indian colleague is the son of a businessman and, with his ostentatious gold rings and big, flashy Opel car, doesn't quite fit in with the rest of us, and spends much of his time in the West. The two Ghanaians are princes, the sons of chieftains, and are also not short of money for shopping trips to West Berlin. We are a real polyglot collection and conversations are often very complex and convoluted in addition to the various emotional and psychological conflicts which arise, mainly over girlfriends or injured pride, but in general we all get on very well.

For those students from the Arab countries, from Latin America or Africa the GDR is a sexual paradise. The religious and cultural oppression in their own countries, accompanied by taboos on pre-marital sex and the impossibility of having a natural and free relationship with girls is transformed into its opposite in the GDR. Since the war, because of the lack of men, many women developed a freer attitude to sexual relationships, and marriage is not seen as a necessary goal. Couples living together in so-called 'Lebensgemeinschaften' (common law partnerships) are very usual, and the GDR, despite being very puritanical in many other spheres, is here extremely tolerant. If any student strikes up a relationship with a girl it is not too much of a problem to get permission to live together in a student flat. In my first year I fall in love with a student in the acting faculty. I visit her in her room which we nick-name the 'telephone cell' because it is an attic cupboard with just enough space for a single bed. When you first fall in love room for a bed is all you need, but we do begin to feel that life in bed, as pleasant as it is, does become a little limiting if the relationship is to develop and mature.

We are soon given permission to move together into a bigger room. The girls in the GDR at this time have an aura of innocence about them which has long ago disappeared in the West. They are 'unspoilt'. Sex education is unheard of (which doesn't mean young people know nothing about sex, but they do know little about contraception); there is no sexually titillating literature or porno, and boys and girls all go to mixed schools, inter-relating very naturally with each other. There are few cosmetics or fashionable clothing available, and the girls therefore appear country-like and fresh. Even contraceptives are scarce and abortion at the time unavailable – the GDR has a desperate need for children to replace the population depleted before the wall was built. The result is that illegitimate children are not rare, because childcare facilities are readily available and such children are not considered a stigma; those that want an abortion take a cheap train trip to Poland where abortions are readily available (abortion was legalised in the GDR only in 1972). Most opt to have the children because, even for students, it is quite easy to obtain places for children in the kindergarten.

At this time, too, there are many articles in the papers about solidarity with the liberation struggles of Africa and Latin America so that students from these countries are seen as heroes, and winning over the hearts of the girls is not a difficult matter for them.

I think we are lucky to be at the film school at the height of its development. It has just come through the worst of the Stalinist period where such expressions of 'bourgeois individualism' as growing beards had been forbidden as had the wearing of jeans and western-style parachutists' jackets, or American badges. I am told on various occasions that I am quite a nice person but why do I have to grow a beard! In the provinces, further away from Berlin it is even worse. In the busses or trams I am laughed at, pointed at and asked by pure strangers if I can't afford a razor. And all this despite the fact that Marx, the spiritual founder of the country, had one of the world's most famous beards and even their own state leader, Walther Ulbricht sports one!

Although things are obviously loosening up a little by 1965 everything is still very much controlled from above by the party. We have two film-history lecturers who are enamoured with the new Italian film movement around Fellini and Antonioni and who try to introduce some new thinking into the narrow concept of socialist realism. They are soon dismissed from their jobs. Of course at the time we never heard the reasons for their departure, simply rumour. We didn't reflect on it, we were too pre-occupied with our own work. My own professor, Dr. Wilkening, the administrative head of the DEFA feature film studios, is a typical narrow-minded apparatchik. In our first year we have to complete a series of photographic studio portraits to illustrate different lighting techniques. I do a number with very subdued light and little highlighting, my model dressed in black. He is not impressed and complains that they don't sufficiently reflect socialist optimism and the bright future! He only comes into the college on rare occasions and is greeted with the sort of subservience still reserved for professors and doctors, even though, in the new socialist state, they are now nominally 'comrades' like every other mortal. He disperses a few hackneyed phrases about socialism and then leaves in his chauffeur-driven car.

We film students are a very privileged group. Throughout the country watching western TV or listening to western radio is still banned but we are allowed to watch West German TV 'as part of our film training'. Each week we also have the opportunity of seeing recently released western films which have been offered to the GDR for sale and which are shown to us before being returned to the distributor in West Berlin. One day some students come into the common room to watch TV and find that the adaptor which makes it possible for us to watch West German programmes has been removed. A whisper goes around that we will no longer be allowed to watch these programmes and everyone speculates on who is responsible and why it has been done. No one, of course, goes up to the rector and confronts him with the situation, demanding an explanation. Years of acceptance, of discipline, of unquestioning has produced this subservience. I have been brought up in a different tradition and believing in Communist democracy, have no compunctions about protesting, and so, together with some other students, we write a letter demanding that it be restored, pinning the letter up on our wall newspaper. The result is that within a day the adaptor is restored and we are again able to watch western TV programmes. We never receive an explanation, though, of why it happened in the first place.

Our lecture rooms look out over the lake which divides the GDR from West Berlin. We often stare out of the window watching the police boats patrol the invisible line in the centre of the lake; over the tree tops we can see the tall spire of West Berlin's TV tower. It is like looking out at another planet. I often wonder what people on the other side feel, looking over to us. The fact that our college is in the border zone means that we can't show any of our films to friends and guests from outside. The GDR is paranoid about foreigners and the possibility of spies entering the country or 'corrupting' the minds of the people and it is almost impossible for outsiders to visit schools or factories without government permission. For us, having our college in such a sensitive area, it is even worse, and the receptionist on the door is a real Cerberus who wouldn't even let a fly in without its identity card.

To overcome this problem we clandestinely book a room in the Johannes Becher Cultural Centre in Berlin and invite our friends, including some from West Berlin, to see the films we have made. We have to do it secretly because we would never receive permission from the rector to invite foreigners. We all arrive at the centre on the appointed evening and sit down to watch the films, the lights are dimmed and the first film, about the Vietnam war begins. Suddenly the doors burst open and the lights are switched back on and we find ourselves confronted by a group of security men in their long

25

overcoats demanding to see our identity cards. They write down everyone's details, name, address etc. They must think we were going to show porno or secret anti-state films. How disappointed and flabbergasted they must have been when they saw that all those works to be shown were pro-socialist and non-controversial! There are no further repercussions from this even though we are all severely reprimanded and I almost lose my prize of a trip to the Moscow film school. As foreign students we are undoubtedly allowed more rope than our GDR colleagues and our misdemeanours are tolerated, albeit grudgingly. The saddest thing about it is that one of our student colleagues has obviously shopped us to the security forces. We know this because we had kept it very secret and only informed a small number of student friends. We are reasonably certain who it is but never know conclusively.

At the height of the Vietnam war the film school students organise collections on the street but the rector doesn't approve of this because, he says, 'it smacks of the nazi period when people were pressurised into giving for the cause'. We manage to collect quite a large sum of money, though, before we have to stop. People on the streets give readily and generously, probably because they realise it is a genuine student initiative and not something organised by officialdom. Following on from this we decide to organise a demonstration to the US military mission in Potsdam. This has never happened before; demonstrations were either organised by the party or didn't take place. The students are thrilled to be organising their own demo. We paint posters and make banners and even persuade the local army barracks to let us use their lorries to transport us. The neighbouring teachers' training college joins us and the demo is a huge success. We stand in the gardens of the mission, plant out banners on the lawn and chant 'Amis raus aus Vietnam'. The expressions on the officers' faces behind the mission's windows are a sight: They don't know whether this is an attack, a joke, a provocation or what. The next day we have a high-level visit from the Potsdam FDJ (the local branch of the Free German Youth, the youth wing of the SED), wanting to know how we'd organised it and why we'd done it without informing them. They have obviously never heard of grass roots activity and are very embarrassed by the whole thing although at the same time proud that it has taken place in their district.

Another amusing story in connection with the Vietnam war occurs a few months later. As part of my course work – we have to complete several short films each year – I decide to make a film about an American mother whose son is sent to Vietnam and doesn't return. I have to borrow an American uniform from the DEFA costume department and one of the students from the acting faculty plays the soldier. We are half way through filming and need the uniform for a few more days but are told it is no longer available. I tell them I can't complete the film without it, I have to have it. All my pleading is in vain, and the film is never completed. I learn some time later that some bright spark had hit upon the idea of borrowing the uniform and had jauntily walked through Checkpoint Charlie and stayed in the West! As Berlin was still under four-power control, allied soldiers could cross the border back and forth without being checked and he'd taken advantage of this loophole. I cursed him for ruining my film though.

The summers are idyllic in Babelsberg. The woods are a cascade of bird sound: nightingales, golden orioles and wood warblers abound. The lakes are warm and usually deserted during the week. A group of us would regularly take a few sandwiches and towels and spend the day sunbathing and swimming or wandering through the woods. It is marvellous not being confronted by 'Private – trespassers will be prosecuted' notices everywhere as so often in Britain. Although one day we are innocently walking near the lakeside when a foot-patrol of border police challenges us. We have strayed into the border zone. Our protests of ignorance don't help us. We are arrested and taken back to the guard house. The soldiers are very friendly and ply us with cups of tea but can't let us go, they say, until our trespass has been clarified. After ringing the college and checking our story we are released after a couple of hours and there are no further repercussions.

The grant I receive from the GDR government is not a lot but I can live on it if I budget carefully. Food and accommodation is extremely cheap and there isn't much else to spend money on in Babelsberg. In my second year, though, I find a surprising source of supplementary income. The local documentary film studio has been given the job of producing a series of English language programmes for the schools. I am the only full-time British student in the GDR and Britons of any sort are a rare species, so I am offered regular parts in the series and am paid a handsome 100 Marks each day I work. I become a sort of minor celebrity as a result and am recognised in trams and on the streets by gaggles of school kids. I also have a tiny part as a RAF officer in a big feature film about the development of the V-2 rockets, called *Gefrorene Blitze*. One of my compatriots in this film is John Peet, the flamboyant ex- Reuters correspondent who defected to the East at the end of the war. He is still the archetypal Englishman with his deer-stalker, officer's moustache and upper-class accent. His monthly news sheet in English, *German Democratic Report* was obligatory reading for any journalist wishing to come to grips with East Germany. I spent three years at the film school and enjoyed every minute of it. The opportunity of making our own films, watching all the classics – Eisenstein, Dovchenko, Pudovkin, Vigo, Pabst, Renoir etc. and many of the nazi films, none of which I'd had an opportunity to see before; to experience the invigorating discussions and exchanges between the students, particularly because each brought his or her own country's experience to bear on the subjects debated, was all extremely thought-provoking and enriching.

One short series of lectures was particularly stimulating, delivered by the well-known North American film critic Jay Leyda, who paid a short visit to the school. He had studied with Eisenstein in Moscow and been hounded by McCarthy in his home country. He showed us some of Leni Riefenstahl's Olympic Games newsreels and asked us to comment on them. Of course, the first thing that hits you is the superb visual imagery, the technical perfection of the photography and the innovative style and it is precisely this which has given her films a new cult value in the west recently. Jay Leyda, very cleverly persuaded us to look behind the dazzle and think about the content of the images. What were they purveying? He made us realise that within this imagery was a basically anti-human and fascistic ideology: in her films the human body became a machine, was worshipped as a machine. There was none of the pain, frailty, disappointment, tragedy, none of that real human emotion which accompanies every Olympic competition, only 'Aryan' heroism and perfection. As the only English-speaking student I did the translating for him. I'm sure my primitive German at that time could scarce do his lectures justice, but I hope I managed to convey something of his penetrating and provocative thinking. We had our own club in one of the old villas, with a bar, and many a party was held there until well into the early hours.

The Latin Americans were the best party people and if even only one of them was present you could bet there would be dancing and a fun atmosphere in no time. They knew how to enjoy themselves.

The fact that we were relatively isolated from large towns and other student establishments, forming a small enclave of our own, meant that a very intimate atmosphere developed and, although in a sense artificial, the lack of outside diversion produced a concentration which was nevertheless at the same time relaxing and enjoyable.

CHAPTER 2
Return to the other world

My time to return home to Britain comes all too quickly. Although I relish the idea of now being able to make films for a living I am also a little apprehensive of leaving the comfortable student existence and of what I will find in Britain on my return. I've been away for four years and have only been home twice on short visits, so am very out of touch with the life and changes which have taken place. For all these years I have hardly spoken a word of English, have lived in a totally different environment and now return to a country I no longer know. For some time I feel like a foreigner in my own country.

I know it won't be easy to find a job in the British TV and film industry, particularly as I don't yet possess the necessary union ticket. So, before I leave Berlin I decide to write to GDR TV asking if they would be interested in employing a correspondent in the UK. I don't hear from them for some time but then out of the blue am asked to come for an interview in a downtown hotel. I stand in front of the lift doors in the empty, hospital-like lobby, watching the numerals of the floors light up sequentially as the lift descends. My sore throat is really plaguing me in the heat and on top of that I'd felt obliged to wear a tie 'to make the right impression'. I feel as if my neck is in splints. I enter the metal cubicle, the doors jerk together like a nervous couple having sex for the first time and I press the button for the 6th floor. I read the notices in the lift, smiling at the Prussian thoroughness of it all: 'Es ist verboten..., Es ist unerwünscht...' and then the unintentional humour of the English translation next to it: 'It is not recommended to step out of the lift backwards while in

30

motion'. The GDR still has enormous problems finding good translators, particularly for little jobs like lift notices.

I begin wondering what they will offer me, if anything. I certainly don't fancy the idea of going home to make cigarette or sun-tan lotion commercials or work on soap operas so I really hope I will be offered something challenging. I am imbued with the art of cinema, inspired by people like John Grierson, Santiago Alvarez and Joris Ivens, all three of whom I'd met in Leipzig during the annual documentary film festival. I realise the potential of film, how its language could be used to inform and inspire people but also misused as a soporific to cocoon them. I know that this interview can decide my future.

I knock confidently on the door although butterflies flutter in my stomach and my throat is like emery paper. A male voice bids me enter. In the small bedroom there are three men, one I already know from the correspondent department of TV. One of the others is sitting stiffly on a chair looking rather like a distraught hamster; he is introduced to me as 'the director', and the third lies, like a fat puppy in his vest, on the bed. This small rotund man on the bed is shouting into the telephone: 'I've been on to you three times already and you still haven't brought me the cold water I ordered. What sort of hotel is this. If I don't get it immediately I'll take the matter to a higher level'. He slams the phone down cholerically and introduces himself to me as 'the inspector'. The director proceeds to ask me a few informal questions about my training, my intentions and the sort of salary I expect. It appears I am being offered a job. I am told that as soon as I return to England I can start work as their British correspondent. Having been away from Britain for so long and having little idea of current salaries I naively suggest £25 a week to start with. This is readily agreed to. I little realise that this is hardly above a subsistence wage

Although I am happy to have a job offer I still want to try British TV companies because my intention has always been to make films in Britain for a British audience, films which would inform people about the nature of their society, about social processes and of their own creative potential. I am under no illusions that this would be straightforward but I am willing to struggle. After arriving back in Britain I write off applications to all British TV companies but only Granada gives me an interview. I am told that without a union ticket I can't be employed but they are prepared to offer me a traineeship if I wish, as a means of 'getting in'. I feel I have enough training and now want to work properly so I reject the offer.

During this time I sign on at the Labour Exchange in order to get my unemployment pay. I am living with my father for the time being, in Coventry. The labour exchange there is like all the others, an indifferent pre-war office block with wide entrance doors marked with big letters: A-G, H-N and O-Z. Inside on the wooden benches an assortment of 'benefit recipients' sits and waits: the apathetic, the lethargic, the poor and depressed. Several are being dealt with at the counters, whispering their case histories to the clerks, desperately trying to maintain some sort of privacy in this public hall. I join the waiting ones until my turn comes. I explain that I am an unemployed cameraman, just returned to the UK. The clerk smiles and confides that she doesn't think she'll be able to find me a job in that field but she'll take my details anyway – I never did get a penny or a job offer out of the Job Centre. After six years of study I am desperate to start work, I can't hang around waiting any longer so write to the GDR and say I am willing to start immediately.

My wife and I meet the delegation at London's Heathrow airport. The distraught hamster is there and so is the small chubby inspector, in immaculate suit and smelling as if he's tipped the whole bottle of aftershave over himself. With him is another short-cropped, beefy, affluent-looking West German. My wife, the ex-drama student from Babelsberg, is showered with bunches of flowers and expensive perfume from the duty free and my hand is pumped in good German tradition.

It is 1968 and the GDR is still not recognised as a legitimate state outside the socialist world. Its citizens cannot travel on GDR passports. The few that are given entry visas to western countries, after long waits, are still viewed invariably in the West as 'communist agents'. Because of these difficulties and the fact that journalists with other passports can travel more easily to capture the hot news items, the GDR is obliged to rely on a roundabout way to obtain its news items.

We all squeeze into a taxi and drive to their hotel in central London. We must look an incongruous bunch, like a gang of sophisticated bank robbers in a George Raft film. If MI5 was watching it would have been convinced we were part of a clever communist conspiracy to undermine the democratic system: me, the tall skinny, bearded Englishman wedged between the bullet-headed German and the worried hamster, my wife, the Slav-looking moll and the roly-poly godfather with the fat wallet. The management has come over to London to offer me a contract.

After a quick breakfast we quickly get down to the details of contract and money, it is all concluded in an hour. I leave them that morning with very ambiguous feelings. On the one hand the euphoria at having a job, one month's advance salary and the money to buy a new car in my pocket, but on the other the fear of finally leaving the womb of studenthood for the unknown world of work. At last I am now leaving the stifling boredom of Coventry for the big metropolis which is as foreign to me as Japan or Greenland. The search for a place to live is a demoralising process. First we ask friends and acquaintances but draw a complete blank. We then traipse around the flat agencies in town, well furnished offices with well-groomed young women in suits and blouses, but on asking for something around £4 or £6 (prices I'd imagined were normal) are given polite, condescending smiles and told that there is nothing in that price category available. We buy the *Evening Standard* and scan the 'To Let' columns but don't realise that the 'Evening' Standard comes out in editions beginning at ten in the morning and if you don't buy the first edition you can forget it.

After spending a fortune on telephone calls someone eventually tells us about the early edition. We then travel by tube all over London, from Chiswick to Wood End and from Clapham to Islington, to view flats. We are invariably interviewed, although 'grilled' would be a better term, by the landlords about our marital status, whether we have children, whether my wife is pregnant, what our jobs are, what our wages are etc. and all this just to rent a grotty room or tiny flatlet. We go around the shady little flat agencies in attic rooms, where crooks make money out of the chronic housing shortage and people's desperation. After paying our 'key money' and one month's rent in advance we take a flat in South Wimbledon for £40 a month. We are exhaustedly happy that our search is at an end. The flat, in an old Edwardian terrace is not even self-contained. To reach our bedroom from the living room we have to cross the communal corridor which also serves the upstairs flat where a Sri Lankan family lives. Our kitchen is damp and the walls covered in mildew and the toilet is an outside one but it is a flat of our own at last!

We live there for the first six months and settle into the routine of work. According to my contract, I am obliged to shoot 15 items a month. This is an arbitrary figure and I usually manage nine or ten but sometimes, amazingly more than 15. I have none of the usual journalistic contacts, few friends, a total ignorance of London, apart from the underground tube stations, and not a very clear idea of what sort of items are required. To begin with I work alone, using an Arriflex standard 16mm camera; sometimes my wife helps me and we record sound using a Mayak mechanical wind-up tape recorder. Much of our early work involves the search for sympathetic interview partners who are willing to declare publicly their support for and recognition of the GDR as a state; the higher their status, so much the better – MPs, like Ian Mikado, Konni Zilliacus, Renee Short, trade union officials and businessmen. One MP always willing to give us a sympathetic statement is the avuncular Will Owen, a seemingly very ordinary and unpretentious man. A few years later we are shocked to hear that he has been brought to court by MI5 and accused of being an agent working for the GDR!

We are still in the cold war period but the GDR is pushing hard for recognition as a sovereign state. West Germany maintains its position of being responsible for all Germans and sees the GDR as a temporary aberration. While our colleagues in the Federal Republic are ferreting out former Nazis, now occupying influential positions in the West German establishment and trying to cover their tracks, pretending to be born-again democrats, we complement their work in Britain. We interview and become acquainted with lawyers, like D. N. Pritt QC and Platts-Mills QC, who expose the role of former Nazis in West Germany and support the establishment of a truly de-nazified German state in the Soviet Zone. Every voice raised in this way constitutes pressure on the international community to recognise the socialist German state. In the early seventies this long campaign culminates in success when one after the other the western nations, and finally the United Nations, grant diplomatic recognition. The enormous economic success of the GDR, its political stability and the key role it plays in European affairs can no longer be ignored.

The early years shooting a dozen news items a month introduce me intimately to life in my own country in a way which would have been impossible otherwise. Basically our job is to demonstrate the inequalities and injustices of capitalism in order to bolster socialist ideology in the GDR. I have no problems with this concept because I recognise the iniquities of the capitalist system and want to see a socialist society in Britain too. At this time, in the early seventies, the British media are hardly touching social problems and films like *Cathy Come Home* (a sensational film at the time, exposing the heartbreak of homelessness, and leading to the creation of the national charity SHELTER, to aid the homeless in Britain) are exceptions.

We are often the only ones to be covering the demonstrations, strikes and squats. We film and talk to families desperately trying to make ends meet in East End slums, with pensioners demonstrating for higher pensions, with striking workers from a myriad of industries, student campaigns for higher grants, with homeless families. Our work rubs our noses in those problems, we identify with those struggling for a life of dignity, free of fear; we are forced to examine workers' grievances and 25 their reasons for protesting. We have to burrow and ferret out the hidden corners of deprivation and misery because, apart from the *Morning Star*, hardly a newspaper covers these issues or if they do it is invariably in a dismissive or trivialised manner – the problems simply don't exist in the minds of most people. But although they are 'hidden' we realise that they are far from marginal or exceptional but surprisingly widespread and, even where they are unique cases, the pain and humiliation is not therefore minimised. Like the couple with two small children in Norfolk, evicted from their tied cottage and forced to live in a tent in winter; the family at the Worlds' End site in South London living in a car park in a makeshift cardboard hut; the Asians scarred by the knives of National Fronters and too frightened to report to the police because they know they will receive no support; the pensioners vegetating alone and in fear on miserable pensions. The list is long. Marxian concepts of capitalism are constantly affirmed and underlined by the realities confronting us in our work, whether in the narrow, crowded terraces of Manchester and Liverpool, the blighted valleys of South Wales or the deprived inner cities of Glasgow and Belfast. We witness the daily economic struggles of ordinary working class families to achieve a life of dignity for themselves and their children, and also their courage and determination in struggle against the employers.

We glimpse the other side too when we cover the smoked-salmon and champagne gatherings at Ascot or the super-rich at the sale of Mentmore House, bidding millions for antique clocks or vases with less deliberation than many a family does before spending a few pounds on groceries. We follow the rise of racism in the mid-seventies, the increasing volume of marching boots and swirl of union jacks as the National Front grows nationally, abetted by the media and Tory right wing.

The many small items we shoot in those early years serve to hone my camera skills, training my eye and speeding-up my reactions. I travel the length and breadth of Britain, getting to know my own country, exploring beneath the glossy patina, digging and probing. On occasions we are really hard put to convey a particular social problem in visual terms when those involved or taking part in a public demonstration are so few and ill represent the enormity of the problem. One particular instance is a pensioners' march in Holborn. It is well advertised but only four people turn up, one of them the legendary East End Dockers' leader, Jack Dash. This really taxes my filmic abilities: making four pensioners look like a mass demo! We do it by interviewing Jack as he walks up and down with his poster. He is a really colourful figure with a good turn of speech, embellished with cockney humour. We use the other three to intercut the interview, using close-ups of their posters, their faces and feet.

Then, as now, many pensioners live close to the poverty line and their demand for a living pension was not only justified but was supported, albeit passively, by a majority of the population. Demonstrations, as proved here, are not necessarily a true indicator of concern about problems or injustice. One of the great achievements of the British democratic system, cemented by the media, has been to paralyse peoples' active participation in politics, to make demonstrations and positive action appear pointless and to view the bringing about of political and social change as a preserve of those elected to govern.

The enormous demonstrations and activities against Barbara Castle's Industrial Relations Bill present us with the opposite sort of problem: how to capture the immensity, the colour and euphoric sense of united strength in a few shots? The streets of London resound with shouts of 'kill the bill', miners' brass bands blast the bastions of financial might and the bright union banners make a carnival of Fleet Street.

In those early years with the help of comrades from the *Morning Star* and the Communist Party we built up a very useful network of contacts in the trade union and labour movement and this was invaluable for our work. Ironically, because we were often the only journalists covering the struggles and battles of working people it was often thought that we must be working for MI5 or the police and it was these many friends and comrades who vouched for us, allaying suspicion and sometimes saving us and our equipment from physical attack!

Covering so many stories here in Britain we often feel very frustrated that our reports are not seen here, but console ourselves with the thought that someone somewhere is watching them, is being moved by them, identifying with the victims and being informed about the causes. The early seventies bring a spate of 'work-ins' by workers defending their jobs and demanding the right to work. The first is the now famous Upper Clyde Shipbuilders takeover in Glasgow. The shipyard that had built some of Britain's biggest and most famous ships, like the Queen Elizabeth, is to be closed and all jobs lost. Clydeside was synonymous with shipbuilding. Generations had worked in the yards and the closure decision comes as a traumatic shock to the people. The occupation is led by the Communists Jimmy Reid and Jimmie Airlie, together with other militant shop stewards, and it very soon captures the imagination of the whole country which sympathises with the workers' aspirations. UCS is followed by the occupation and worker takeover of the Fisher-Bendix engineering factory near Liverpool and of Briant's Printers in London. With Tony Benn's support Fisher Bendix becomes a workers' co-operative, as does Triumph Motorcycles in Coventry. We are in at the beginning of all these events.

We have to rush up to Glasgow in order to film the momentous vote to occupy the yards. A work-in was something never attempted before in the history of the British working class. Our first daughter, Galina, is six months old and we have to take her with us, having no one readily at hand to look after her. While we are clambering over the piles of sheet steel to find a vantage point from where we can film the vote, she is in the shop stewards' office being entertained with Scottish folk songs sung by a couple of hardened and burly workers.

Clydebank is redolent of the atmosphere of British manufacturing in its heyday. The enormous cranes hold out their extended jibs like gallows waiting for the victims; grimy, windswept sheds house the ribs and keels of unfinished ships, bursts of white flame spring up and splutter like candles in the dark corners of the hulls and a deafening hammering and clatter reverberates from the thin walls;

rusting rails run between the cobblestones and the Lowry-like figures emerge from the sheds and workshops, converging on the meeting. It is a celebration of the British manufacturing tradition – the workshop of the world as Britain used to be called – a time to recall the great ships built there but also a commemoration of its demise. Of course at that time no one could have dreamt that within less that two decades all British manufacturing industry would have disappeared or be in the hands of foreign multi-nationals, that in these yards, where father and son had served their time and given of their health, it would be silent and still.

Jimmy Reid gives a short stirring speech, emphasising the historic importance of the decision and its message of hope to all those threatened by redundancy. Hundreds of welders, caulkers, painters and boilermakers gather in the yard, framed by the tall and gaunt derricks, their beautiful faces, lined, scarred and wrinkled by their hard but dignified lives, listen intently to what he is saying. Nowhere else in Europe can you see such faces: a mixture of Norse courage, Anglo-Saxon stamina and Gaelic canniness. They banter with each other, eyes twinkling with humour and optimism despite the dire threat to their livelihoods. When asked to support the shop stewards' decision to occupy the yards all hands go up and everyone roars hooray, a sense of relief brightening up the stern faces – now something concrete is being done!

The occupation lasts several weeks and tremendous solidarity from throughout the world is engendered. We spend a fortnight up there in the yard and in the homes of the workers. Their warmth and humour, which they never lose throughout the occupation, is a constant reminder of what the break-up of this community would mean in terms of de-humanisation. Even though the work itself broke the health of many a worker – caulkers we spoke to who lost their hearing working in the double hulls hammering off the excess metal, welders whose lungs were destroyed by the toxic fumes and men who'd lost fingers or been scarred for life by falling girders or sheets of heavy steel – the social process of production forged a strong human bond between the men and their families. In the end the workers manage to negotiate an agreement with a new boss and save most of the jobs. Sadly this solution only holds for a short period while the oil boom lasts and rig-building is in fashion. The yard is now permanently closed.

In 1972 there is a big dock strike and five dockers leaders are put in prison by the government – the so-called Pentonville Five, named after the prison in which they are placed. Such action is unheard of since the war and the British trade union movement rises up in anger. That same evening London is hit by spontaneous walk-outs. In Fleet Street, the centre of London's newspaper publishing, every printing press is brought to a standstill. The government is so taken aback by the workers' response that they release the imprisoned dockers and we are able to film them as they are carried victorious on the shoulders of the waiting crowds away from the prison. This is the highpoint of worker solidarity and strength and is a lesson to the employers that the trade union movement has to be smashed.

The following decades see that process take place. What was brought home to me particularly clearly while covering these occupations and struggles was the enormous waste of indigenous talent and expertise the capitalist system entails. The inequalities in basic education and the lack of opportunity for further education and training condemns thousands to dead-end jobs or no jobs at all. People like Jack Spriggs, the trade union convenor, who later became managing director of the Fisher Bendix Co-operative, or Jimmy Reid and the other shop stewards who proved that they could run a whole ship-yard without the bosses, Bill Freeman, organiser of the Briant occupation – they all showed amazing talent, organising ability, social consciousness and an intelligence far beyond the demands of their jobs. They are continually put down, dismissed as mere manual workers, rejected, and treated as wage slaves with no right to join in the decision-making processes or even to be informed about matters which affect their very lives. Capitalism continually accelerates the process of alienation, destroys organic, cohesive and supportive communities built up over generations, communities which are warm and alive. A wedge is driven between individuals and their societies, preventing real participation and taking away the most important attribute of any human being, their dignity, their sense of belonging and sense of purpose. At this time I don't realise that in the socialist societies as they exist in eastern Europe a similar alienation is taking place.

Today, in the nineties, to look back on those last decades is to realise that we have been present at the sick bed of a dying way of life. The Thatcher years have led to the almost total destruction of British manufacturing – once the 'workshop of the world' and now the beggar of Europe. Most of the coal mines have closed, the South

Wales valleys are now green again with only the rusting remains of the pit-winding towers to remind us that there were once pits there; the steel works have gone, the car factories, the shipyards and docklands. The skills which once made Britain a leading industrial nation are no longer required. Thatcher has reduced Britain to a centre for financial deals, profiteering and speculation, she has created a pocket of relative affluence in the south-east where the financial centres are based, but blighted the rest of the country, destroyed communities, peoples' sense of dignity, their sense of social responsibility, of caring and solidarity and replaced it with a rapacious individual greed, where material wealth has become the sole criterion of success. She has denied that there is such a thing as 'society', only groups of individuals and it is this philosophy which has marked the last decade.

CHAPTER 3 – BEHIND ENEMY LINES
Greece – a visit to the colonels

In the early seventies it was decided to extend our coverage to countries other than the immediate neighbours and Britain. Our first assignments were Greece, Spain and Portugal.

All three countries were, at that time, in the hands of fascist dictatorships and we could only film there clandestinely. Our financial resources were still very modest and it was made clear to us that we shouldn't be too adventurous or do anything which could involve the confiscation of our valuable equipment.

In 1971 we went first to Greece, which was languishing under the brutal dictatorship of the colonels, who took power after the bloody suppression of the Athens student protests in 1967. They imprisoned and tortured leading communists, trade unionists and democrats, creating notorious concentration camps on isolated islands in the Aegean. The famous Greek composer Mikis Theodorakis was one of those sent to an island prison. We met others who related how they were tortured and maltreated during their imprisonment. Some had been through it once already under the fascist dictatorship after the Second World War.

This report from Greece was very important because the western media had virtually ignored the country since the coup: the danger to NATO and to "western democracy" posed by the upsurge of left-wing forces had been avoided, so everything in the garden was again lovely. The harsh oppression and lack of basic human rights like the right to join a trade union or belong to a political party were, apparently, of no interest to the western media. Greece was again firmly in the Western Alliance and that was all that mattered. The western powers react very differently when socialist governments come to power as in Grenada or Nicaragua, then they are branded as totalitarian and must be removed. This army dictatorship was acceptable.

As it is our first assignment we don't want to take any undue risks, but will be pleased if we can smuggle out some sort of report. I normally sport a beard and have done since my youth, hating the idea of having to shave at least once every day. My beard had become part of my personality and I would feel naked without it, but for the first time in my life I felt it was necessary to shave it off. In the wake of the student revolt throughout Western Europe beards and long hair were associated with left-wing views and, for the military, such hirsute symbols were anathema. By the time I ha cropped my hair and taken off my beard, leaving only a short military style moustache I looked the archetypal fascist, but it almost became my undoing towards the end of our trip. My colleague Klaus and I book a cheap package tour to Athens. On arrival we hire a small Volkswagen to get us around. Our equipment consists of a tiny innocent-looking Beaulieu 16mm camera, a small tape recorder and a few rolls of film and tape.

The colonels had taken power in 1967 to prevent elections taking place which would have probably returned a left-wing government. They claimed it was to stall a 'communist revolt', but evidence for this was blatantly lacking. A left-wing government would not have been to the liking of NATO and the USA either, because they have large bases on the Peloponnesian Peninsular.

The Acropolis, our first subject to film, stands defiantly, in view of the whole city – a monument to democracy, one of the most treasured concepts the Greeks bequeathed us. We then shoot as much as we can in the city itself which would convey the atmosphere of junta rule. We observe the life of the port workers in Piraeus and then the contrasting wealth of Glyfada, outside Athens, the home of the wealthy. Here the white villas, framed by purple bougainvillea and green vines look out over the harbour where sleek yachts glint in the sun.

We only have a week to film and are busy virtually from dawn until sunset. The heat is oppressive and in our little Volkswagen we literally boil. After sunset we are relieved to go into the Plaka, beneath the Acropolis, slake our thirst and relax in the noise and bustle of the market.

One amusing thing happens to us before we leave Athens though.

We park on one of the big squares, ignoring No Parking signs because we are foreigners, and do some filming in a side street. On returning to our car we can't believe our eyes; the number plates have been stolen! We stand there wondering what to do, obviously looking totally perplexed, when a helpful passer-by with a few words of English explains that this is how the police here stop illegal parking. We have to go to the local police station, pay a fine and collect our number plates, which then have to be bolted back on.

According to our information some political prisoners are held on the island of Aegina, just off the coast of Athens so we decide to take the ferry over and see if we can film something. On arrival in the picturesque little harbour we kit ourselves out with straw sombreros – not exactly Greek national costume – hire a tandem and cycle around the island, playing the innocent tourists. We don't catch a glimpse of the concentration camp but are able to film the prison. We pretend to film each other in the vicinity of the prison itself, which is in the centre of the town, but actually shooting the prison only.

To film the army presence in and around Athens we remove the back seat of the car and I sit in the back covered by the upturned sea and my colleague's large coat and can now shoot through a narrow slit. We are almost discovered when a policeman strolls by just as my colleague is burying me in the back of the car, but the policeman obviously has other concerns and continues on his way without noticing our activities. Ironically we are arrested some time later after filming what we thought was an innocuous sign, but which happened to be near a sensitive military area. The arresting officer refuses to accept that I don't understand Greek because of my dark appearance and Greek-style moustache. That fact delays our release somewhat. Fortunately his chief is less suspiciously minded and does in the end accept our story that we are ignorant tourists and that we hadn't filmed anything other than the sign. He lets us go with a warning to be more careful in future.

Before we leave Greece, as if on command, eight ships of the US Sixth Fleet, including the destroyer Albany sail into Faliron harbour on a courtesy visit and we are able to shoot their arrival. We realise what we have shot is not a sensationally revealing film – that wasn't our intention. Our images will serve to visually underline a commentary explaining the present situation; it will give our audience an inkling of the country and its people. We include an interview with a member of the Greek resistance, but shoot this in Germany where there is no danger to him.

We leave Greece separately, I carry the tape recorder and the 'harmless' cans of film and my colleague takes the 'hot cans' with the illegal shots. He is able to mingle with a group of American tourists who are already checked in and so slips through the controls without a hitch. I am not searched either, but my heart is pounding as the border guard examines my passport. In the plane winging our way back to Berlin I am exhausted but exhilarated that our first foreign mission has been successfully accomplished. The only remaining question is whether the film has been properly exposed and shot. The wait until we have confirmation from the laboratory that everything is OK is always a tantalising time. My anxiety is unfounded though and the item is shown and given priority treatment.

What in retrospect may seem exaggerated caution was, at the time, appropriate. Even accredited correspondents were under threat. Not long after we had left the West German correspondent Edmund Gruber and his cameraman were arrested at Athens airport; only the intervention of the BRD ambassador secured their release.

In 1974 I was to return again to film the release of political prisoners after the collapse of the colonels' rule. This time we go there with a different feeling, no longer having to disguise ourselves as tourists and with the joy that this abhorrent regime had collapsed upon itself because of its incompetence and the resistance of the Greek people.

The prison is an enormous building on the outskirts of the city, difficult to reach by public transport and standing all by itself, surrounded by parched wasteland. The newspapers had announced that political prisoners would be released on a particular date but no time was given. We, along with a whole number of relatives, wives and mothers dressed in their traditional black, brothers and sisters with flowers arrived at the main gate early in the morning, but the guards said they couldn't tell us when the prisoners would be released. We waited a whole day in the vicious sun, with the tense relatives outside that notorious prison. There were no cafes to buy a quick drink, no shade to sit under, only the huge prison wall towering above us and reflecting the heat of the sun like a hot pavement. Eventually, just before dusk, as we were almost giving up with exhaustion and the feeling that we had perhaps been tricked by the government, the gates were swung open and the first prisoners came out – like those first members of the chorus in Fidelio, slowly emerging, uncertain, to freedom, from the shadows of the wings. They were embraced with tears and emotion by their still unbelieving families and we were able to capture the jubilation of the people as they carried their heroes home on their shoulders. Among them was the veteran seamen's leader and communist, Tony Ambatielos, who I'd known in London during his long period of exile and to whose mother I had taken a parcel of clothes on my first visit to Greece. He was now in his sixties, but that hadn't stopped his jailers torturing him during his imprisonment. In elections the following year he was elected as MP for Piraeus. Also among those released with him was a young, skinny-looking West German journalist called Günther Wallraff, relatively unknown then, but later to become one of West Germany's best known investigative left-wing writers and journalists. He had been imprisoned for chaining himself to the railings in Athens' main square as a lone gesture to draw attention to the brutality of the colonels' rule. He gave us a spontaneous and inspiring interview, testifying to his indomitable and courageous spirit.

In 1973, one year before the collapse of the Greek dictatorship there was an adventurous attempt by a right-wing Greek officer, Nikos Sampson to stage a coup in Cyprus and return the island to Greece. This gave the Turks the long awaited opportunity to invade Cyprus with 40,000 troops under the guise of giving protection to the Turkish population there. The fact that this brought two NATO members, Greece and Turkey into conflict and almost to war with each other, created fear and confusion in western circles.

We were sent out to Ankara immediately to enter Cyprus in the wake of the first Turkish troops and cover the invasion. We had not reckoned with Turkish bureaucracy and procrastination! Along with a whole posse of other journalists we sat in Ankara for a fortnight, as virtual prisoners, as there were no means of leaving, putting pressure on the authorities to let us go to Cyprus, traipsing along each day to the government press conferences which, like all such press conferences, gave a rosy-coloured government viewpoint with not a real fact to be seen or heard. Correspondents tried desperately to make something out of nothing and send reports back home. Herr Pilz, a West German TV presenter, had his telephone report interrupted by the censor and told to continue in English because they couldn't understand his German! Most of the time we spent sunbathing around the hotel pool or drinking raki – the Turkish national aniseed flavoured drink, and kicking our heels in boredom. In the end we gave up and took the first available flight out, after the relaxation of the war emergency. One Lufthansa plane was allowed in to pick up stranded tourists and journalists.

Only a whole week later were we able to fly into Nicosia airport and see for ourselves what the invasion of Cyprus had done to the island. There were no hotels available any more, they were all packed with refugees from the Turkish occupied part of the island or journalists looking for stories. Eventually the receptionist at the Hilton hotel took pity on us and offered us a camp-bed, along with a group of other journalists in the hotel lobby. Even if it weren't the Hilton's usual standard of luxury, we were more than happy to accept. To hire a car – and there weren't many of those available either – we had to sign an agreement that we would accept all risks ourselves i.e. we were not insured and if the car were damaged or wrecked we would have to pay for it all! The Turks had laid lots of mines and already one TV crew had been blown up on one of the roads – so car hire firms were taking no more risks.

Cyprus had always been a bone of contention between Greeks and Turks. The Greek population made up over two thirds of the whole population and was largely more prosperous than the Turks, being, in general, like the Jews or Indians, a very business minded people and very industrious. Because of this business prowess and having strong lings with Greece the Turkish population had been at a distinct disadvantage.

Although the two groups had lived relatively amicably side by side for decades, the British occupation of the island after the collapse of the Ottoman Empire in 1878 changed all that. There was an increasingly vocal and then violent rebellion against British rule after the Second World War, by the Greek speaking population and led by the guerrilla organisation EOKA. The British, using their well-tried tactic of divide and rule, played the Turks off against the Greeks and fomented nationalist hatred which then festered long after independence in 1959. The Turkish invasion was simply a culmination of this hatred and bitterness, cementing the divisions between the two communities. Although Cyprus has been independent for many years now, it still has large British bases on it.

This beautiful island, which has been at the cross roads of so much history, is still redolent with it today: Moorish fortresses tower above Byzantine churches, memorials to the crusades next to mosques. It was here that Othello set up base for the Doge of Venice and where, according to mythology, Aphrodite rose from the waves of Paphos; the trading boats of Phoenicians, Greeks and Arabs called regularly at its ports. The snow-capped Rhodos mountains look out over fertile vineyards and orchards and idyllic little ports like Kyrenia enclose the crystal clear amethyst waters of the Mediterranean sea. In past times the narrow streets of Nicosia resounded to the hammering of coppersmiths and blacksmiths, the sewing machines of back-street tailors or the cries of shopkeepers and the two communities commuted freely all over the island. Since the invasion so much of this vibrant life has been lost, the ports of Kyrenia and Famagusta have become run-down and drab, the two parts of the island completely cut-off from each other and a permanent Turkish army of occupation installed in the Turkish section. I felt very unhappy returning to an island where I had only happy memories of friendship and hospitality from both Greeks and Turks, to find now only tension, fear and bitterness and a massive refugee problem – 200,000 Greek-Cypriots were made homeless by the Turkish invasion.

The first time I visited Cyprus I had the good fortune to meet that wily and capable diplomat, Archbishop Makarios, who steered his newly independent country through its first difficult years. That was in 1972 en route for Israel on a rusting old Greek passenger ship taking us and a group of pilgrims to the Holy Land. At that time we could travel the length and breadth of the island freely, speaking to Turks and Greeks.

In 1972 we were filming material for a short news item on the Munich Olympics when a group of Israeli sportsmen and women were massacred by the extremist Palestinian Black September group. In the aftermath we decided it would be useful to produce a report from Israel on the situation there and, if possible, provide some background information on the Israeli-Palestinian conflict.

We flew to Nicosia and took a cheap sea passage to the Israeli port of Haifa. The ship was for the cheaper end of the pilgrim market and life on board was a caricature of a 'cruise'. The restaurant with its wood panels and columns had seen better days. The ship was carrying well over its normal capacity and passengers had to eat in three shifts. If you arrived a few minutes late you missed the first course. Plates were swept off the table before you had finished the last mouthful because of the time pressure, and the food was barely edible. Our cabin was tiny and oppressively hot– it must have been originally designed for the cabin boys. I refused to sleep on the top bunk because of a big whirling fan, which I thought would decapitate me in the night, so close did it swing over the bed.

We spent a fortnight in Israel visiting the main cities and the vast sprawling Palestinian refugee camps. To wander around the old cities of Jerusalem or Bethlehem is to be transported back into biblical times: the narrow streets lined with small stores, selling carpets, embroidered dresses, pots and pans; handicraft workshops with sewing machines or small smithies; the sweep and swish of ankle-length clothing as the women pushed by with shopping on their heads, and the old orthodox Jews with their black hats and curls chatting in the shade of doorways. Here both Jews and Palestinians lived side by side, but the tension was underlined by the patrols of Israeli soldiers. In one of the back streets of Jerusalem I was filming an old Arab, crouching in his long white shirt and skull cap, slicing old tyres with a deadly sharp knife and making them into sandals. Someone must have whispered to him that I was filming because he suddenly jumped up and began menacing me with his knife, an expression of anger and insult on his face. I backed off quickly, apologising. Many people, particularly in Islamic countries, don't like being filmed (it is religiously offensive to make images of anyone), but such a reaction was unusual and perhaps underlined the tension and bad feeling in these sensitive areas. In the Gaza strip the wrecks of armoured vehicles from the Six Day War in 1967 were still scattered at the roadside and there were continuous Israeli check points.

The Palestinians here saw the Israelis as an army of occupation and their government as an alien one for the Jews only. So many of the laws and regulations were aimed against the Palestinians, they had few rights and were treated as second class citizens in their own country. Their land was taken from them, their agricultural produce was not allowed to compete with Jewish produce and their own elected representatives were either ignored or, if they became too vocal, deported.

We didn't even try to obtain accreditation because after the Munich massacre the Israelis were in the grip of a spy and terrorist paranoia and we would have had little chance of getting it, or at best been attached to an army press liaison officer. We were aware that our intended 10 minute report could never do justice to the complexities of the Israeli-Palestinian conflict. That was left to later years when, with the help of the journalist Hans Lebrecht and the courageous Israeli lawyer Dr. Felicia Langer, we were able to look at the situation in more depth.

We were lucky, on this occasion, to smuggle our film safely out of the country because only a few years later, in 1978, a friend of ours, the Cypriot journalist, Paniotis Paschalis, was arrested and given a five year jail sentence for taking photos, it was alleged, 'for the PLO'.

CHAPTER 3 – BEHIND ENEMY LINES
The Autumn of the Patriarch

Franco Spain, along with Portugal, was the last remaining vestige of pre- war fascism in Europe. Franco's bloody war against his own people, aided and abetted by Hitler Germany, had left the country traumatised and on its knees. The iron grip of his Falange party was still as firm as ever in 1973 when I was asked to go there after our successful assignment in Greece. Our task was to contact the underground opposition and report on the situation inside the country.

During this early period of working for the GDR solidarity with those peoples struggling for liberation was a top priority. This attitude was to change later as 'Realpolitik' or policy pragmatism took over and only subjects with a direct economic or political relevance for the GDR were of interest. A number of the then GDR party leadership had fought in the Spanish Civil War so a film from Franco's Spain found ready sympathy. I am to work with the same, older, West German colleague who accompanied me to Greece. He has a wide experience of underground work in the illegal German Communist Party after the war.

We meet in Paris where the Spanish opposition in exile is based. In a small office in the Quartier Latin we are welcomed by the widow of Julian Grimau, the anti-fascist leader who had been garrotted by Franco. She worked together with Marcos Ana, a leading Communist and poet who had been badly tortured and had spent 23 years in Franco's jails and was twice condemned to death. A poem he wrote in prison reveals the mental torture he went through:

'Tell me what a tree is like,
Tell me of the song of a river
When the birds lie upon it
Speak to me of the sea, speak to me too
Of the smell of the fields
Of the stars
Of the air
Talk to me of the horizon
Without bolts and without keys
Like the simple cottage of a poor man
Tell me what the kiss of a woman is like
Find me the word
For love; I have forgotten it.
Are the nights still perfumed
With the passion of lovers
Trembling under the moon?
Or is there only this pit,
The light of a grave
And the music of steps on stones?
Twenty-two years...
I have not forgotten
The size of things, their colour, their smell
I write
Falteringly – 'sea' – 'fields'
I say 'woods' and I have lost
The geometry of a tree.
I speak only to speak of the things
That the years have washed away.'

Today, seeing him, still working for the anti-fascist cause in his modest way it is impossible to believe that this slight figure with thinning hair has been to the edge of the abyss, but has not lost his faith in a better world. His eyes are large and dark like Picasso's and his face is taught with an expression of nervousness. He is already informed about our project but asks us for a few more details of what we wish to do and how we plan tackling it. He listens in silence while we explain our ideas, nodding approval and proceeds to jot down a couple of addresses for us. One is a lawyer in Madrid, and he says we should be careful not to be followed when we go to his office; the other is a former political prisoner who has been released following

Amnesty International taking up his case. "He is in no more danger," he tells us, "they will leave him alone now. He is old and in poor health but he can give you useful information."

We take Marcos Ana's advice, catching the overnight 'Costa del Sol' express from Paris down through Biarritz. He says that many wealthy tourists travel this way and the customs will be less likely to be as thorough as on the roads. His assumptions are correct: the guard takes our passports but our luggage, including my Arriflex camera, carefully hidden in a specially made leather brief case, is not looked at as we sleep peacefully in our bunks during the border crossing. We arrive in Madrid in early January and it is still very cold. We hire a small car, a Volkswagen beetle, and set out to locate our lawyer contact. We find his flat in a suburb south of the city. We park a few streets away and walk to the flat, making sure we are not followed. Sr. Lavanderos, as he is called, is a member of a young progressive lawyers' co-operative, specialising in cases of injustice at work or where small peasants are in conflict with large landowners. He welcomes us into his flat, furnished in the traditional style, simply and uncluttered, with sideboards and chairs of carved dark wood on a tiled floor. He indicates that he doesn't want to discuss our project in the house but will take us out somewhere where we can talk freely. He drives us to a small rustic restaurant near the centre of Madrid where, to the accompaniment of crispy sucking pig and a couple of bottles of Rioja we discuss details of our filming.

Our first risky task is to take shots of the infamous Carabanchel prison where most political prisoners, including the legendary trade union leader, Marcelino Camacho, are held. The day is swelteringly hot and our beetle hasn't the luxury of air conditioning. We drive out to Carabanchel on the outskirts of Madrid to do a reconnaissance. Klaus, my colleague, drives at a leisurely pace around the enormous complex so that I can work out where we can get the best shots. After we've done that, we drive some way away and into a quiet side road so that I can slip into the back of the car, get the camera ready and allow myself to be buried under a mound of clothing, made up of our coats and a blanket, as we had done in Greece. I can poke the camera lens through the coats and shoot as Klaus drives past the prison. I try to make myself comfortable, but it is impossible, and Klaus drives back towards the prison. To talk to me he sings in a mock-opera voice – a man talking to himself would look very suspicious! I think to myself that it is a good thing no one can actually hear him because he doesn't exactly have the dulcet tones of a Fischer-Dieskau. The journey back seems to be taking an eternity. I am dripping with sweat in the back and becoming impatient. "What the hell's the matter?" I ask. A rather apologetic song drifts back to me, "I think I've lost the way, I can't find the damned place anymore," he sings. After a fruitless drive down various streets and a good half an hour later I demand to be let out before I die of suffocation. Klaus relents. The next day, after I'd forced him to study the map closely again, we try once more and are successful this time. Through the camera I can clearly see the guards in their look-out towers staring in our direction – a very uncomfortable feeling.

We drive north through the mining area of Asturias, famous for its resistance to fascism and for the small town of Guernica which the Nazis razed to the ground. After the unsuccessful rebellion of the miners there in 1934 thousands were brutally murdered and 30,000 interned. The area is dominated by slate-grey hills and the slag heaps from the coal mines. The winter skies probably make it look darker and more depressing than it normally would be. It is still obviously poor and there is no colour to relieve the monotone of the view; even the people wear almost entirely black. On our journey through we are not able to estimate whether there is any resistance still today, but what is noticeable is that in every small village and on all the main roads into the towns there are Guardia Civil, with their typical black leather hats, their capes and machine guns, patrolling, always in twos.

In Barcelona comrades from the Catalonian party take us under their wing and make sure we are protected. One of them is a Catholic priest. We visit him in his church and find him undressing after the mass. He says he would rather not talk to us in the church, because the police have been visiting his masses again and may still be around. He tells us to come to the home of a lawyer friend of his where we can talk freely. "I don't see a contradiction in being a Communist and a Catholic at the same time", he says. He doesn't accept materialist philosophy but finds sense in Marx's economic ideas and the principles of economic justice. We film him in shadow so that his face is not recognisable.

On the last Sunday of every month patriotic citizens of Barcelona gather in the evening on the main square in front of the cathedral as a form of protest at Franco's suppression of their language and culture. Our friends offer to take us to watch and to film. We walk there through the narrow streets leading to the square and the comrades with us point out the green-grey buses parked ominously in all the side streets leading off the square. Inside are the notorious riot police, cooped up for hours like animals, waiting hungrily to be let out for the hunt. As the sun is setting knots of people begin coming together, then link arms and begin a traditional Catalan dance. The rhythm becomes more and more excited and the stamping more determined, then clenched fists are raised and from nowhere a banner appears calling for Catalan independence and slogans are shouted. We watch fascinated, shooting as much as we can, oblivious of things happening outside the immediate confines of the square. Suddenly I feel a thumping on my shoulders and our friend urges us to flee immediately. He points: from the side streets ugly groups of riot police, with their plastic visors down, shields and truncheons at the ready, are gathering, preparing to charge. As they begin to run so do we, clasping camera and tape recorder, down the first narrow, cobble-stoned alley-way where we dive into the first doorway we come across. Inside it is cool and dark. We find ourselves in a small chapel where we will be safe from the police. Through the closed door we can still hear the chanting of small groups and the stamp of running boots on the cobbles. With bated breath we wait a good hour until all is quiet outside so that we can emerge and disappear back to our hotel.

The person whose name Marcos Ana had given us in Paris, Miguel Pineda, lives in Valencia. His release from prison a year earlier had been due to international pressure initiated by Amnesty. He is now in his sixties and in obviously not very good health. We visit him in his small apartment in one of those enormous grey concrete housing complexes on the outskirts of the city. He is very willing to be interviewed despite the danger to himself. "They won't do anything more to me now", he says. His wife hovers, nervously in the background and is obviously of a different opinion. We see that he is no longer a physically strong man and the Spartan furnishings tell us that he does not live well on his meagre pension. We decide there and then to relinquish the idea of interviewing him. We don't feel it would be fair to risk his safety even if he is courageous enough to do so. We explain as best we can why we feel it is better not to film, thank him and his wife warmly and depart. Our return journey takes us through the Jarama Valley, that bare, wide river bed where the International Brigades strove to keep Franco out of Madrid in 1937. It is difficult now to imagine that over this red, rocky landscape thousands of young men from around the world gave their blood to defend a people they hardly knew, whose language few of them spoke, but whose struggle represented a fight for human dignity and freedom. Today as we drive through only the sound of insects cracks the silence and the clear blue sky looks down in pure innocence.

We take all our exposed film and tapes to the left luggage office of Madrid's main station. Klaus hides the luggage ticket in his shoe. Before leaving the country, if all goes well and we haven't been picked up, we will be able to collect it and leave, as we came, on the express train back to Paris via Biarritz. All our notes and the film list Klaus writes as separate letters couched in innocuous tourist chat to his wife. They can be disentangled and 'de-coded' on his return.

Like all our assignments we are so involved in shooting what we need that there is little time left to see the tourist attractions or to visit places we would like to see. We are determined, however, to fit in a quick visit to the magnificent Prado gallery in Madrid before our train leaves. We have literally two hours. It is impossible to see everything in that time and we decide not to try. We spend those two hours in fascinated contemplation of Goya's etchings, *Los Desastres de la Guerra* and are shocked, horrified and deeply moved by his incredible portrayal of man's inhumanity to man. We feel that in our miniscule way we are also contributing to that tradition with our modest film report.

CHAPTER 3 – BEHIND ENEMY LINES
Ireland – a war without end

The civil war in Ireland is a very complex one to fully understand and has dragged on for so long, that the rest of the world has forgotten about it. For the Irish, however, it is part of their daily lives and the fact that an army of occupation has been on the streets of this province since 1969 with still no political solution in sight, is something everyone in Europe, but particularly in Britain, ought to be ashamed of. The success mass civil rights movement of the sixties led to the army being called in and a bloody civil war followed.

Ireland has been occupied by the British for over 800 years, used as a cheap source of food for the mainland and as a source of cheap labour for British industries. It is a country in its own right with a distinct national culture more than 2,000 years old and its own Celtic language. The British, particularly since Cromwell, have used the Protestant church as their power base and discriminated against the Catholics. Traditionally, the landowners were British and Protestant, the peasants and workers, Catholic. English landownership was established in the Tudor period when the English tricked Irish Chiefs into incurring the confiscation of their estates, followed by massive clearances of peasants from the land. The Protestant Reformation in Ireland had merely meant the robbing of the church of its treasures and land, handing them over to English landowners. In the ensuing centuries the indigenous Irish population was subjected to virtual genocide: tens of thousands died in the famines created by English ownership of their land, thousands of others were forcibly evicted and turned into beggars or emigrants. Those remaining were second class citizens in their own country, prevented from full participation in the affairs of government and the economy by discriminatory laws.

In an attempt to head off the total loss of Ireland in face of the growing armed rebellion of the population the British government granted independence to the southern 26 counties, but retained control of the more industrialised and richer north, where the majority of the population was Protestant.

After partition in 1922, when the Irish Free State was created, the Protestants dominated the province of Ulster, still under British sovereignty. The Protestants in the north represented a privileged class: they owned most property, occupied the best jobs and ran the administration and police force. The Catholics were discriminated against in all areas of life and, until the early seventies, didn't even have the automatic right to vote – only householders could vote and most Catholics were tenants. Thus, although outsiders are told it is a religious war it is very largely a class war overlaid by religious bigotry and allegiance. Shortly after the British Army was sent over in 1969, the sovereign Northern Ireland parliament at Stormont was dissolved and Ireland again ruled directly from Westminster, thus effectively disenfranchising the population.

We went over to Ireland on filming assignments regularly during those early years of out and out civil war on the streets of Belfast and Derry. We worked closely with leaders of the Civil Rights movement like Madge Davison, a courageous young Communist who worked flat-out and non-stop over many years for this movement, advising victims of army violence, comforting the bereaved and giving political leadership to the struggle. She worked alongside Edwina Stewart, General Secretary of NICRA (Northern Ireland Civil Rights Association), and also a leading Communist. Both commanded wide respect, despite the strong religious convictions of most of the population, simply for their obvious devotion to the cause of human dignity and liberation. We valued the help given us by Betty Sinclair, Secretary of the Belfast Trades Council and one of the initiators of the first trade union conference on civil rights in Belfast where, for the first time in their lives old Catholic workers told their Protestant trade unionists what it was like to be second class citizens.

In those early days, in the late sixties, before the waves of bombings had begun, Belfast was quite a pleasant town, characterised by Victorian imperial buildings in the neo-classical style and its streets alive with an industrious people going about their business and its pubs and clubs at night packed with jovial customers, the banter of men relaxing after a day's work and the strains of that melancholic music so typical of Ireland. Even then, though, the Protestants kept to their part of the city and the Catholics to theirs. There were a few mixed marriages and families who refused to be locked in their own ghettos, but these were later driven out by the fire-bombers, the vigilantes and sheer fear. The Falls Road was the main Catholic street and the Shankill the Protestant one, an invisible wall divided the two areas – later the British army erected a real enormous corrugated tin 'wall' between them. The tree-lined better middle class housing suburbs were Protestant and the outlying, sprawling council estates Catholic. On the latter were hundreds of men without work. We met families where several generations had known nothing but the dole.

The Protestants were determined to maintain their privileges, rather like the whites in South Africa, they weren't interested in progress or democracy. They looked back with nostalgia to 1690 when their hero, the Protestant King William of Orange, landed in Ireland to defeat the Catholic army of King James II. They couldn't see their own psychological dilemma of being Irish but pretending desperately to be British, worshipping the Queen and the English way of life. Their hatred of Catholics, 'the popists' and their bigotry, expressed in their uniforms, their marches and bands, had much in common with the nazi movement. Although many of our friends and helpers were of Protestant background they identified with the progressive sections of the Catholic community and often with the IRA, which was fighting British occupation.

In our reports we tried to clarify the background to the conflict, to explain it in terms of the history of Ireland and British colonial domination, to show how the IRA, however repugnant one might find its methods of struggle, was a logical product of the oppression and was a genuine expression of the people's determination to be free, enjoying widespread support amongst the people. The way all the other media portrayed the conflict was as a religious feud or simply a series of terrorist killings, totally out of its political context. Under the pretext of "objective reporting" the western media described the bombings and killings, the demonstrations and counter demonstrations, but hardly attempted to put all this in a context that would help their audiences understand what was going on, that there were genuine grievances in Ireland, ignored by successive British governments and that now the sores of these grievances had burst. Already by the early seventies, in the aftermath of the Bloody Sunday massacre of 13 innocent civil rights marchers by British paratroopers, on 31 January 1972 open war had broken out.

When we arrive there is a thick fog and Belfast takes on an even more unreal character: people loom suddenly out of the grey, cars travel slowly like hearses and the army's Saracen armoured cars rumble up the narrow streets like dinosaurs emerging from the swamps. Belfast has become the front line and we find ourselves rushing from one incident to the next or hiding behind the barricades of burning buses while the army shoots their deadly plastic bullets wildly at anything that moves. These bullets, supposedly meant only to hurt after being aimed at people's legs from a long distance, have been responsible for the most horrendous maiming and deaths of civilians after they have been shot in the face at short range. We are given several of these plastic and rubber bullets as 'evidence'(It is illegal to have such bullets in one's possession).

Because of its brutality towards the civilian population, the British Army is hated by the Catholic section of the population and by those who believe in a united Ireland. Madge Davison, the Assistant General Secretary of the Northern Ireland Civil Rights Movement, takes us to the Turf Lodge housing estate to meet children of interned parents, now being cared for by relatives. The parents of these children, some still toddlers, have been picked up by the British Army, off the street or direct from their houses and the children left with no one to care for them. These parents are worried sick about their children and despite appeals to the Army to at least let them telephone friends or arrange for the children to be looked after, they are held incommunicado and then interned under the notorious 'imprisonment without trial' laws of Northern Ireland. Without the excellent and supportive network of neighbours and relatives in the Catholic areas these children would be left to fend for themselves, often without knowing where their parents are or when they would return. It is these kinds of incidences, and the one described here is no exception, that cause the hatred to fester.

Everywhere one goes in Belfast there are crowds of kids on the streets. The excitement of soldiery and 'war' keeps them away from school, away from parental care, playing at war games on the streets. The biggest thrill is to hurl stones at the British armoured cars and then run as the soldiers pour out and start firing rubber bullets.

These children have known nothing else but civil strife and killing on their streets and the incidences of bed-wetting and more serious forms of psychological disturbance are worryingly high. Knowing only violence as children, they see it as a solution to problems in adult life too and thus provide the IRA or the British Army with a steady stream of recruits.

The Europa hotel where we stay has already, by 1972, been bombed innumerable times and is now surrounded by a high barbed wire fence and tight security on the gates. Each time we wish to enter our bags are searched and our identity checked, but even this isn't sufficient to prevent the IRA from penetrating the area. Shortly after midnight during one of our stays there we are awoken to a loud explosion and a shattering of glass, as our windows cave in under the force of the blast. Luckily we aren't hurt but breakfast has to be eaten elsewhere as the dining room is a sea of glass fragments. At night time driving around Belfast is also, a risky business because most of the street lamps have been smashed and the British Army armoured cars career through the narrow streets without lights. We have several narrow escapes from being crushed by one of these beasts. There are shootings each day and going to funerals becomes a daily occupation for us.

The urban war in Northern Ireland is unlike a traditional war where there are clear front lines. In the cities the army can be and is sniped at from roof-tops, windows or side streets. This makes the army very nervous and trigger-happy. Once we are following an armoured car; the army drives with the back doors half open and two soldiers sit, their guns cocked in the open door, ready to spring out at short notice. We want a travelling shot of this, so I raise the camera and film through the windscreen while my colleague drives close behind the army vehicle. When you are looking through the camera viewfinder you become so concerned and pre-occupied with the aesthetics of the picture, the framing, the focus, the movement, that the reality as such becomes secondary. That is why I am unaware of the fact that one of the soldiers sitting in the back feels threatened by my camera and raises his rifle and points it directly at my head. Only the intervention of my colleague pulling the camera down and telling me to stop filming brings about the realisation of the danger. A camera can look somewhat like a bazooka to the untrained eye, and who knows what that soldier thinks I am doing; in situations like this they act first and ask questions afterwards!

After two years of continued conflict Belfast now resembles a real war zone. Gone are the relaxed citizens, the welcoming pubs and shops. Everywhere is boarded up, shop fronts covered with wire mesh, houses and businesses gutted by fire, central shopping streets cordoned off with barbed wire and checkpoints, soldiers with guns at the ready running from street to street or watching from sandbagged sentry posts. The people themselves now rushed everywhere, had no time to stop and chat, their faces tense, drawn and bitter.

On this occasion we hope to be able to present both sides of the conflict in some depth, in order to help our audience understand what the issues are. By letting leading spokespeople from both sides of the divide articulate their philosophy and aims, and by showing the consequences of the fighting, we hope also to communicate the feelings and emotions involved.

To interview the para-military organisations is not an easy task. The UVF (Ulster Volunteer Force) is the most difficult because we have no good contacts in that direction. The UVF has just issued a press statement, saying they will kill innocent Roman Catholics as well as known IRA members, in answer to IRA threats. After knocking on a number of wrong doors, we eventually find Mr. McKeague who publishes *Loyalist News*, a right wing Protestant paper, and promises to bring us to the UVF. It takes a few more visits before he gives us a firm appointment. We arrive at the agreed spot and are taken by car through a maze of darkened streets to the Protestant part of the city. We are on our way to the military council HQ of the UVF, but for the last section of the journey our eyes are bound so that we can't see where we are going. The UVF is now a banned organisation and they don't wish to risk discovery.

We are led through a hallway, into a big room. Behind a table two commanders of the organisation are sitting and are prepared to answer our questions, above their heads a painting full of pathos of a fallen protestant soldier; the atmosphere is stiff and unfriendly. They explain that they are totally opposed to the integration of the six counties of Northern Ireland into the Republic and will resist it with all means. They are prepared to fight all subversive forces, whether the Provisional IRA, Official IRA or Communists. Communists have no place in a Protestant country they say; everywhere the Catholics rule is a breeding place for Communism. Although the Communist Party in Ireland is respected it is very small, with little influence. Here the extremist Protestants reveal their basically right wing position. Many of their organisations have close links with the neo-fascist National Front in England and are characterised by their bigotry and racism. The interview is over and Klaus asks me if everything is in the can. I check the camera and realise I have forgotten to put a new roll of film in the magazine. It couldn't have happened at a worst time. Luckily our UVF commanders are willing to go through the questions again for us and this time I make sure there is enough film.

The Northern Ireland police and the Ulster Defence Regiment have always carried arms and been the military arm of the Protestant ruling class, and it is only when they seem incapable of controlling the deteriorating situation that Protestant extremists form organisations of their own outside these official bodies, but at the same time having close links with them. Many members of the UDA (Ulster Defence Association) or UVF are also, at the same time, members of the police or armed forces. Both the UDA and UVF are involved in the bloody individual acts of assassination against either individual Catholics or suspected members of the IRA. At that time the IRA was more accessible. It was keen to achieve publicity for its cause, to be seen as a credible and effective military organisation.

Almost every progressive Catholic family has members or relatives either in it or with close contacts to it. Martin Lynch, a good friend of ours (today an acclaimed Irish playright) who lives on the Turf Lodge estate takes us into one of the bars frequented by leaders of the IRA. Here we are introduced to a number of legendary figures, many of whom are now dead. On estates like Turf Lodge and Andersonstown built on the outskirts of the city, away from the affluent Protestant middle class, there is mass unemployment and deprivation. It is on estates like these that the IRA has its strongholds and in fact, for a time, it literally controlled them as 'liberated zones'. When the British army went in it was with the utmost brutality; we are shown houses which look as if wild animals have gone berserk in them: curtains and bedding torn, doors splintered and smashed, record players broken, pet dogs shot, all in the name of searching for terrorists or suspected weapons stores. It is no wonder the people feel resentful and see the British as an occupation force.

Our friend takes us to interview the Provisional IRA. We are led through narrow streets behind the Falls Road and into one of the terraced houses. There in the attic room we are greeted by three young officers. They refuse to have their faces filmed so we throw our light onto the wall behind them with a poster on it showing the brutally battered face of a prisoner in Long Kesh – the infamous British internment camp for Irish prisoners. These three officers give us an impassioned picture of the occupation, reiterate that Ireland is a separate country with a separate culture and only when British troops are removed will peace be restored, they say. The following day Martin takes us to Derry (the Protestants prefer to give it its English name Londonderry) on the north coast. Here the IRA has created a 'no-go' area for British troops, called Free Derry. The area is marked by huge painted signs on the walls of the houses. To enter the area we are issued with special press credentials as if we are entering a separate country. With our press cards we can wander freely and talk to the Catholic families living in the Bogside. The tiny streets and long terraces of narrow houses with their small back yards look very much like those northern industrial towns of Britain that Engels wrote about almost a century ago. Even the people look as if they belong in a past era.

On 6 February, a month later, we are again in Northern Ireland, this time there is to be another massive civil rights march in answer to Bloody Sunday. Everyone expects another massacre or at least a bloody conflict and so the world's press is here and the country is like a fortress. On every street corner armoured cars, sentries and barbed wire. On every road cars are stopped and checked. Shopkeepers have boarded up their shop fronts and there is only the odd person on the streets. It is still wintry and cold. I am wearing a Basque beret and Klaus. a fur hat with a blue, red and white scarf. We are naively unaware of the symbolic significance of our clothing, but in times of passionate conflict and nationalist fervour colours and symbols have a very important role to play. In Ireland this is particularly so. Anything green is automatically Republican, anything orange is Protestant.

An army patrol stops us on the way to Newry, where the march is to take place and tells me to remove my beret because it looks like part of a Provisional IRA uniform. Shortly afterwards Klaus is told to remove his scarf by some civil rights workers because it contains the British colours and some people might get the wrong idea and take offence. Again a soldier challenges us and asks Klaus if he is Russian because of his fur hat. We end up freezing in the cutting wind, but feel safer without our inappropriate pieces of clothing!

Before the march is due to start the army brings up dozens of armoured cars and unrolls lengths of barbed wire alongside the road.

Although it is broad daylight the soldiers in the barracks are having their faces smeared with black paint, making them look fearsome and war-like. They take up positions from vantage points along the way. It is hard to believe that this is ' peaceful' Europe in the 1970s, it is more like Vietnam. Here are a people marching for rights which others in Western Europe take for granted and the British government sends in a huge army, prepared to shoot and kill.

We stick a large T and a V on to the side of our car with gaffer tape so that we are clearly recognisable as press. Eventually there are 40,000 people marching. They are asked by the stewards to keep absolutely silent in memory of the dead of Bloody Sunday. There are a few skirmishes, but no shooting – the march is a huge success. We are happy with our material. We have good interviews with the civil rights leaders and with Bernadette Devlin, the 19 year-old firebrand of the republican movement and Britain's youngest MP. We have lots of footage of the army of occupation and of the march itself, we can now return to our hotel and have a good night's sleep – if the bombers allow us to.

What most people have failed to understand about the British occupation of Ireland is that the problem could have been solved years ago with the political will. Can one believe, too, that the whole might of the British state and armed forces is not capable of defeating a small, amateur armed group like the IRA? No, the truth lies deeper: for Britain, Ireland is an ideal training ground both for the police and the army. Where else in the world can you provide raw recruits with a taste of real war and give them experience of controlling civil disturbances? So much of modern policing methods in mainland Britain today have been tried and tested in Ireland, particularly the refined means of surveillance and control. It is a sad reflection on the attitudes of successive British governments which have always used and abused the Irish people over centuries.

CHAPTER 3 – BEHIND ENEMY LINES
The gathering of the veterans

Our colleagues in the Federal Republic were slowly becoming known in neo-Nazi circles and were finding it more difficult to penetrate their organisations. So we were asked, as a 'London firm' to undertake an important job. On the North Sea coast of the Federal Republic, not too far from Hamburg, is a large monument dedicated to the submarine crews who lost their lives in the Second World War. This monument is looked after by a monument preservation committee and is a favourite place of pilgrimage for former nazi officers, many of whom are now securely ensconced in prominent positions in the West German hierarchy. Each year they have a commemoration service, where 'old comrades' come together, where the Swastika is openly displayed (although its public display is against the law) and old memories and aspirations re-ignited.

We write an official letter to the monument committee, saying that we are preparing a series of films on war monuments and would like to make a pilot programme about this one and interview a few old soldiers. I didn't see it as necessary to explain exactly what we intended doing because it would have resulted in a point blank refusal to film. As a journalist one's job is to ferret out and expose injustice and malpractice and to provide information on which the general public can make assessments and decisions. If certain organisations, governments or institutions prefer to hide things from the general public, then I will see it as my duty to break that wall of secrecy. Nothing that is ethical, legitimate and in the public interest needs to be kept secret. If there is nothing to hide, there is nothing to fear from genuine journalistic investigation.

RED REPORTER
COVERT CORRESPONDENT FOR EAST GERMANY

We know that there is a special ceremony planned for this year, where many old nazis, former officers from the Wehrmacht and SS men will come together to reminisce over old times. So that when the committee replies to our request, saying they will be only too glad to accommodate us, but wish to know a few more details about our project, we tell them that we will come over, introduce ourselves and perhaps film something of the ceremony at the same time.

The monument is on a wind-swept stretch of the North Sea coast and even under normal circumstances not a very inviting place to be. The monument committee has its headquarters nearby and we are invited to meet and have drinks. I feel very uncomfortable amongst these old men, asking penetrating questions. I always have the feeling that I am transparent, that they will see through our camouflage, but as usual they are soon put at ease by our guarded but straightforward answers. We are taken into their confidence and are told that it was a great pity that England and Germany didn't fight together against the real threat, the Russians. Hitler never really wanted to fight England, they maintain, it was a big mistake. They proceed to tell us stories about the war, how they torpedoed English cargo ships or escaped the destroyers which were tracking them. One of them tells me what a great time he had in an English prisoner-of-war camp and how he cheated the guards by sewing pound notes into the hem of his jacket so that they wouldn't be found when he was allowed out. For these men, it seems, the war was one big game, which they temporarily lost.

The monument itself is a tall granite stone structure rising sharply upwards into the sky, reminiscent of a submarine periscope, below is a dimly-lit, bunker-like chamber with the names of fallen sailors inscribed on the walls and suitably heroic inscriptions. On the day of the ceremony this vault is decorated with the old nazi banners, their swastikas prominently displayed. Those who arrive for the ceremony, in their black leather coats and with suitably stiff expressions, march into the chamber to pay homage to their fallen, accompanied by the music of old marching songs.

The atmosphere is uncanny, surreal almost, of a forgotten past still alive down here in the bowels of the earth. Back on top the faithful then gather around the screw of the German battleship, Prinz Eugen, which was sunk off the coast of Argentina and the hulk was later taken by the United States navy to the Marshall Islands and used by them when testing their atomic bombs on Bikini Atoll. Several of the men had brought along model battleships, carefully painted with names, flags and swastikas, which they placed alongside the bronze screw of the Prinz Eugen. They stand around and chat to each other in subdued voices.

Although we have been allowed to film the ceremony, as the only journalists present, some veterans are not been too happy to see us here; they undoubtedly have much to hide from prying reporters. Others, though, are quite willing to talk and we are able to obtain some useful interviews which reveal clearly that there are still a large number of people in West Germany who have drawn no lessons from the war and the defeat of Hitler. They still dream of a powerful Germany, conquering the 'lost lands', but are of course very circumspect about the methods that should or could be used to realise their aims. Some of them still hold high positions in the West German establishment or have connections to it. There has been little real denazification here, the wolves have simply donned sheep's clothing.

This little story had its epilogue. As luck would have it someone from the monument committee happened to see the programme, made from our material, and was understandably upset. They wrote to us asking if we had sold the material to the GDR. We replied politely and truthfully that the sales side of our work was dealt with by our Scandinavian agency and that they should approach it if they wanted further information.

They were not satisfied with this and got in touch with WDR (Westdeutsche Rundfunk), telling them the story. We later received a call from the WDR correspondent in London who tried to pump us about who we worked for and where our films were sold. We told him the same thing. In the end a report was shown on West German TV purporting to reveal a GDR media conspiracy. A member of the monument committee was interviewed and a copy of our letter to the committee, on our headed note-paper was shown.

The report itself was surprisingly weak and without real evidence; no attempt had been made to talk to us directly or to follow up the leads offered. There was the usual smear, picked up from an old *Bild-am-Sonntag* (a leading West German Sunday paper) story, of trying to link us with the Staatssicherheit (State Security), maintaining that our material went straight to the Stasi headquarters, implying that we were spies, not journalists. Some time after the programme was shown I heard from one of my friends, a former student colleague in Babelsberg, now living in Vienna, that he had been approached by the programme makers and asked about me and what I was doing. How did they get such leads? It appeared more likely that it was they who were working closely with their own security services and that the shoe was on the other foot!

The forerunner of the above incident took place in 1977, but had more far-reaching repercussions. At the time inter-German relations were at a low point. Towards the end of December 1976 the GDR had expelled Lothar Loewe, a well-known TV presenter, from East Berlin. A short time later *Der Spiegel* accused the Verfassungschutz (West German Special Branch) of illegally spying on the atom physicist Klaus Traube. *Bild am Sonntag* came to their defence by hitting out in the other direction with a strident headline: "Red reporters camouflaged as Swedes" and with the sub-heading: GDR television has a Swedish firm working for it in the Federal Republic – these films are also used by the Ministry for State security in East Berlin." One could search the article in vain for any evidence to support their accusation. "Security experts are convinced that their material and their knowledge is evaluated by the East Berlin Secret Service" – that was all they had to support their story!

In Sweden the story touched a sensitive nerve and there was a demand for an apology. The Swedish magazine *Lektyr* questioned Nordreporter's director about his being called "Spy Chief" in the article, and described him thus: "He is approaching retirement. A smallish man with greying hair and a slight German accent, although he has lived in Sweden for the last 34 years. He lives with his wife and daughter in a very ordinary rented flat in Aspudden, just outside Stockholm. If anyone told the neighbours that this small, shy man they may bump into on the stairs is the boss of an international spy network they would probably collapse in a fit of laughter or see it as a very poor joke".

Our director explained to the journalist interviewing him that he was a businessman and that if the East German security people wanted to watch his programmes, they were welcome to do it for days on end if they so wished. "I sell programmes to East German TV", he said, "and I get paid for them and that is all that interests me". The journalist, Per Johansson tried to explain the background for his readers: "In today's West Germany spies are being demasked everywhere. On almost every street corner you can spot agents. Outside observers say that the country is in the process of becoming a first class police state and – as far as spies and terrorists are concerned – is in the grip of a permanent psychosis."

CHAPTER 4 – NEW APPROACHES TO FOREIGN REPORTING
The series *Everyday Life in the West*

Our real boss, as I indicated earlier, was not the nominal director in Stockholm but the 'inspector'. He was a short, rotund Bavarian in his mid- forties, hyper-active, a chain-smoker and someone who always needed to be going somewhere. Most of his life was spent sitting in aeroplanes between Zurich, Berlin and Stockholm or racing down the autobahn in his Mercedes.

In a rare moment of intimacy he told me that he had been called-up into the nazi Wehrmacht shortly before the end of the war as a raw 16 year-old. He had been detailed to a firing squad, but had refused to shoot a Russian prisoner. For this he had been court-martialled, but escaped a death sentence himself because of his tender age. I don't know how far this story was true but I heard it from others too. After the war he joined the young communists, the Free German Youth – an organisation banned in the Federal Republic. He was arrested several times and beaten up by US troops for hoisting the GDR flag on public buildings or handing out leaflets in front of the bases. His bravado and keenness obviously captured the attention of the party in the GDR and he was asked, in the early fifties, whether he would be willing to shoot news footage for the infant GDR television. He began with an ancient Arriflex 16mm camera and a battered beetle Volkswagen and that, in essence, was the beginning of the company.

During those early years when the GDR was a pariah among nations and suffering a harsh economic blockade anyone, including journalists, who worked for it faced harassment and even imprisonment. This applied particularly to those working in the Federal Republic. Our boss, along with other progressive journalists suffered regular harassment: flats broken into and searched, being threatened and beaten up and documents sequestrated. His services were also used by other sectors of industry in the GDR as a means of by-passing the embargoes. With his double citizenship he could travel easily throughout Europe, obtaining materials, spares and equipment sorely needed in the war-ravaged GDR. This work gave him an almost 'untouchable' status. He had connections to the highest organs of party and state. These connections were to serve us well in the early years of our work, when we often had to fight censorship and the sheer cowardice or fear of television department heads, in getting our films shown. On many occasions he had to go right 'to the top' to ensure us a place in the programming.

The constant sniping and persecution of journalists working for the GDR by Western countries made it impossible for them to continue their work, and for Adlershof (where GDR television headquarters were) the urgent question arose: how to maintain the supply of news material from the other side? The West Germans spoke openly about a "war of the air-waves" and they really did go to war against the GDR's fledgling media.

This situation forced a solution: co-operation between a friendly firm on neutral territory, which could employ its own journalists and cameramen and sell its film material to the GDR. This would afford the teams a certain protection by giving them a sorely needed legitimacy, as employees of a neutral and respected country. Franz, 'the inspector', found a partner in the form of an Austrian businessman who had settled in Sweden and become a naturalised Swedish citizen.

The latter was looking for new business opportunities and the idea of running a small TV agency appealed to him. The business was duly registered with the Royal Patent and Registration Office on 22 August 1962. Nordreporter AB, Auth. Press and TV Agency, was launched with headquarters in Stockholm. On the firm's notepaper it boasted offices in the FRG, Rome, Amsterdam and London, Brussels, Paris, Geneva and Oslo, and this was true even if most of those offices consisted of one free-lance cameraman. In later years this number was severely reduced by economic exigencies.

People were recruited to the new firm from among activists in the peace movement and left politics. A positive attitude to the GDR was, of course, also a prerequisite. All of us apart from me were self-taught. Some had a little journalistic experience or photographic knowledge, but in the main knowledge and expertise was picked up as we went along.

The severe problems faced working on 'the other side', the tricks one had to use, the subterfuge and brazenness, were one side of the coin, the other comprised the difficulties faced by those in Adlershof who were responsible for completing the editing and putting their names to the finished product: the fear of deviating from the Party line and of facing disciplinary proceedings for negligence was a constant preoccupation of programme editors and meant that only those reports or films approved by the Party's Agitation and Propaganda department were given the green light without problems.

Every other item had to go through the 'Abnahme Komitees' (vetting committees) where anything which could possibly offend or be open to question would be eliminated, ensuring one anodyne 60 programme after another, where every interview partner, whether priest or conservative, sounded like a mouthpiece of the Socialist Unity Party. The worst thing about this system was that those in responsible positions became increasingly censorious and less flexible the farther down the hierarchy they were, interpreting policies 250%, and the only way of circumventing them was to appeal right to the top – a means open to very few.

A number of our best programmes and those which found most resonance amongst audiences were often only given a programme slot because Franz, using his status, by-passed the normal channels and was granted permission from someone near the top. Because of our involvement on the ground, actually producing the material and our commitment to what we produced, knowing it to be true and journalistically sound, we played no part in the internal battles over editing and programming. We left all that to Franz and he, intentionally, kept us very much in the dark about the Byzantine methods used and battles waged. Only later did it become more apparent and the implications clearer.

Despite the existence of the National Front (a body comprising all the 'democratic' parties – CDU, NDPD, Peasants Party and LDPD) no one ever questioned the fact that it was the SED which called the tune and determined the policies of television. Each department had its party organisation, which included almost all employees, because if you weren't a member you could virtually forget promotion into a responsible position. Much of each department's time would be taken up with party meetings, party schools or lectures, but all decisions or course changes came from above, to be carried out by those below. Almost everyone complained and bellyached about the restrictions, pettiness and fear, but in the end almost everyone went along with it; those that didn't suffered the consequences. There were those who lost their jobs in Adlershof, other film-makers like Frank Beyer, went from one banned film to another or Jürgen Böttcher who spent months without being allowed to make a film; Hans Bentzien who was demoted from Minister of Culture for allowing a questionable film through the tight censorship; others were simply sent into the wilderness altogether.

It is perhaps difficult to understand why so many allowed this situation to continue and became willing accomplices to it. I feel, as in my own case (although I was not party to the internal debates and struggles), that the idea of a better society, a more humane one, built on social conscience not on greed and rampant individualism, kept people going and led to an acceptance of 'temporary' deviations or minor injustices for the greater cause.

I always found it very difficult to understand how, for instance, the news programme, *Aktuelle Kamera*, could be so boringly bad and monotonous and that nothing was done about it. Everyone saw it as a catastrophe; the standing joke was that it was watched each evening by two people only: Erich Honecker, the party leader, and the 'Mann vom Dienst' (the person responsible for checking the programme output). It served only to encourage people to watch the West's alternative Tagesschau and appeared to be tailored to achieve just that. A western agent couldn't have done a better job if he had been in sole command.

The endless items of State visits, interminable protocol, Honecker shaking hands or giving speeches; his congratulatory birthday telegrams to various obscure heads of state would be read out in full and so it went on. The *Aktuelle Kamera* became a sort of court report. The top party and government people would watch it with stop-watches, timing their appearances and complaining if someone else had more coverage. Honecker once had a cameraman hauled over the coals because he had filmed him looking pale and off-colour whereas another member of the Central Committee (who'd just returned bronzed from holiday) appeared in the same news brimming with health and vigour.

Willi Stoph, president of the Volkskammer (State parliament), had a whole stack of videos at home, of himself taken on various state occasions, like a collection of holiday snaps. The news, like the party newspaper *Neues Deutschland*, was usually vetted personally by Honecker before it could go out and this is why late, but vital news items were often omitted because they came in too late for the vetting process. If unapproved things did slip through then the head of the Department of Agitation and Propaganda in the Central Committee would be on the line immediately afterwards demanding scalps! This situation became increasingly worse and entrenched in the later years of the Honecker regime.

In 1974 Franz managed to find the partner in Adlershof we needed in order to break out of the narrow field of short news items and allow us to deal with issues in more depth and in a more adventurous way. He had won the co-operation of a young ex-student from the journalistic department of Leipzig University, who had just completed her doctorate on television documentaries. Her name was Dr. Sabine Katins. The relationship between Franz, the man of action, and Dr. Katins, the one with the necessary theory and knowledge of film making, proved to be very fruitful for all of us.

In the early years and the initial period with the "Katins' Group" there was little time to reflect on our working relationship or on the wider questions of socialism and media policies in the GDR, because we were filming and travelling almost non-stop. Initially I was deeply satisfied to be able to cover the struggles of ordinary people for work, dignity and human rights, to communicate the tragedies and exhilaration of the liberation struggles.

With each year the demands on us increased, the areas we covered expanded, our freedom to operate effectively was extended and we progressed from making short news items to full length documentaries. 1973-77 were the years of our big reportage films – 40 or 45 minutes, like *The Men of Kent, South Africa – the divided country*, and *What does the West German citizen know of the GDR*. In this sense we didn't have much cause to question the whole basis of media politics in the GDR, of which we were only vaguely aware. Our area of responsibility was also relatively unproblematic; we could report things as we found them.

Those responsible for internal coverage or reporting from the other socialist countries were continually walking a bouncy tightrope. Franz often told us that we were lucky not to be on the front line and to have to go through the debilitating process of dealing with the bureaucracy of television and the party, to emerge from the bitter ideological struggles and in-fighting and still have the energy to keep going.

We were kept in the dark about the struggles Franz often had with the hierarchy in getting some of our films transmitted. *What does the West German citizen know about the GDR* – a series of interviews with a cross section of people from the FRG was one such film, which was only shown after Franz went to the top and got Honecker's approval. Each film or programme had to be fought for and Franz was only able to win by using his valuable connections or dubious machinations, methods which were fraught with dangers and which, in the end, proved his undoing.

I was unwittingly involved in one such effort when Franz asked me to spend a week in Geneva as chauffeur and general assistant to Frau Adamek, wife of the director of GDR Fernsehen, who was shooting some scenes for her own drama with Renate Richter from the Berliner Ensemble and a Soviet actress. There were only a few scenes, to be shot in the United Nations building and they could have just as easily been done in Berlin, but obviously the opportunity of a week in Switzerland was too good to be missed. She seemed to spend much of her time shopping in the big stores (to which I had to drive her in a large hired Mercedes) and very little directing the actresses. This was just one of the 'services' Franz felt obliged to provide in order to maintain credit in the ruling circles.

Such methods are only effective as long as the connections remain in place, but in the meantime create not a few enemies. The death of Werner Lamberz in a helicopter crash in 1978 was a severe blow to the Katins' Group because he was one of those to whom Franz had ready access and who was apparently less of a bureaucrat.

Many of the petty frustrations or problems involved in getting our films shown were spared us, the makers in the outside world, and we were thus unaware of the often primitive level of discussion involved, of the narrow-minded attitudes, the censorship and arrogance of those in power. Our film-making skills were improving, our films were becoming better and better, under Katins' leadership we were winning and retaining an audience, which recognised our commitment, honesty and originality. We were optimistic about the future, about the steady improvement of life for people in the GDR, of the expansion of freedoms and democracy.

Towards the end of 1975 Franz surprised us with a new concept. We were to supply ideas and material for a new bi-monthly series, beginning in January. Each programme would be 30 minutes long and the series would be called *Alltag im Westen* (Everyday Life in the West). We had no time to prepare a few programmes in advance. For our small group (four two- person teams only) it was an enormous amount of work and a real challenge. We worked flat out, following with avid interest what was happening in our immediate environment – special events, personal stories or problems, anything which we felt would make an interesting, informative and entertaining half-hour.

Even in the FRG the series Alltag im Westen won recognition: *Der Spiegel*, the respected West German political weekly magazine, in an extremely critical report on GDR television called, *My arms fall asleep, I'm falling asleep*, said that only the productions of Dr. Sabine Katins were excluded, "The films produced by her for the series *Everyday Life in the West* are of an admirable quality".

Reports such as 'What does the West German citizen know about the GDR' – a collection of opinions, "are, even with their one-sided commitment, sensitively made, and have helped GDR television achieve a rare political success with the public." (*Der Spiegel* Nr. 35/1979). What gave our films their special character was our preparedness to let people themselves speak and give their views. We kept commentaries to an absolute minimum.

Most documentarists – at that time anyway – used people often as visual backdrops for their own opinions and commentary. We let people tell us what they wanted to say. Of course it had to be edited, but it had much more a ring of authenticity about it than if we had just mediated. Thus we made a virtue out of necessity – because we had to be anonymous and couldn't appear in front of the camera as commentators, we were obliged to rely much more heavily on first hand accounts by those who appeared in our films. Franz had the ability to fire one's enthusiasm. At the end of every conference we had he would give us a pep talk on the international situation and the urgency of our work and how important it was in building a strong socialist GDR. He would stress the international solidarity aspect and the global implications of the ideological struggle. I returned back home each time with new enthusiasm and energy. It is clear that our divorce from everyday reality in the GDR, the bitter bureaucracy and sectarian struggles enabled us to overlook the problems of 'real existing Socialism'. Because we were on the front line, immersed in and confronted by the harsh battles against capitalist injustice in all its forms, we pushed uncomfortable GDR realities into the background.

In retrospect this was undoubtedly wrong, but who is not wiser with hindsight?

I had, through my mother who lived in Potsdam and was an English lecturer at the teachers training college there, and through my wife's family in Berlin quite close links to GDR reality. Through my mother I met many of her colleagues, students and neighbours. I also spent lengthy periods in the GDR with my wife and children, so I did have a taste of everyday life. Through my mother particularly I met many outstanding SED members – not the mass of careerists and opportunists, although I met these as well – but those who in their everyday lives and in their relationships with others tried to behave as communists. My contacts and acquaintances were, though, limited and to a certain extent selected and there was much that remained hidden to me, as it did to many others, even those living permanently in the GDR.

In Adlershof the success of the Katins Group had also created enemies. Its innovative style, its apparent ability to circumvent much of the petty censorship all programme makers had to undergo, had given it the reputation of having privileged status. This was compacted by the fact that the door to the department was always permanently locked and no outside people had access. Franz himself was very free with his largesse and it appeared that he had no shortage of money. This and the fact that all our films were made in' western' countries, costing rare hard currency, led to rumours of our unlimited resources, some of which other film makers would have desperately loved to get their hands on. As always when truth is withheld, rumours gain currency. It was believed that we earned enormous salaries and led lives of luxury. The fact that we worked incredibly hard, produced more films than any of our colleagues in similar departments, were always conscious of keeping costs to a minimum because we knew who was paying the bills, and were always paid below the current western rates, was never disclosed.

We were shadowy, anonymous figures, never seen. For many years even those colleagues in the department who edited our work never knew our names or could fit a face to the voice on the sound tape. Our isolation from our colleagues in Adlershof was justified by the genuine need to maintain our security, but was also a means of keeping us away from the decision-making centres and prevented us from forming bonds with those responsible for editing and completing the films. It gave Franz a formidable power by allowing him to divide and rule.

CHAPTER 4 – NEW APPROACHES TO FOREIGN REPORTING
The shadow side

The fact that the GDR was not recognised in those early years meant that we could not have functioned as official GDR correspondents. To have done so would not only have made our work much more difficult, but would have closed many countries and many doors to us as journalists. If some of the people we spoke to or interviewed had known that our material was being shown in the GDR they would probably have refused to talk to us or spoken in a different manner, either out of fear of being misused or of being labelled as communists in their own countries.

Our status as independent film-makers allowed us to avoid having to lie; we possessed the rights to our material which we could sell to any interested parties, as long as it was not to be misused. We did in fact sell a number of items over the years to a several TV stations, but in the main they were not interested in the subjects we dealt with and in films unequivocally committed to the struggle for socialism and liberation.

We also had the additional problem that the film stock we normally used (ORWO, the GDR's own film stock to begin with and only later, AGFA) did not guarantee the quality required by most western stations. We were still shooting on black and white, for instance, long after they had gone over to colour. Of course in those countries where people's lives were at stake we told them clearly that the films would be shown in the socialist countries and asked whether they would have any problems because of it; often we filmed them with their faces masked if necessary.

We were, though, film-makers not business people. We neither had the ambition or the time to devote to selling and marketing. This could have been done by our company, but our director, it seemed, had little inclination to conquer new markets and the GDR itself didn't offer the necessary logistical back-up and real interest was lacking. During the Katins years most of our films were transmitted throughout the socialist world via Intervision. Under Herlt even this was rarely done. A narrow, purely GDR view of the world then became almost the sole criterion for our work. Right from the start it had been made clear to me that I should resign from the party and cease public activity on its behalf, and it was emphasised that I should talk to no one outside our group about the work we did, I should on no account have anything to do with people from the GDR as this could jeopardise our work. With hindsight I'm sure much of this enforced secrecy was insisted upon by Franz in order to keep us dependent upon him, as the only official link between the group and our TV contractors in the GDR. However, remembering the state of the cold war at that time and the paranoia about communist spies, his insistence on discipline and secrecy was probably well founded. The accusation made about our work by WDR and *Der Spiegel*, mentioned elsewhere, is evidence of this type of smear tactic.

Whenever we went to the GDR in the early years we would always have a visa waiting for us at the border checkpoint to obviate getting GDR stamps in our passports. For some countries including the USA, Israel and many Latin American countries such a stamp could mean refused entry. Customs were instructed not to search us when we went through. We would never meet at TV headquarters in Adlershof in case anyone saw us. Franz was as cautious of GDR citizens as he was of those in the West. We were for many years thus kept at arms length from those people who we were supposed to be working with, the programme editors, who completed the montage of our material into the final programmes for transmission. For them, we were also anonymous, shadowy figures who simply supplied material. As producers our group met regularly, viewed the edited material, discussed, commented and evaluated it. Views and comments were relayed by Franz back and forth.

Again in the early years we came together perhaps twice a year, but always outside the GDR, maybe in Vienna, Munich or Copenhagen. When meetings were arranged we used code words over the telephone for places and for names of colleagues.. We knew that our telephones were almost certainly tapped and so we avoided giving gratuitous information which could be used against us, or endanger our assignments. Later, under Herlt, in an internationally less hostile climate, this charade ceased and we began meeting regularly in the GDR, getting to know our colleagues in Adlershof for the first time, something we had long demanded.

It was far from easy, working for over ten years producing material and sending it off and having no more influence over the final product. I felt as if I was handing over pieces of my own life, but perhaps a better metaphor is of a painter having to paint blindfold, never being able to see how his picture gradually takes shape; he knows his paint tubes and how to wield his brush, but the finished painting, when he has the blindfold taken off, is a surprise to him. Of course we communicated our idea or concept for the finished film, often in a detailed manner. We made suggestions for editing, we sent extensive background material and information for the commentary, but it was still frustrating having to leave the work half way through, so to speak, for someone else who had not partaken of the experience to finish it off – and then not even being included in the film credits for security reasons. It is surprising, despite this total separation of the two sides of the film-making process, that so many films of quality were produced. It also, though, explains why a large number failed to achieve the quality expected. How could the programme editors who had never been to the West, had little access to western information and media, understand or be able to put themselves in a position of someone living in, say, Chile or Zimbabwe. The last film we made on South Africa in 1983 under very difficult circumstances was put together by the editor as if it were a report from a European democracy, with a bland commentary which made no reference to the dangerous and almost impossible circumstances of filming there or of the courage of those appearing in the film.

Of course, for us too, it was a permanent preoccupation trying to put ourselves in the position of our prospective audience, trying to see through their eyes, but at the same time using our own critical faculties, brought up as we were within the capitalist system. For those living in a country the realities are always very different from those merely visiting, even as critical or interested visitors, and we didn't just see the problems we actually lived them. We had continuous and heated discussions about the *Alltag* series. What is *Alltag*, how can it be communicated without it being boring, unexciting or uninteresting? Can a dramatic case or an exceptional case still reflect day to day realities? We constantly attempted to avoid simplistic black and white portrayals, but we didn't always succeed. Sometimes that was our fault, but was very often due to the dictates of those higher up.

The semi-conspiratorial way we were obliged to work over the years brought with it quite a number of problems and difficulties. Although the work itself was often exciting, dramatic and very rewarding, it also took its toll on private and family life. Because we weren't supposed to talk to anyone about our work, not even friends and relatives, we felt very frustrated. We were cut off from colleagues within the TV and film industry in our own countries as well as in the GDR and it meant that our work brought with it an acute sense of isolation. Even though I largely ignored the restrictions as far as close friends and relatives were concerned, and continued doing political work of a non-public character, I still missed the friendship and solidarity of colleagues and the support a workplace group can offer. One can imagine the curiosity of friends who wanted to know where we had been and what we did and, of course, where the films were being shown. Colleagues from the film and TV world wondered where we raised the finance for such assignments. This industry is notoriously full of freelance technicians, all looking for new work and curious to know where and when films are being made and how they are financed. To avoid having to answer (or refuse to answer) these questions we were obliged to keep very much to ourselves.

To break out of the frustration of not being able to communicate our experiences and the information gleaned from our film work, I wrote articles for the *Morning Star*, the co-operatively owned Communist daily. I did this under a variety of pseudonyms, thus maintaining my anonymity and ensuring that the articles could not be associated with our filming. In this way I hoped to reach a wider audience and make more use of the material we had collected.

During those years where we tried to respond rapidly and effectively to world events – and this was to the credit of Franz, who realised that if we were to win and capture an audience we had to be as quick as the western media in reacting- life was very hectic. A late night telephone call could mean taking a flight the next morning to a distant country, without having the time to carry out research and not knowing whether the job would take a day or a fortnight.

My wife and I worked as a team on many of the projects, but this was made difficult when, in 1970, our first daughter was born and then one and a half year's later our second – so that we found ourselves looking after two small children in the busiest period of our lives. In Britain there were, and still are, precious few, if any nurseries, forcing us to find our own solutions. Without incredibly understanding and willing relatives we could never have managed. Our chaotic and disruptive life style became transferred to them too. Our children were ferried from grandparents, to aunts or baby-sitters in those years at a moment's notice or the relatives had to come to us, all the way from Berlin, and take over. A normal life was impossible, no date could be made with friends or for a visit to the theatre with the certainty that it would be kept. We were obliged to take free time when it was available, in between assignments and try to pack things into that space and enjoy the company of the children, trying to make up for the long periods of absence.

In 1975, when the children were five and three years old we were asked to spend a number of months in Lisbon to follow the process of the April revolution. Franz had arranged with the GDR embassy there for us to have the children in its own kindergarten. This was an ideal solution and we packed all the necessary things, took the ferry to Bilboa and drove down to Lisbon. We had told the children about their new kindergarten and they were very excited.

On arrival we were shocked and disappointed to be told it was no longer possible – it had been vetoed by Berlin! The fact that my wife and children were also GDR citizens made no difference, apparently the fact that one lived abroad, in the West, apparently presented a danger that our small children might infect the embassy staff with capitalist bacilli. We were never given a real reason why they weren't allowed to go to the kindergarten. So my wife had to take the first plane to Berlin and dump the children on her long suffering mother.

In 1978 just before Christmas we were sent to Iran to cover the last days of the Shah. The people were massing on the streets every day and huge demonstrations were shaking the peacock throne on its pedestal. The fear of the Shah's secret police SAVAK was still there, but was diminishing each day as people's power became more tangible. We did not know whether we would be back in Berlin for Christmas day and had left our children in Köpenick with my wife's family. We worked hard and did just manage to get a flight back from Tehran on 23 December, arriving in Berlin on Christmas Eve. The Germans celebrate Christmas on the 24th, when the tree is decorated and presents are given out. I came in through the back door of the house, dressed in a coat with a big fur collar and a Father Christmas mask over my face and the children didn't even recognise me or my voice – they had probably already come to terms with the fact that mummy and daddy weren't going to be there. The joy on their faces when they did recognise us was wonderful to see, but at the same time gave me a feeling of deep sadness that we might not have made it and caused me to think of the many times we hadn't been there when the children may have needed us. It did worry me often what effect this gypsy life would have on the children's lives, even though I knew they were always with loving and caring members of the family. A foreign correspondent's job, I'm now convinced, is for the young and single, not for those with families.

Although from the outside the life of a foreign television correspondent can appear very glamorous (even though I would dispute the term and the assertion), it does, like all jobs, have its negative side. It can be a very solitary existence. One often spends weeks in a foreign country, not speaking the language, knowing no one and the only home is just another small room in an anonymous hotel. This is the other side of the 'glamour'. Often I woke up in my bed and looked at the basic furnishings around me, wondering for the first few seconds where I was, searching for a clue as to which country or in which city I was in, wishing only to be home near my family and friends. I look at my black camera, somewhat battered and worn, sitting there on the table or desk, a neutral instrument for making pictures, but once it contains exposed film it becomes a witness, a vital historical piece of evidence, it has already been involved in decision-making, selecting and choosing. It has accompanied me on so many journeys, been in so many tight situations, been hidden, confiscated, attacked, had sun-stroke, been frozen and clogged by desert sands; it has become part of me, an extension of my eyes and hands, a means of communicating the lives, hopes and aspirations of others. I love it almost like a baby. In these moments I reflect that it is perhaps all worth it, that it is a vital job, a socially useful one.

CHAPTER 4 – NEW APPROACHES TO FOREIGN REPORTING
Britain on the picket lines

Up to now the films we shot had either been for 2-3 minute items in the *Aktuelle Kamera*, or 10 minute reports for the current affairs magazine, *Objektiv*. In the very beginning I was shooting much of this material alone and then later my wife joined me and we became a two person team. Often I worked with one of the other colleagues, particularly when the children were small and it was difficult for us both to take long trips together. It was a rare luxury to have additional help or a second camera. We were responsible for doing all our own research, maintaining and operating our equipment and every other aspect of the shooting side of things; the company couldn't afford additional manpower. Such a situation is not usual; most TV crews are larger and have back-up assistance. Being such a small team, though, did have advantages on occasions when versatility was called for. In intimate situations a larger crew would have intimidated our interview partners or drawn unnecessary attention to us.

In the early seventies our department became more ambitious and embarked on the first 40/45 minute features, following these it introduced a new fortnightly series of films intended to expose and illuminate the iniquities, deficiencies and injustices of the capitalist system. This was the *Alltag im Westen* series (Everyday Life in the West). In these 30 minute films we were able to explore in more depth some of the problems we had already been dealing with as news items. Some of the more memorable ones we made were: the Meccano factory work-in in Liverpool, the Lee Jeans occupation in Greenock, the fight to save the Elizabeth Garrett Anderson women's' hospital in London, the famous Right-to-Work marches from north to south, and a portrait of Dan Jones, the East End artist and trade union activist.

The first of the long reportage films was on the big miners' strike in 1974 which brought down the Heath government. The Tories thought that the strike had no support amongst the people and so went to the country on the issue. The people gave their verdict, and Labour was returned to power. This film set the tone for the many which followed, establishing the reputation of the Katins Group for lively, informative, honest and entertaining documentaries.

For this report on the mining strike we spent a couple of weeks with the miners of Kent, a small, isolated mining community on the south-east coast, following their struggle day by day in intimate detail. The miners there live in small ghettos separated from the more affluent, largely middle-class communities surrounding them. The picturesque Kent farmland is an incongruous place to find pits but the coal here is some of the best in Britain. Miners were brought from all over the country to work, and in the bath house Yorkshire accents vie with Lancashire, Welsh and Scottish ones. Some of the most militant communist miners' leaders were sent into 'exile' here and ironically created one of the most militant coalfields in the country. The locals treated the miners as gypsies to begin with, ostracising their children in the schools and having nothing to do with them. We were welcomed into their homes and their welfare club and made many a firm friendship during that strike. Again I was impressed by their indomitable spirit, their sense of solidarity and their organising ability in face of the concerted attempt to cow them. Our film *The Men of Kent* was a tribute to their determination and stamina. Sadly this unique community no longer exists because the pits that brought it into being are now closed

The one struggle which perhaps captured the imagination of working people most of all during the seventies was the Grunwick strike in 1976. Here a notorious employer, running a photo-processing business, had pushed his workforce too far and they had gone on strike. He employed mainly Asian women in almost slave-like conditions – they had to ask permission to go to the toilets, were obliged to work long hours of overtime and were paid a pittance – and they, inexperienced as they were of trade union struggle, decided to strike. This small group of courageous women, looking fragile and vulnerable in their colourful saris as they stood picketing the factory gate, captured the imagination of the British labour movement. Workers from all over the country came to help picket the gate and support these women: miners from Wales and Yorkshire, shipbuilders from Scotland and dockers form the ports. The strike held for two years before it was called off, but only after the whole force of the media, the Conservative Party and the police had been mobilised to break it.

To be in Chapter Road, north London at 6 o'clock in the morning during July of 1976 was to experience the exhilaration of working class strength. At the height of the picketing there were over a thousand people at the gates and it was at this time that the police tried out their new strike-breaking tactics for the first time. The newly formed Special Patrol Group was used as a battering ram to clear the pickets from the gates, brutality was not spared and hundreds of arrests were made. Anyone who still believed in the myth of the kindly English bobby was soon disabused of that notion at Grunwick's. The Conservative Party and the business community could not afford to let this strike be won because it had become a symbol throughout the country for workers' rights, for women's rights and for those of ethnic minorities. A victory here would have sparked a country-wide movement in the same direction; the workers had to be taught a lesson!

Although the strike lasted two years, the strikers were not able to overcome the combined strength of a united employers' front, fully supported by the government, the police and the law courts. The leaders were refused their jobs back and had to look elsewhere, and many of the others refused to go back to work for such a company. The lessons of struggle are sometimes bitter, but as Dolores Ibarruri said, "It is better to die on one's feet than be forced to live on one's knees".

Although the 1974 miners' strike did have a certain amount of sympathetic reporting in the British media at the time – low paid miners, working in dangerous conditions deep in the bowels of the earth have always had substantial sympathy amongst the wider population – strikes are, nevertheless, always condemned as being instigated by unscrupulous union bosses and harmful to the well-being of the country as a whole. The real issues or causes of strikes are rarely dealt with. The subsequent miners' strike in 1984/5 was dealt with in a much more vicious and uncompromising way by the media. The Grunwick strike had received little sympathy either and the police-induced violence on the picket lines soon captured and dominated the headlines, clouding the original issues. In our reports we attempted to come to grips with those issues by allowing those involved to tell us and not simply impose our own interpretation. This latter aspect characterised most of our films: letting the protagonists tell their own stories, put their own case. In most TV documentaries the omnipotent commentator tells you what the people think and gives you, the audience, his or her interpretation; seldom do you see programmes where those being filmed are allowed to speak at length or where there is minimal commentary i.e. minimal manipulation.

The Men of Kent and *Grunwick* were just two of the many films we made in Britain for the series *Alltag im Westen*, but perhaps the most important ones were those on the Portuguese April revolution of 1974 and on the struggles in the so-called Third World. This year was a turning point in world history because it not only heralded the collapse of the last remaining colonial power, Portugal, and the consequent liberation of Angola, Mozambique, Guinea Bissau, Cape Verde, Macau and Goa, but also saw a rising tide of liberation in Central America, Namibia, South Africa and the Far East, it saw the liberation of Greece from the army dictatorship and, shortly afterwards, the victory of the Vietnamese people.

CHAPTER 5 – VICTORIES OF THE LIBERATION MOVEMENTS
Namibia/South Africa – the last outpost

In 1974 our crews made a two-part documentary on Namibia – a film used by Nobel Peace Prize winner Sean McBride in the United Nations to illustrate South African abuse of its mandate in Namibia. This film, *Wer hat Angst vorm Schwarzen Mann*, also won the Golden Dove at the Leipzig Film Festival.

Namibia, formerly the German colony of Suedwest Afrika, became a virtual appendage of South Africa after Germany's defeat in the First World War. Despite demands made by the United Nations and a decision taken by the International Court of Justice, declaring South African occupation illegal, nothing was done to speed Namibia's independence. No doubt the presence of Uranium mines (vital for the West German nuclear industry, as well as for other western countries) and rich diamond fields were factors delaying this process. SWAPO, the South West Africa Peoples' Organisation, founded in 1960, became so impatient with the lack of progress and the obvious foot-dragging by the western powers in forcing South Africa out, that they took up the armed struggle to liberate their own country.

South Africa made no pretence about South West Africa being a separate country; it was administered as a province and all South African laws applied. Coming from Europe it is impossible to imagine what racial segregation really means in terms of the destruction of human relationships, fear and degradation. Aaron Mushimba is SWAPO National Organiser in Namibia at the time, and during our stay he is our guide and, in effect, our film director because he suggests the best things for us to film and organises everything for us.

After wasting two days of regular strolls up and down the main street in Windhoek wearing a red tie – this was the identification signal agreed in London –I would be met in the street by a SWAPO representative. Our contact didn't materialise and it took us a further two days and a lot of risk-taking before we were able to establish proper contact with Aaron. We found out later that the man who was supposed to meet us hadn't taken the instructions very seriously and had gone to a football match instead. Our European preoccupation with time and punctuality is not always understood elsewhere, as we discovered to our cost.

Aaron lives in the black township of Katatura, outside the capital Windhoek and when we need to meet we have to go through a convoluted series of contacts and arrange meeting places in out of the way places, where we won't arouse suspicion. Simply to go to his house or for him to visit us in our hotel is out of the question. Any white seen with a black, other than a servant carrying groceries or one sitting in the back of his pick-up truck, would immediately cause raised eyebrows.

Once during this trip we have to translate some Nama dialogue and choose a quiet lay-by off the road, where we sit with Aaron's brother-in-law listening to the tape and transcribing interviews. Within minutes a police car appears, drives slowly by, then backs up to ask whether we 'need any assistance'. Needless to say we have already hidden the tape recorder under the seat and tell them we've just stopped for a rest. When travelling in the country Aaron insists on driving because, he says, "a white man chauffeuring a black person in a saloon car would attract attention because it is not common." Every time we stop for a drink or a snack (and that is quite often in the excessive heat and the long distances we have to traverse) we are able to go into the cafe or restaurant and sit comfortably at a table, but our friend Aaron is only allowed to go around to the back to buy a drink from the kitchen window. We refuse to accept such imposed roles and therefore decide to eat in the car together. It is impossible to behave naturally in public, one is always under the physical as well as psychological constraints of the apartheid laws. It is impossible to show affection or behave as equal friends in public.

Aaron is determined to show us the breadth of support SWAPO enjoys amongst the people because the South Africans insist that it is an unrepresentative small terrorist organisation financed by international communism. Everywhere he takes us SWAPO is strongly organised and people readily come out and greet us, telling us of their hopes for a free Namibia and of their support for SWAPO. In a township near Swakopmund we spend eight hours hidden by a family in their tiny shack so that we can film a SWAPO mass rally through a gap in the curtains. The place is swarming with South African police and we can only cover the rally by arriving before dawn and leaving at dusk. For the family sheltering us the risks are far greater than for us. On another occasion Aaron takes us deep into a part of the Namib Desert to visit a small Nama village where everyone is a SWAPO member. Unfortunately on our first attempt to reach the place we get stuck in the sand – our Ford Cortina is not meant for desert driving. Aaron insists on doing all the physical work of trying to free the wheels. He makes it clear to us that whites can't be seen doing such dirty work when there is a black man there. We are stuck in up to the axles and can find no stones or wood to lay under the wheels. Aaron spots a thin spiral of dust on the horizon and soon recognises the jeep approaching. He warns us to make sure we address him as 'boy' and he will call us 'baas' and 'ma'am' – a piece of play acting for the visitor. As irony would have it, the owner of our rescue vehicle is a member of the security forces. He is, quite naturally, curious and we only manage to extricate ourselves from the situation by pretending we are European pastors visiting a church (Just before the security man has drawn alongside us Aaron, perspicaciously gives me the visiting card of a Pastor Wagner who had been to Namibia some weeks before).

People here in the desert areas live miles and miles apart from each other because the sandy earth is so poor that every family needs an enormous area for their herds of sheep to wander and feed. The sheep herds are their only means of livelihood; no crops will grow here. They live, no longer in their traditional adobe huts, which are cool in the summer and warm in the winter, but in corrugated tin shacks, the cheapest building materials available.

In order to spend a day and talk to the Nama families living there we have to arrive in the evening and stay overnight. Aaron, my wife and I all sleep together under one blanket in one of the small shacks and I have never frozen so much in all my life. Despite being fully clothed I shiver and shake all night and it takes a couple of hours in the morning before the strong sun has penetrated to my bones again. During the day the huts are like ovens, the tin becoming too hot even to touch and are sweltering inside. Despite the enormous distances people live from each other, about twenty of them, overwhelmingly women, turn up to talk to us the following morning, all resplendent in their bright colourful dresses and SWAPO stickers. One of the women tells us, after losing her inhibitions, that for her to invite a white person into her hut is like taking in a poisonous snake; but she is happy we have come to hear about their oppression and their struggle and trusts us to take their message back to the outside world. A sheep is slaughtered in honour of our visit and we are given enormous platefuls of rather tough, boiled meat with mealy-meal porridge and sour sheep's milk, the staple food.

At that time, in 1974, no one has yet filmed with the SWAPO guerrillas operating out of northern Angola and our aim is to accompany them during training and exercises, to show them as a real liberation army and not just a small group of terrorists, as South African propaganda would have the world believe. Our biggest problem is to enter Angola and liaise with the SWAPO liberation forces without the South Africans getting wind of us. To reach Angola we have to first pass through Ovamboland, the most northern province of 'South West Africa'. Ovamboland is under military jurisdiction and banned for tourists. We have to apply for a special transit permit from the 'Bantu Administration' in order to travel through. The obese, khaki-uniformed official in Windhoek who gives us our permits wants to know why we wish to travel into Angola. On telling him that we are interested in filming the birds and other wildlife he says we are mad. Angola, he tells us, is in the hands of bandits and we are risking our lives by going there. We feel secure because our SWAPO friends have arranged to meet us in Otjiwarongo and accompany us unobtrusively over the border.

The permit is a two-page document listing the things we are not allowed to do while traversing Ovamboland: "Under no circumstances is the permit holder to interfere with the domestic affairs of the native", whatever that means! "The wearing of ultra mini-skirts or shorts by women in the native areas is prohibited, as is the taking of photos" etc. etc. We are able to ignore the latter stipulation because Ovamboland is an arid bush-covered flatland with a very low population and we can keep a good look-out while we are filming, to make sure no whites are observing us. On entering Ovamboland there is a large sign warning all travellers that this is a special zone and stopping or leaving the main road is not permitted.

Unfortunately our SWAPO contact man doesn't show up as arranged in Otjiwarongo, the small town on the Ovamboland border. We think, aha, this is a repeat of our initial experience. So after waiting for two hours, we decide to carry on alone and try to make contact on the other side. Our second-hand, mud-brown Volkswagen is the only vehicle travelling to the border and we feel very alone and vulnerable. The blue-uniformed South African border officers stamp our passports, give us a pitying look and wave us through. On the Angolan side young, black soldiers with Kalashnikovs slung over their shoulders examine our passports carefully and let us pass. Here the climate is already more tropical, the vegetation more dense and the humidity high. The road to Ngiva is totally deserted, only the insistent chirp of insects and the odd squawk of a bird disturbs the hot silence. After a few kilometres we see a lone soldier by the roadside, waving his gun for us to slow down.

The warnings of our 'Bantu administrator' come uncomfortably back to us. He asks for a lift – we can't afford to say no – so we load him into the back, next to our bags. I try to strike up a conversation with the few words of Portuguese I can remember, but he doesn't seem keen to respond so we spend the remaining hour of our journey in tense silence. We pass no cars, people or villages, only the impenetrable bush on either side of the narrow road, begrudging us even the solace of an open landscape. We have already read a report of western scientists being killed by uncontrolled elements in Angola and, for this young peasant soldier in our car, we must appear like rich South Africans. To get rid of us and take our belongings would have been an easy matter, but our fears are unfounded; he gets out just before we arrive in Ngiva, much to our relief. Aaron had told us that they work closely with UNITA in southern Angola, so we ask a passer-by where the UNITA office in the town is and drive there.

During the war of liberation against the Portuguese colonial occupation there were three liberation forces, the main one being the MPLA, supported by the majority of the people. The FNLA is a tiny group supported by the Zaire dictator Mobutu and the other is UNITA, based on the Ovambo tribe in the south of the country. UNITA had been used by the Portuguese secret service, PIDE, to combat the success of the MPLA, but it was a genuine liberation organisation, even though a tribally based one. For SWAPO to operate in northern Namibia (also dominated by the Ovambo tribe) co-operation with UNITA is absolutely essential.

We enter the UNITA office and are immediately surrounded by curious onlookers and a number of would-be translators attempting to interpret our request. We have naively underestimated the level of chaos and disorganisation left in the wake of the collapsed Portuguese war and the suspicion that would be aroused by foreign whites in a South African registered car arriving in this small border town asking for SWAPO. The result of our innocent questions is that we are arrested by UNITA officers and accused of being South African spies.

In a sense it is not surprising that UNITA over-reacts, because the South Africans are continually trying to present SWAPO's struggle as outside interference and accuse Angola of instigating the resistance. The fact that the colonial border between Namibia and Angola – like so many arbitrarily drawn colonial borders – goes right through the middle of Ovamboland is ignored; the fact that a once united tribe is forced to live artificially separated in two different countries is never mentioned. It is therefore perfectly logical that the SWAPO liberation army, based in Ovamboland should straddle the border carry out much of its training in the safety (at least it was considered to be safe then) of Angola. What an ironic situation it is for us, though, to be accused of being South African spies! In other circumstances I could perhaps have seen the funny side of it but this is deadly serious and we feel no urge to laugh.

To begin with we are interrogated by two leading officers in a small room of UNITA headquarters in the centre of town. The door is guarded by heavily armed soldiers, as if we are dangerous criminals. Our chief investigating officer is a nervous, paranoid character who has apparently (as we learned later) been imprisoned and badly tortured by the Portuguese and has no love of 'white colonialists' of any nation. We understand next to no Portuguese and he no English, so everything has to be translated by a captain. At one point our investigator indicates that he wishes to write something, but has no pen. I immediately offer him mine. After he has taken it, the captain sitting next to him says something and he flings the pen in panic across the room. The captain then retrieves it and slowly takes it apart to examine its contents. This paranoia doesn't bode well for us.

After an hour's interrogation in the hot and stuffy little room it is clear to us that our story – a pretty unlikely one we have to admit – is not being believed. We are told we are under arrest. Our car is to be parked in the main square where it is under observation. As we leave the building we are thrilled to see the SWAPO van draw up and Rueben, the man supposed to meet us in Otjiwarongo, get out.

We greet him with relief, as our saving angel. We are then horrified to see him arrested immediately too, bundled back into his van and driven off.

Luckily we are not kept in a prison cell, but in the house of a coffee plantation owner and we have to report each morning to the UNITA office in the central square, where we are made to sit on a bench in front of the office, to be viewed and gawped at by every curious passer-by, as if we are infamous criminals waiting for the hangman. I am a bit worried about our film material in the car, which is standing in the full sun all day. I decide to move it a few yards so that it will be in the shade of a big wall. No one seems to worry about my walking over and moving the car, but when our interrogator comes back he is enraged and begins yelling at me and then hitting me, there in the middle of the square. I think I am in for a real beating, if not worse, but my wife intervenes on my behalf and he stops and simply storms off. We are ordered back to sit on our bench in front of the army post. We have nothing to do, nothing to read and hardly speak to each other, we are drained of feeling and full of a fear which we don't want to make any worse by communicating it to each other. We feel completely abandoned, there is no embassy to contact, no friends or acquaintances.

This small border town is still incredibly tense in the interim period after hostilities between Portugal and the liberation forces have ceased, but no new government yet established. The heat is unrelenting and the population seems to have nothing constructive to do. The men hang around on the streets or in the bars, the Portuguese troops still drive up and down like victors in their jeeps but no longer have power to do anything. Each evening just before sunset each of the liberation organisations marches through the main square, their party anthems blaring from loudspeakers and every vehicle has to come to a halt, drivers and passengers disembark and everyone stands to attention. The FNLN unit consists of a motley bunch of about 20 assorted youngsters in colourful clothing, marching around the square with an Africanised version of the Portuguese goose-step. After them comes the MPLA, a little better organised and then UNITA, obviously the decisive force in the town. We, of course, also have to stand to attention as each contingent marches past.

We eat lunch in a big cafe and bar on the square. It is always packed full with men drinking, flies settle everywhere and the 'toilets' are a sea of putrid urine. A few Portuguese officers drink here too and one day while we are eating our small plate of rice a fight erupts between a drunken Angolan and a white Portuguese soldier. Within minutes bottles are being thrown and tables overturned; the Portuguese slashes the Angolan's face with a broken bottle and blood pours from the wound. Just arrived from South Africa, where an incident like this would have brought out all the frustration and erupted into a race riot, we are very frightened and feel completely vulnerable – we are already 'criminals' and a situation like this could be used to finish us off too. However, here in Angola, despite years of brutal war, racial feelings are not the same as in South Africa. The Portuguese have mixed freely with the indigenous black population and have never pursued strict Apartheid policies like the Boers to the south. The incident is thus kept within bounds, the injured man carted off to hospital and life goes on as before.

The main evidence for our presence in Angola centres around our instructions from SWAPO's European office in London. We live in the hope that they will hear of our fate and do something to get us released, because no one else knows that we are here. We are totally cut off from the outside world.

Late one afternoon, during our arrest, a jeep full of armed soldiers drives up to us and tells us to get in our car and follow them. This is it we think. They don't want to shoot us publicly in the town square and are taking us off somewhere to do it. We don't dare tell each other our secret fears, but we both think the same thing. Eventually we arrive at a clearing in the forest and are waved down by the vehicle in front. They dismount, come over to our car and start unloading our belongings. All the soldiers appear to be very young, in their early teens, looking awkward and uncomfortable with their big heavy weapons. Their faces are expressionless and indifferent – we don't feel we can expect much sympathy and we can't even talk with them. Then suddenly one of the soldiers starts talking to us in a thick Bavarian accent! We are so relieved that here is someone we can at least communicate with on a person to person level. It appears he has spent some time in Bavaria on a training course and learnt the language there. All our fears turn out to be unfounded: after searching the car for weapons or illegal material they take us back to the village again.

Luckily SWAPO in London has been contacted by our captors and eventually confirms by telegram that we are in fact working on its behalf. Thus, after four days of captivity and uncertainty we are released, given an armed guard and taken back to the border. I never thought I'd feel happy and relieved to be entering South African controlled Namibia again, but I do on that day.

Before we leave the country we give our car, a second-hand Volkswagen which has served us well in the dust and desert sand without breaking down, to SWAPO. To hire cars in South Africa is exorbitantly expensive and it was cheaper to buy a second-hand one and re-sell it at the end of our stay. By giving it to SWAPO we feel it is recompense for their invaluable help and co-operation and will be very useful to them.

For our Namibian films we had two teams in the country and while we worked with SWAPO our other team concentrated on the white rulers, the fossilised German population which still flew the Kaiser's flag and lived in a bygone age alongside the latecomers who fled the ruins of Europe after the Second World War and who retained their beloved nazi literature on their bookshelves and still harboured the same theories of racial superiority.

Aaron our guide and helper was arrested not long after we'd left, but totally disconnected with our visit. Later, in a frame-up trial he was badly tortured and condemned to death for the murder of a puppet chieftain in Ovamboland. Because it was proven that an employee at his lawyer's office actually worked for the security police, he was later released on a legal technicality based on this discovery. We met again, years later, in Warnemünde, when he was studying with other Namibian freedom fighters and families in the GDR.

During his trial our names had become linked to the case and when I was once again asked to go to South Africa in 1983 I realised that I would have to travel under a different name if I were to get into the country without being arrested on arrival. Our experience working in South Africa had taught us how efficient and incredibly well-organised BOSS, the South African secret police was. Their expertise, ruthlessness and sophisticated net of informers made them one of the most efficient security services in the world and they were particularly active in London, where the ANC had its European headquarters. An added, and almost insurmountable difficulty when working in South Africa is the effect of the total separation of the races: as a white team you stick out like a sore thumb in a black area and for a black team in a white area it would be the same, so that trying to move about and work without drawing attention is hardly possible.

Red Reporter
Covert Correspondent for East Germany

So I go through the process of changing my name by deed-poll, taking my mother's maiden name, and obtain a new passport. I start preparing for the trip. This time, particularly, I want to be extra careful and to prepare scrupulously so that, despite the difficulties ahead, we will be able to shoot some unique material. It goes without saying that for all our trips to South Africa we had to enter as tourists and film clandestinely; we would never have been given press credentials.

The following weeks we spend establishing proper contact with the ANC people here in London. I do all this through personal meetings and avoid the telephone or talking to office staff, feeling quite certain that BOSS and MI5 work closely together and knowing that BOSS has its spies within the expatriate South African community in Britain. I meet our contact, a former political prisoner in South Africa, in a small pub in Upper Street, Islington to discuss our plans and ideas with him, asking his advice about our itinerary. He gives us a number of names and addresses and sends a message to South Africa to ensure that we obtain help on arrival.

It is 1983 and although in the meantime there have been a number of films made about South Africa they were overwhelmingly shot from a liberal viewpoint, where whites were the chief spokespersons: mere moral condemnations of apartheid. Virtually no films had attempted to portray the struggle of the black organisations, particularly the vital and popular role of the ANC or the unions in the country. Most of the films had been made by accredited correspondents for big television companies, under South Africa's censorship regulations, very few by small underground teams, probably because of, on the one hand, the great difficulties of working in South Africa and, on the other, the draconian punishments threatening those caught.

Our aim is to document as much as we can about the underground struggle in South Africa, its strength and effectiveness and at the same time to communicate what apartheid means in terms of people's daily lives. Our dilemma is to capture on film as much as possible without taking undue risks and being caught, but at the same time to risk enough in order to bring back useful and informative material.

We leave London's grey dampness a few weeks later, myself and a female colleague – a couple is never so conspicuous as two men travelling together. We hide our few contact addresses, memorise other details and reduce our equipment to a minimum so that it can, at a push, be passed off as tourist gear. My hobby is ornithology and in my passport I am described as a zoologist (I have a degree in zoology from

Bristol University, so it is not entirely untrue), and with a few books on South African birds in my suitcase I can argue convincingly that I am only interested in South African wildlife should I be asked by immigration.

We fly direct to Johannesburg with South African Airways. I rarely if ever watch the in-flight movies because they are seldom worth watching, the sound and picture quality is atrocious and they are always interrupted by screaming babies, or passengers going to the toilets. I usually prefer to read or sleep. This time I try to sleep but, perhaps with premonition I keep my eyes half open to watch the first images: I think I'm having a nightmare! There flickering on the tiny screen are the famous black and white newsreel images of East German border guards jumping over the wall, and others laying the barbed wire. I feel very uncomfortable, as if I have been recognised as a secret GDR emissary. Is this a warning, an omen? They are showing the film about a real-life story of a family who built their own balloon and escaped in it to the West. I decide to watch the rest of the film out of curiosity. It is a badly made film, laden with clichés and images of the GDR from the fifties. It could have been made with more verve, a keener sense of authenticity and really got under the skin, but Hollywood's involvement precluded that. Seeing this film, though, doesn't help dissipate my feelings of anxiety.

Our arrival in South Africa is uncomplicated, as it turns out the authorities ask no questions and after a fleeting look duly stamp our passports with a visa which states: "purpose of visit may not be changed", and wave us through. Jan Smuts airport in Johannesburg is scrupulously clean and spacious. Black men are everywhere with brooms and dusters cleaning continuously, the white men are in RAF-blue uniforms, short trousers and sporting clipped moustaches, invariably with an air of indifferent arrogance about them. My immediate feeling is that I am entering a large jailhouse, I am now in the hands of the enemy and one false step can mean a harsher sentence.

Our first undertaking is to hire a car and find a hotel near the town centre – I haven't booked one from London for security reasons – not a difficult task because tourists are thin on the ground still. Johannesburg reminds me of a mini-New York with its skyscraper banks and office blocks. On the outskirts the large tips of yellow slag from the gold mines are a stark reminder of where the wealth has come from.

RED REPORTER
COVERT CORRESPONDENT FOR EAST GERMANY

The name of the person who will help us in Johannesburg is Beyers Naude, someone very famous or notorious here, depending on which side you are on. He is a protestant churchman and Director of the Christian Institute in South Africa. He comes from an elite Afrikaans family, is a former member of the Broederbund and now committed to the struggle for a free and non-racial South Africa. He is still under a banning order when we visit him. We first drive past his house in a leafy, white suburb of the city, just to make sure there are no obvious security people about. The acacia trees are in full bloom and stand out unnaturally stark against the cobalt sky. The streets are quiet and completely deserted. The lawns and gardens beautifully laid out and cared for. If anyone is watching the house we will be noticed immediately.

We park a few streets down, so that the car is out of view, and wander back to the house, making sure no one is following us. We ring the door bell and are let in by a maid and asked to wait in the hallway. A tall man with glasses emerges from the living room, says goodbye to a visiting German priest, apologises for keeping us waiting, then welcomes us warmly and says he is expecting us. We are relieved to learn that the message from London has got through. "Let us talk in the garden," he says, "walls have ears here". Under flowering apple trees we sip tea and tell Beyers our plans. He is a busy man and not one to waste precious time, so we get down to business immediately. He wants to know exactly what we have in mind and for each of our suggestions he offers ideas and names of people he knows who will help. His network of friends and acquaintances seems enormous. Although businesslike, he nevertheless radiates a humanity and concern about our work and our safety as if that were his prime interest.

Over that weekend we follow up the Johannesburg contacts he gives us and others we were given in London. We decide not to rush into filming before we have established a proper plan of action, so as not to become conspicuous too early on. This all takes much time because people have to be visited personally – we still don't want to use the telephone– and often they are not in, so a second or third visit becomes necessary. Only once do we use the phone and that is because one of our contacts in a human rights office calls us. After we leave the country the security forces visit this office enquiring about us and refer to this telephone call, so our vigilance is not pure paranoia.

Our friends tell us to go straight to East London, where there is a big bus boycott going on. We will get some good material on the struggle, they tell us, and establish useful contacts with the trade unions there. We stay in the Holiday Inn and are met soon after our arrival by one of the black trade union leaders. Since my previous visit to the country blacks have now been allowed into many hotels and meetings like this between white and black people are no longer so unusual as to cause suspicion. He tells us to come to the township of Mdantsane very early the next morning to film the bus boycott. People now either take the overcrowded trains or walk to work: the buses remain empty. They are protesting about recent high price rises by the monopoly bus company.

We leave the hotel before sunrise, our camera and tape recorder hidden in leather bag, and drive out to Mdantsane. East London, where all the industry is and where the black population works, is in South Africa, but the suburb of East London, Mdantsane, where the blacks live, is now deemed to be in the 'independent' homeland of Ciskei, so the workers have to cross 'the border' each day to work. We arrive at the wire border just as dawn is breaking. It is 5.30 in the morning and the mist still hangs over the hills which are densely covered by rows of tiny concrete or brick boxes, as if a child had laid its building blocks out on a carpet. This is the township. From these boxes people are streaming along the paths, like ants from an ant hill, towards the railway station, just inside the Ciskei. Notices warn outsiders not to enter the Ciskei without a permit. We park near the railway station as arranged and wait. No other whites are about at this time in the morning and those blacks who pass by look at us but, in the way they have learnt, remain expressionless, ask no questions and express no apparent curiosity; white people spell danger and are better ignored unless you are forced into contact with them.

After a short wait our trade union friend, Tobile turns up and tells us to bring our camera and follow him. We unpack it quickly, lock the car and follow him through a hole in the border fence and onto the platform of the station. By now it is quite crowded and filling up steadily every minute as the people arrive from their homes. We can hardly move in the crush. Tobile, tells us to be ready to film and then disappears. We see him farther along the platform, now together with the other comrades from the union. They are going up and down the platform whispering to the people standing there. Then all of a sudden we hear voices singing and the sound swells towards us like a large wave on a calm sea: "Nkosi sikelel'i Afrika...". Very soon everyone on the platform is singing and then clenched fists are raised in the air. We are frantically filming as much as we can. Everyone simply ignores us, as if we are invisible, they just keep singing with raised, clenched fists, the expression on their faces serious and determined. I feel shivers down my spine as we listen and film the scene. It is as if we are in a church and the incredibly beautiful harmony of the voices carries the whole soul and the suffering of these people out into the empty morning air. The shrill whistle of the train breaks the spell, but they still keep singing as it pulls in and everyone struggles to get aboard, through doors, windows or by simply clinging to the outside of the carriages. As it draws away we can still hear the voices singing and clenched fists are thrust out through the open windows. We don't hang about, but return to our car and drive back to the hotel by a round about route to make sure we are not being followed.

The next morning we plan interviewing Tobile about the bus boycott. I leave the hotel after breakfast, my leather bag carrying the camera in my hand. My colleague, will follow me a few minutes later. As I walk over to the car in the car park I notice one of the cars near our own with a man sitting in it, alone. I immediately feel uncomfortable but keep on walking. As I draw near the man climbs out of his car and saunters over to me. "This is it," I think, my heart beating anxiously, "this is where they catch us". He has the usual short-cropped hair and short moustache and wears a cynical smirk on his face. He introduces himself immediately, in that clipped Afrikaans voice that sends shudders through me: "Good morning sir. I'm Captain Villiers from the security police. Do you mind telling me what the purpose of your visit to our country is?" I reply that we are touring but filming bits and pieces of our trip to show the relatives back home. I decide that it is better not to hide the filming side, after all I have the camera in the bag beside me, and desperately hope he won't ask to look inside it. "How long do you intend staying," he then asks," and which other places are you visiting?" I give him a list of the main cities and tourist spots. This seems to satisfy him. He wishes me a pleasant stay, walks back to his car and drives off.

This is obviously just a gentle warning but I feel drained and defeated. How, despite the most stringent precautions, have they tumbled us and found out where we were staying? We only just started filming yesterday! We hold a hurried conference, not knowing whether to pack it all in now or to try and continue. We talk it over with our trade union friends who suggest we keep going until they actually stop us. We still keep up our vigilance. We swap hotels and think it will be a good idea to change the car because they now obviously have the number. We drive out to East London airport, thinking it will be better to change it there rather than in the city centre – travellers come through and hire cars often on spec. I leave my colleague in the car with the equipment and go into the airport lobby.

The AVIS girls are very friendly. I say we are having problems with the engine, which appears to be overheating, and can we change the car. No problem, one of them says, making a quick phone call and then handing me a new set of keys and telling me which bay the car is in. We are just transferring our cases from the old to the new car when two burly policemen come rushing over and in a state of panicky excitement shout, "OK you are under arrest, come with us". "Why," I ask. "Don't argue, komm," one of them orders us. We are taken to the small local station at the airport and told to sit down. One of them then makes a telephone call in Afrikaans. I gather something about "we've caught them" but can't follow the rest of the one-sided conversation. After this short phone call he comes over to us and says, angrily, "OK you can go now". I demand to know why we have been arrested, but he says it is a mistake and we can go, refusing to divulge any further details. I imagine the car rental people had been asked to let the police know if we changed the car and this over-efficient officer, instead of reporting the incident, has arrested us instead.

We really feel low after this and know we have little chance of doing a disappearing trick. We nevertheless decide to be stoical about it and plug on as best we can. Surprisingly, perhaps, the security forces leave us alone after this last episode and, although still being extra cautious, we manage to shoot some good material. They are obviously not sure who we are or what we are doing because, as I discover after I return home, they have been enquiring in London about me, pretending to be a credit card company.

We film an excellent interview with six members of the East London trade union leadership about the day-to-day problems of trying to organise while at the same time being harassed not only by the South Africans but also by the Ciskei police. Most of them work for big companies that are household names in Europe, like Johnson and Johnson, Metal Box or Mercedes-Benz. They tell us that they never sleep in the same house for more than one night for fear of being attacked or kidnapped. We talk to a family in Cape Town about their son on Robben Island. We can only visit them after dark because a car and white people at the house during the day would only invite more trouble; we have a moving interview with a student leader, Johnny Issels, who has been tortured and imprisoned and is now under a banning order – his talking to us is forbidden and could mean his return to jail for breaking the banning order but that won't deter his speaking out. We meet the emergent United Democratic Front and film a public demonstration of theirs, where everyone is arrested. With the help of a courageous young white student from Cape Town, who drives us through the security gate into Cape Town harbour, we are also able to film from the car the relatives of prisoners on Robben Island boarding the boat which leaves each week for the island. He then takes us to a vantage point above Pollsmoor prison where Mandela is being held, and where we are able film the whole complex – even filming prisons in South Africa can carry a ten year sentence.

From Table Mountain there is a magnificent view over Cape Town itself and the inhospitable Robben Island can be discerned mistily in the distance, encircled by a white halo of breaking surf. On Table Mountain, surrounded by meadows of red protea flowers, symbol of South Africa, looking out over the rugged but soft-coloured hilly landscape you realise how beautiful this country is. But there in the middle of this breath-taking panorama, just below the mountain itself, is the obscene excrescence of Crossroads, the shanty town where many Cape Town blacks are condemned to live.

The beaches on this lovely coast are, incredibly, divided into four different sections and are signposted as such: the first and best is for whites only, then one for the Asians, followed by one for the coloureds and farthest away for the blacks. Infringements of another race's bathing area is strictly prohibited. This sort of petty racism is used to divide the people and to prevent dialogue and possible co-operation. No white, for instance, is allowed into the 'homeland' areas or black townships without a special permit. This means that the whites never know how the black population lives, how the women and children vegetate, starving and in abject poverty in the desert wastelands they have the audacity to call 'homelands'. In the biggest movement of people since the Jewish exodus from fascist Europe, hundreds of thousands of Africans have been forcibly repatriated to these areas. In this way they are denied South African citizenship, are declared foreigners in their own country. Most of the men are obliged to live hundreds of miles away from their families in the cramped hostels on the outskirts of the big cities where the work is.

We finish our filming as quickly as we can because we know BOSS will not be far behind us, and leave our exposed film with friends in Johannesburg to smuggle out to us at a later date. We have booked our return flight for two weeks hence but, after safely depositing our film, we go straight to the airport and, without pre-booking, take the plane leaving for London that day. This must have taken the security forces by surprise because we are not even questioned or our luggage checked. We certainly feel relieved to be sitting in that plane winging our way over the continent of Africa on our way back home.

As a postscript, about a fortnight after returning safely to London I receive a phone call in a perfectly good English accent from the 'security department' of the HMV record shop in Oxford Street, saying someone has used my credit card and they are just checking up that it was me. They say the name on the card is 'Rudyard', the name I used in South Africa. "That's funny," I say naively, "I don't use that name here and have certainly bought no records in your shop recently". Only after I've put the phone down does the penny drop! I ring the shop immediately to check. "No," they say, "we have no security department and can't recall making any call to you". This was the second phone call and this time I fall, for the trick. So, the South Africans are still trying to find out who I am and have obviously obtained copies of the credit card with which I paid my hotel bill.

Although our film is eventually shown in the GDR it doesn't reflect the severe difficulties and special conditions we had to work under in South Africa. It doesn't attempt to reflect the tension, the fear, the daily horrors of a police state. We are not involved in the editing and the indifferent way the film has been put together makes me very angry. This is not intentional, it simply reveals a total lack of imagination about working under such restrictions and above all what it means for the black population to live as oppressed outcasts in their own country. It is therefore particularly galling to have those hard won cans of film treated in such a light manner.

CHAPTER 5 – VICTORIES OF THE LIBERATION MOVEMENTS
Mozambique – from liberation to new suffering

In order to make our first assignment to South Africa in 1972 economically more effective we decided to make additional short reports on the two neighbouring countries of Mozambique and Zimbabwe (then known as Rhodesia). Mozambique was in the throes of a protracted colonial war and Rhodesia was under the iron fist Emergency Regulations of the Ian Smith minority white government, but still nominally a British colony.

In Mozambique we attempted to show the impossible situation of the Portuguese occupation in face of an increasingly effective guerrilla struggle led by Samora Machel and in Zimbabwe the continued oppression of the black opposition, at this time still attempting to achieve change through peaceful means.

My main memory in Mozambique is of Lourenco Marques, the capital, now known as Maputo. It is a typical colonial port with sprawling shanty towns, bars and cafes, markets and teeming with life. Brothels proliferate around the docks, where indigenous women and girls offer themselves to the white sailors for a few Centavos. Although 95% of the population is black you only see whites in the bars and cafes. On the streets beggars in rags accost the tourists, many of them maimed by leprosy or eye diseases, often without arms or legs, propelling themselves over the dangerous roads on little wooden trolleys, on crutches or simply on filthy stumps. Old ladies with shrivelled up faces sit in front of their shacks tying tobacco leaves, while young girls congregate around the rare water spouts with old tins for carrying the precious water.

Not far from the centre is a big open-air 'restaurant' where the building workers, servants and labourers eat. Women stir food in big oil drums, on open fires, filled with whole cows' heads and mealy-meal porridge. For two centavos each customer is given a few scrapings of meat from the head and a dollop of mealy meal. Beside, the women, in the little shade that is available, enveloped in the smoke from the fires their children sleep, their faces swarming with flies. The humid heat and lack of hygiene contribute to an incredible infant mortality. We accompany a family carrying their dead child in a small cardboard box to the city cemetery for blacks. Here there are hundreds of graves, marked only with numbers and instead of gravestones each little mound of earth is decorated with a tin of Johnson's baby powder, under the firm's name a laughing, healthy face of a podgy white baby – what bitter mockery! I presume the parents saw this product of white civilisation, with its image of bursting health, as a good omen for their own babies to come.

On the outskirts were the big colonial mansions and hotels, like the luxurious Polana, set in its own grounds with swimming pool, palm trees and black waiters to attend to your every whim. It is here to Lourenco Marques that South African male tourists came to enjoy the cheap life and indulge in sexual adventures with black women – something illegal and severely punished at home. In front of a large white church, not far from the centre of town, a group of Portuguese ladies are selling sweets and cakes in aid of a church hospital where their soldiers maimed in the war can convalesce.

To the north of Lourenco Marques we manage to interview some young Portuguese officers in the field. They are resting against their new Mercedes armoured cars eating South African provided rations. They are quite open about the fact that they can never win the war. They are only just holding their own, they say, particularly now that NATO is not supplying them with the same amount of weaponry as before. Of course many of these young officers are the cream of the Portuguese middle class and have been conscripted into the army much against their will, and it is precisely these officers who are in the front line and losing their lives. It is this decimation of their ranks by the guerrillas and the increasing dissatisfaction with an unjust war, creating severe economic hardship back home in Portugal, which leads, two years later, to the April Revolution of 1974.

When the Caetano regime was overthrown the colonial war collapsed and the Portuguese pulled out leaving behind them a chaos and misery for the young revolutionary government of Samora

Machel. They had educated no indigenous people to run and administer the country. When the Portuguese withdrew they took all skilled personnel with them. The young Mozambique began its new independent life with about three doctors, perhaps two engineers and a handful of teachers. It is to the honour of the Portuguese Communist Party that, immediately after their own country's liberation, they sent trained comrades out to help the emergent republic – doctors, architects, teachers and engineers.

When I return to Mozambique for the last time in 1987 to show the immense struggle being waged against the South African backed RENAMO terrorist bands I am horrified at the destruction and mayhem they have managed to cause there. Everything the Machel government has achieved is being systematically destroyed by the terrorists. They don't often attack the army but murder and maim teachers, doctors and engineers, burn down schools and clinics. We speak to one such teacher from the north who'd had his ears and nose cut off by RENAMO, (The Mozambique National Resistance) simply because he works for the government.

Maputo is now cleared of the brothels and sleazy bars, there are no longer the beggars and lepers on the streets and, despite the scarcity of consumer goods and obvious lack of many facilities, people here in the city appear to be adequately fed, clothed and with a new dignity. It is sometimes difficult to comprehend the enormous consequences of such a protracted and disruptive war, aimed as it was at the economic well-being of the country, in order to take the pressure off South Africa and to prove that socialism can not work. I remember talking to a GDR fishing expert in the port of Beira, who was doing all he could to help build up a fishing fleet and train young Mozambiquan fishermen, but who commented, "Es ist unmöglich hier, überall in Afrika ist der Wurm drin. Es klappt nichts, Geraete verkommen, werden nicht gepflegt, keiner uebernimmt Verantwortung" (It's impossible here, everywhere in Africa there is a grub in the core, nothing works, machinery is not cared for and rusts, noone takes responsibility). This was his first-hand experience, but he seemed to ignore or be unaware of the legacy of decades of colonial rule and the vicious war being waged by South Africa against Mozambique. There were quite a number of GDR aid workers in Mozambique – teachers, trawlermen, mining engineers and doctors, working under extreme conditions.

We visit a small hospital in Chimoio in the north of the country, on the Beira Corridor, where some of these GDR doctors and nurses worked alongside others from Vietnam and Cuba helping to treat those who would otherwise have no medical help. It was almost impossible to find anyone to take us along the road to Chimoio, renowned for the number of terrorist attacks and ambushes on it, but in the end we locate a grizzled old Portuguese settler who is willing to do it for a suitable sum.

We arrive at the hospital after an uneventful, but tense journey, past shrapnel-scarred villages and burnt-out vehicles, just as night is falling. We introduce ourselves to the two GDR doctors and their wives and are just explaining what we want to film when there is an almighty commotion in the entrance. A family is brought in on stretchers, blood is everywhere and the mother is screaming, clutching her baby to her blood-drenched breast. The doctors jump up immediately, don their white gowns and go into the operating theatre. It transpires that this family, travelling only minutes behind us, has been attacked by the bandits. The father is badly hurt, but will be saved, we are told, and the baby has a bullet wedged in its bottom. This, says our GDR doctor friends, is a daily reality here.

The next day they show us around the hospital: in almost every ward there are men, women and children without feet, legs or arms, blown off by mines or injured by heavy calibre bullets while working in their fields. The GDR staff spare no efforts to help these patients and are prepared to accept the harsh working conditions, cut off from friends and families for long periods and with scant material reward. I can, in all honesty say, that everywhere I went – and not only here in Mozambique, but in almost every Third World country – the GDR had the best reputation of any country for its solidarity, the commitment and support given by those sent out to work in these countries and for the training it has given to thousands of students who would otherwise have been condemned to lives of ignorance and poverty. This is a reputation of which every GDR citizen could be proud and despite the distortion of socialism and the idea of international solidarity by the ruling clique in the GDR, this will remain for many a vital achievement.

Zimbabwe, or Rhodesia as it was called when I visited it in 1972, is very different from colonial Mozambique. More whites live there than in Mozambique, although still a minority of the population: 280,000 to six million blacks. Despite sanctions and a state of emergency it still conveyed a sense of relatively relaxed colonial charm. Salisbury itself reminded me of an English spa town with its white Victorian civic buildings and its wide tree-lined boulevards. Outside the cities, though, the guerrilla war was making its mark and most white farmers travelled around in comic-looking, high-wheeled, armour-plated vehicles which were mine-proof. Ian Smith, the white minority prime minister, was cracking down on the increasingly active and vocal ANC (not to be confused with the South African ANC, but modelled on it. It later split into ZANU and ZAPU factions). Many of its leaders were either in prison or under house arrest. The black majority was allowed no voice at all and the burgeoning trade union movement was being viciously suppressed. This repression led, a few years later, to open guerrilla warfare as the only means of struggle left open. Robert Mugabe, the present prime minister was in one of Smith's jails and his friend and fellow cabinet minister, Eddison Zvobgo was under house arrest – not allowed to leave a ten mile radius of Salisbury. We interviewed Eddison at his house – although he was not allowed to talk to the press – and filmed him walking to the police station where he had to report everyday. He was allowed to leave the house only between 9am and 6pm. He has already spent six years in detention and in the ten years he has been married he has only been with his wife for 14 months of that time. He was not cowed by the restrictions and was still able to carry out political work behind the backs of the police.

When we returned in 1980 to cover the first free elections in the country we found it still under a virtual state of siege. The white farmers only travelled around in high, inelegant and high-wheeled armoured vehicles to shield them from land-mines and snipers. Many had their own little private armies to protect their estates from guerrilla attacks. Ian Smith had in the meantime illegally declared the country independent from Britain in order to avoid majority rule, but the UN-imposed sanctions were only half-heartedly implemented by the western nations and his regime appeared well able to maintain itself with help from South Africa until 1980 when it collapsed. The high costs of waging war against the unrelenting guerrillas plus its increased international isolation made its position untenable and compromise was sought. Nowhere in the country was safe – Mugabe's ZANU(PF) was attacking from the Mozambique border areas and Nkomo's ZAPU(PF) from Zambia.

Despite numerous attempts by the white minority in Zimbabwe to find an Uncle Tom from among the black leaders to co-operate with them and prevent a Patriotic Front victory, the majority will was not to be frustrated any longer. ZANU(PF) swept to a clear victory in the

1980 elections, held under British supervision with international observers. The party of Mugabe and Zvobgo had at last, after years of bitter struggle, won power and the people danced in the streets waving the ZANU cockerel symbols above their heads in jubilation. Years of senseless resistance by the whites to majority rule had been overcome and the 'dangerous terrorist Mugabe' became a very reasonable politician; there were no acts of revenge, no mass killings, the whites still live amicably in the country, have lost none of their property and are treated as equal citizens.

In 1987 we found ourselves in Zimbabwe once more while making our film on the Beira Corridor railway – Mozambique's vital link between Harare (formerly Salisbury) and the port of Beira on the Indian Ocean. Zimbabwe, a land-locked country depends on this railway link for trade; without it the only feasible route is through South Africa and using this would leave Zimbabwe open to blackmail. Zimbabwe has a highly developed industrial infrastructure, a wealth of raw materials and an abundance of agricultural products, particularly tobacco. This development and the associated higher standard of living is in direct contrast to the underdevelopment and extreme poverty of Mozambique which relies on the tariffs from the Beira Corridor railway to supplement its national income.

We were keen to find Ian Smith again during our stay in Zimbabwe because, although he was no longer in power, he had during his time as Prime Minister been instrumental, together with the Portuguese secret service in setting up RENAMO, the mercenary force now fighting the Mozambique government. We tracked him down on his large farm in central Zimbabwe, still as cantankerous as ever, bitter that the rest of the world had not listened to him. He lived by himself and appeared to be very lonely. To watch his gaunt figure stalk across the fields to his cattle herds, still firing orders to his black labourers in his clipped colonial twang, was to see the stubborn remnants of white rule in southern Africa: doomed, but refusing to admit defeat. He was still convinced that international communism had undermined Western Christian civilisation in Africa and that he was one of the few who saw that clearly. He admitted, in a very circumspect way that he had co-operated closely with the Portuguese in setting up a force to undermine both FRELIMO and ZANU(PF) which was operating out of bases in Mozambique. It was this force which the South Africans had then reinforced with money and weapons and which was now reeking such havoc.

CHAPTER 5 – VICTORIES OF THE LIBERATION MOVEMENTS
Portugal – the carnation revolution

We couldn't believe our ears when we heard on the midday news on the 25 April 1974, that Portugal's dictator, Caetano had been overthrown by young military officers. Europe's oldest dictatorship which had lasted 48 years had collapsed in just 24 hours. When we were filming there the previous year little had we dreamt then that Caetano's regime would collapse so easily.

My colleague Klaus suggested we fly there immediately and Franz gave us the green light. We touched down at Lisbon airport on the morning of the 27th, took the first best hotel in the town centre, unpacked our camera and started shooting. We hardly put the camera down the whole time we were there, apart from when we were sleeping. Already at the airport the atmosphere was charged: crowds of relatives and friends waited for their loved ones to arrive, many exiled for years by the dictatorship. There were ecstatic embraces, laughter and relief. We flew there with a young journalist who had worked for the BBC World Service, and who had for years exposed much of the oppression in the country. He was met at the airport by a friend he had not seen for years. Both of them proved invaluable to us over the next days. We had had no time to arrange an interpreter or study the history, geography or anything else about the country; we came simply with open eyes and ears.

The centre of Lisbon was awash with flowers and jubilant groups on the street. Soldiers and sailors stood in front of official buildings or on street corners, not in a menacing manner, but nonchalantly and relaxed, red carnations in their lapels. You could tell by their rough, open faces that they were ordinary conscripts, peasant boys press-ganged into an oppressing army. They were continually embraced by the ordinary people on the streets, who showered them with flowers and kisses. I have never seen an army so at one with the people. One young conscript said to us, "Yes we now have a unity between the people and the armed forces and we must make sure no one destroys that."

There was so much happening we didn't know where to turn. Every street corner, office and factory was a beehive of activity. Political prisoners, some, who'd been languishing in Caetano's notorious jails, in Caxias and Peniche for ten years or more, were released; the secret police headquarters, the radio stations and government buildings were taken over, trade unions re-established, housing associations and local committees set up and political parties emerged from clandestinity. My colleague Klaus and myself felt instinctively the parallels with the Bolshevik revolution of 1917, particularly as described by John Reed in "10 Days that Shook the World". Here were the same soldiers and sailors, with similar open faces, who'd taken power, here was the ferment and highly charged emotional debate in the smoke-filled rooms, the rushing back and forth with messages and instructions, the chaos, but at the same time an order self-imposed by the citizens and, of course, that indescribable feeling of emerging from a deep, dark pit into the brimming light of freedom. There was an amazing sense of unity and fraternity, of national dignity, with everyone celebrating together. Most of those on the streets appeared to be young, it was as if a whole generation of old fossils had been swept aside.

All the soldiers had carnations sprouting from the barrels of their guns, converting them into flower vases instead of killing tools. The streets were buzzing with knots and crowds of people discussing and chatting animatedly until deep into the night. Every so often there would be a howl of pleasure as people met friends or relatives they hadn't seen for ages, many newly returned from long years of exile; there would be embraces, kisses, back-slapping and tears of joy.

Of course this is always the case after an oppressive regime has been overthrown – everyone is united in their opposition and their joy in victory. It is only afterwards when the real debate over the way forward begins, over the possible solutions, that differences emerge, become bitter and divisive, but in these early days those thoughts were far from everyone's minds.

We pick up information as we go along, taking advice from people we meet, as to where to go, where something is happening. We are dragged off in one direction and then another, not knowing when to stop filming, overwhelmed by the enormity of subject-matter. One of the first places we visit is the former headquarters of PIDE, the secret police. The naval guards on the main gate take us in to the officer in command, who, without any bureaucracy, tells us we can film what we want to.

The whole building is still in the state it was when its inmates fled on that auspicious 25th April day, apart from papers strewn over the floors and drawers left open in haste. Silva Pais, the security chief had clearly left in a great hurry. In his oak-panelled office, with its large oak desk his diary is still open on the 25th, some papers are held down by an enormous plaster penis and a half-drunk bottle of Johnny Walker Scotch stands next to two dirty glasses. On the bookshelf behind the desk is a selection of books: Regis Debray on Che Guevara, ones on the USSR, communism in Africa, a Batista autobiography, a number of books on Cuba and on nazism, one on karate and a gun catalogue. In a recess let into the desk is a hidden microphone and a cassette recorder in a drawer, which the commanding officer shows us. He then takes us to the offices where the files were kept on all left-wing, progressive or simply suspect individuals. Even our interpreter, the journalist from London, finds his own file and photo there amongst trade unionists and communists we know or recognise. We even found the file on Alvaro Cunhal the General Secretary of the Portuguese Communist Party. There are piles of student identity cards, a number of passports, mainly French, police photos and a children's printing outfit, probably used to forge leaflets to incriminate innocent victims. In the basement are the cellars where those arrested were tortured or beaten; there is a room, too, containing a selection of porno films, where the secret police obviously found titillation and blunted what residual sensitivities they may have had to equip themselves for the bloody tasks ahead.

We attend rallies and meetings in so many places that our heads spin. We hear stories and personal histories, each of which would make a fascinating novel and I can only hope that many of these stories will be written down and recorded. In Barreiro, the 'red suburb' of Lisbon, we film the opening of the first legal Communist Party office and the first meeting of the comrades, who still can't get used to the idea that they have nothing to fear. One older comrade who works in the big CUT steel factory nearby insists on dragging us to his small works flat.

Inside, in the Spartanly furnished room, he takes a dusty book down from a high shelf and proudly shows it to us – it is Marx's *Capital*! He explains how he's hidden it for almost 40 years and can now bring it out and read it openly. In the steelworks a few months later there are communist posters everywhere and the workers proudly drive their fork-lift truck onto the factory floor for us to film: it has been covered in revolutionary slogans and has been named V.I Lenin! Cries of PCP, PCP resound from around the works and clenched fists are raised in the air. There is an infectious euphoria.

The young officers who were behind the revolution, and it was primarily the middle ranking younger officers who organised and instigated it, invite us to their barracks to talk to those who'd taken part. It is the Escola Pratica de Cavalaria, the cavalry school in Santarem, which led the march or drive on Lisbon. Their signal was a song on the radio by a well-known, Portuguese singer called Jose Alfonso. The song he sang, "Grandola", conjured up images of Portugal and its people. When this song rang out over the air waves at midnight the officers at the school started up the engines of their old armoured cars and jeeps and headed for Lisbon, 20 km or so away. The coup almost misfired because one of the vehicles leading the column was so ancient that it broke down, but the soldiers managed to repair it. They told us how nervous they were and uncertain whether the coup would come off. The whole thing had to be planned in such secrecy that only a few officers knew about it and no one could be certain how far the other regiments would support their attempt. It is amazing that this pathetic little group of soldiers, with their obsolete vehicles, nevertheless frightened and scattered the dictatorship's demoralised forces. "We had strict instructions not to open fire unless absolutely necessary", one of the majors tells us, "we wanted to avoid the spilling of blood at all costs, so we spoke to the 'enemy' troops trying to win them over to our side. This we managed to do. Only one or two top ranking officers refused to join us and they were arrested".

Most of the soldiers had had enough of the debilitating war in the colonies which was doomed anyway and was eating up the last remaining resources of the country. Over the following days, weeks and months these soldiers, unused to civilian administration grappled uncertainly with the enormous tasks facing them. The Communist Party, despite being persecuted and illegal for over 40 years was the best organised political force in the country and very soon took a leading role.

At the first May Day rally in Lisbon after the coup the atmosphere of the packed stadium was reminiscent of the scenes in the liberated countries after the Second World War. Alvaro Cunhal, the Communist leader, had just returned from his exile in Moscow and stood next to Mario Soares, the socialist leader, returned from Paris, together with soldiers from the MFA (the Movement of the Armed Forces). The Communist Party wished to set up a national coalition of democratic forces to govern the country alongside the MFA, but it wasn't long before party political bickering and in-fighting began. Leading western nations were afraid that Portugal would turn socialist – the Caetano dictatorship had been a loyal member of NATO and European NATO headquarters were in Portugal. They did all they could to slander and isolate the Communist Party to keep it out of power and they financed other parties to gain influence. Mario Soares socialist party had only been formed in 1972, 104 actually in West Germany! The Friedrich Ebert Stiftung was used by the West German Social Democrats to channel large amounts of funding to the Soares' party (see report in the German magazine *Der Spiegel*, Spring 1990) and Willy Brandt was sent over to help and advise them. We caught Brandt by surprise as he arrived in Lisbon, unannounced and unaccompanied and he was obviously very uncomfortable about having to answer our pointed questions at the airport, but he couldn't very well avoid us as we were the only press present.

Mario Soares, the leader of the Socialist Party, a tiny insignificant one at this time, was seen as the man to outdo the communists. Although he offered the people 'socialism with a human face' and toured the constituencies blaring out *The Internationale* on loudspeakers, when his party eventually had power they gave the people in fact a dose of the same sort of economic medicine they'd had for the last decades. The Communist Party was the only one which had existed within the country throughout the dictatorship and at a great sacrifice and cost. During the run-up to the 1975 April elections the party stressed that its 247 candidates for the constituent assembly had between them 440 years behind bars! Once the Socialist Party came to power, though, a witch hunt on the communists began. Ironically almost every one of Portugal's best singers, musicians, writers and many other cultural workers were either in the Communist Party or were sympathisers. Getting rid of them meant emasculating most cultural organisations.

The main bases of the Portuguese Communist Party (PCP) were, apart from the industrial centres in and around Lisbon, in the Alentejo, that broad swathe of agricultural land south of the River Tejo. Here a few large landowners owned enormous estates and employed thousands of agricultural workers, often on a seasonal basis. This agricultural proletariat is unusual in Europe where the system has been more usually a peasant based one with a continuous reduction of land labourers. The struggle for basic rights has been an ongoing one in the Alentejo region throughout the years of fascism, often taking the form of pitched battles between workers and the National Guard. Many of the best leaders were killed or imprisoned but the resistance of the people was steeled and unified over the years and in their overwhelming majority they supported the PCP.

Travelling down from Lisbon we first cross the swirling, muddy waters of the River Tejo, through the rich alluvial plains, past Grandola which gave its name to the song of the revolution, into the heartland of the Alentejo, towards the capital Beja. Here the PCP office will direct us to a new co-operative farm. Since most of the big land-owners were absentee ones or had fled after the revolution, the workers themselves have taken over and formed co-operatives. The land becomes more undulating, rocky and dotted with scrub. The silvery leaved olive trees and the bare mud-red trunks of the stripped cork oaks stand out starkly against the limpid blue sky; in the distance a lone shepherd guards his flock foraging desperately over the parched earth. We pass small fields of desiccated maize or bright yellow sheets of rape fields, splattered with the crimson blobs of poppies. Most of the land is fallow and was used in the past by the owners for hunting.

The co-operative we are taken to in Santa Vitoria is a typical one – a large estate whose owner lives in Lisbon and is rarely seen. It was the first one to be taken over by the workers after 25 April. The chairman, Maurencio, shows us around. In the fields the women and some men are working, planting out the new crop. In the Alentejo both men and women work alongside each other. Two incomes are essential if families are to survive. Women form a large percentage of the work force and their traditional dress of men's dark trilby hats over colourful headscarves, short black bell-shaped skirts, over trousers are a common sight in the fields and farm buildings. This dress is at the same time practical in that it protects the women from the vicious sun while working in the open fields and is also symbolic, stressing their equality with men and their proletarian status. Women have also played a leading role in the struggles and several have died in the process.

The owners of this estate, the Palmas family, employed most of the workers on a seasonal basis, bringing them in when harvesting time came around but discarding them in the winter months. The owners were so stingy that they even refused to allow their workers to draw drinking water from the estate's wells – a very extreme measure in a hot country. We actually manage to interview the couple who own the land in their spacious, down-town Lisbon apartment. They are very keen to express their outrage at the 'illegal' takeover of their land by the 'communist-led gang'. They show us proudly their large collection of silverware, worth thousands of dollars which they have managed to 'rescue' and bring to Lisbon. They don't feel they have much chance of getting their land back because, as they say, "everything is now dominated by the communists and those in Beja are the reddest of them all, this rabble". We are very impressed by the smooth organisation of the co-operatives, their democracy and ideals. Here are semi-literate agricultural labourers with no experience of administration running their own enterprise for the first time in a true spirit of collective responsibility.

In the early years after the revolutionary overthrow of the dictatorship many such co-operatives were formed by the workers, but under the so-called socialist government in the late seventies they were already being broken up and handed back to their former owners. The government was actively sabotaging efforts to make them effective: it had refused to grant import-tax immunity on solidarity shipments of tractors from the Soviet Union and Bulgaria, had refused all help with marketing their produce or giving business management advice. The whole region was seen as a stronghold of the communists and was therefore denied all support.

Many leading trade unionists and communists spent long years languishing in Portugal's antiquated and inhuman jails. One of those was the present editor of the party paper, Dias Lourenco. He was held in the old Moorish prison of Peniche, on the cold and windswept Atlantic coast. Peniche is a typically small Portuguese fishing town, with its white-washed houses, orange tree lined narrow streets, its big open market square and its picturesque port where the gaily painted wooden fishing boats rock gently. The prison dominates the main square where the fishermen's wives sit during the day repairing the nets ready for the evening sailings. From this forbidding, damp stone prison, battered continuously by the rough Atlantic swell Dias Lourenco made his escape in the sixties by springing from the battlements into the sea one cold December day. He almost died of exposure but managed to clamber ashore and live to see his land free. He returned with us to show us where he'd been held and to tell the story of his escape.

The prison was now in the hands of the revolutionary officers of the armed forces and the cells held former PIDE officers. They were kept in very liberal conditions, their cells open all day and they were free to wander about inside the prison, play cards or watch TV in the common room. When we talked to them they expressed no remorse for their actions and arrogantly asserted that they should be set free immediately. It wouldn't be long of course before most of them were set free, without charge or further punishment. For Dias returning to his place of incarceration, but now as a free man was a peculiar sensation. The damp corridors, thick stone walls, the same guards patrolling the battlements. Only the young army officer now acting as prison governor was a recognisable change. The ensuing dialogue between him and Dias Lourenco about the prospects for the revolution formed the core of our film which was called, Lourenco and the Lieutenant. Dias then took this young lieutenant and us to see the cell where he'd been incarcerated for so long. The door was ajar and he looked inside but immediately turned on his heel, his face as white as chalk and refused to talk about it. Only later did he reveal that in his cell, lying on the bed was the PIDE man who'd tortured him when he was first arrested.

Most of the leading communists, including their legendary leader, Alvaro Cunhal, had been held in Peniche. Cunhal, together with a small group of other comrades was also able to make a spectacular escape from this fortress jail on 3 January 1960 by chloroforming their guard, clambering over the outer wall using a rope they'd smuggled in. It was typical of these men – and one of the big problems facing documentary film makers – that they are extremely reticent about telling stories of their own exploits and heroism.

One of the most difficult tasks is to coax these stories from them; often some of the most spectacular ones only come out after one has finished filming! Our interpreter is no exception. He is a shy, rather diffident biochemist who would not look out of place behind a desk in some big government office or bank. We knew he had been a party activist and fled during the dictatorship. Only after we'd finished our filming at the prison did he reveal that he was the person who had supplied the chloroform for Cunhal's escape and driven one of the getaway cars. He refuses point blank to be filmed, stressing that his was a minor role and not worth recording. In the end he did relent and agree to tell it if we promised not to show his face.

It is common knowledge what happened to the April revolution, but not everyone is familiar with the details. We went back regularly in the first years after 1974 and were able to document those tremendous hopes, the potential and aspirations, and then to witness the gradual and systematic destruction of the revolution's hopes and achievements. This was the first time in our filming careers that we had been able to document a whole revolutionary process and it is probably unique. I have lost count of the number of films we made, but it was six at least, covering those years. The films were also, I believe, the high-point of our work, capturing filmically, in the sounds, colours and voices of ordinary Portuguese people a dramatic moment in their history. The gradual betrayal of that revolution was sad to watch. There was the economic sabotage by the powerful capitalist nations and Portugal's own ruling class; the USA sent a new ambassador – Frank Carlucci, who had been their man in Uruguay before the military coup and bloody suppression of democracy there. This sabotage, though, didn't make a halt here: we were shaken out of our hotel beds one night on the Avenida Libertade when a huge car-bomb went off in front of the Lisbon offices of the PCP; we visited the man in Rio Major who manufactured wooden clubs 'for bashing communists', and we saw how the party politicking divided the people, pitting them against each other, sowing suspicion and destroying the unity there had been in the early days.

The Socialist Party of Mario Soares, as the only credible force to counter the Communist Party was being financed and promoted with the help of the Socialist International and capitalist interests which could see clearly that his 'socialism' was a fig-leaf only. The extreme leftist forces, although small, were also very active and disruptive. By attempting to mount a coup before the first elections were held they played into the hands of the anti-revolutionary forces who immediately used it as an example of a communist attempt to seize power by undemocratic means. In the first elections the Socialist Party won most seats but did not have an absolute majority. It refused to work together with the communists, the economy of the country deteriorated, disillusion set in and it was eventually ousted from government. Mario Soares, though, managed to get himself elected as president, with the communist vote, and now happily presides over a firmly capitalist country hardly any better off economically than it was even though it now has a democratic electoral system and is, thankfully, no longer a dictatorship.

CHAPTER 5 – VICTORIES OF THE LIBERATION MOVEMENTS
Grenada – a revolution in paradise

The world's first freely elected socialist government was, surprisingly, in a British colony, Guyana, in the Caribbean. That was in 1964. It was very soon destabilised and brought down by combined US and British machinations because it was considered to be too friendly towards the Soviet Union. The second socialist revolution to take place in a former British colony was perhaps even more unexpected – in the tiny spice island of Grenada. This island with a total population of a little over 100,000 and one of the world's smallest sovereign states, had been ruled by a corrupt and obscurantist dictator, Eric Gairy. Gairy had his own brutal police force, the Mongoose Men, rather like the Tontons Macoute on Haiti, was president of his own 'trade union' from which he pocketed all the dues and became rich on the bribes from foreign businessmen and speculators. He promoted obeah and superstition amongst the rural poor and used it as a smokescreen to hide his own corrupt tracks and laid at the same time an emotive base for violent anti-communism.

In the early seventies Gairy's increasing use of brutal means to put down a burgeoning trade union activity and the successful campaigning of the New Jewel Movement (NJM), a Marxist socialist party, was alienating even the last vestiges of his support. On 12 March 1979 Gairy left for talks with the US ambassador in Barbados, leaving instructions for his forces to assassinate the whole leadership of the NJM. They, however, pre-empted this attempt and in an almost comically simple coup 50 comrades of the NJM attacked the main barracks, scattered Gairy's forces and took over the radio station. Within hours the battle was won and by dawn the people were out on the streets celebrating with machetes, sticks and knives expressing support for the revolution.

In the few years between 1979 and the US invasion of 1983 the New Jewel government had made enormous strides in its programmes of modernisation, literacy campaigns and policies of peaceful development for the Caribbean as a whole. Under the leadership of Maurice Bishop, Bernard Coard and the other NJM members a new era of human dignity, tolerance and progress was opened up. We went out there in 1981 to see what had been achieved, how this tiny outpost of socialism was faring in a hostile environment. Like Cuba before it, the USA had tried to strangle it in the cradle by economic blockade and sabotage, by pressurising other Caribbean countries to cold-shoulder it and to blacken its reputation in the world at large.

To get there one has to fly to Barbados and then either a long boat trip of several days duration or a small ten-seater plane to its only small airstrip at Pearls. From the air the island looks like a small emerald green brooch enclosed on an enormous amethyst blue sheet. On the ground it is a veritable Garden of Eden. It is only about 300 square kilometres, with few roads, which have more pot-holes and craters than tarmac, but surrounded on all sides by a luxuriant growth of ferns, palms and exotic foliage. Huge mango trees drop their succulent fruits literally into the laps of the hungry; women in their colourful dresses sit in front of their wooden huts sorting the crimson cased nutmegs in trays to dry; and the clear, translucent sea laps over clean, white sandy beaches, fringed by slender palm trees waving their windmill fronds in the breeze.

It is no wonder that this was a favourite holiday isle for a select few from North America and Europe. This paradisiacal environment, however, hid a real poverty. Apart from the export of nutmegs and a limited tourism – because of the island's inaccessibility – most of the people carried out subsistence farming or were unemployed. In 1981 when we went there the New Jewel government had already helped establish new farming co-operatives, a new fish-processing factory with fishing fleet and also a canning factory to process the many fruits which grow on the island. All of these projects were only possible with help from the socialist countries; the only western country to offer any real help was Canada. The GDR had installed the telephone system and shown solidarity in other ways.

We wished to show the legacy of Gairy's regime, the backwardness and problems he had bequeathed the people, we wanted to see what had been achieved and to let our audience know what problems the country still faced in its battle to create a better life for the people. Maurice Bishop, the prime minister, gave us an extensive interview with a clear analysis of the situation in the Caribbean as a whole and the role Grenada was playing in trying to develop a sense of responsible independence and national pride, to break out of the stranglehold of British and US imperialism and become less reliant on tourism as almost the sole industry of the region.

We were shown the new co-operatives working the land previously left uncultivated by absentee owners. Here the Bulgarians had given much help and advice. We visited the spanking new canning factory, also installed by the Bulgarians, where the woman director proudly showed us the production line and explained how they could now capitalise on the surplus of fruit which previously rotted on the trees.

As I mentioned above, Grenada had no airport big enough for large jets and this severely restricted the tourist and export possibilities. Cuba had sent over brigades to help build a big new airstrip, designed by one of Grenada's own engineers who had been hindered by Gairy from building it. It was this self-same airstrip which Reagan told the nation was being designed for Cuban or Soviet war planes in order to whip up support for his planned invasion. He said Grenada had no need for such a big airport. Needless to say it is now being used to bring in the sorely needed tourists and there is no more mention of it not being needed. We watched the Cubans building it and talked to two of the brigade leaders. Their unstinting work, their many hours of voluntary overtime and commitment to the job was impressive. The Grenadian engineer said that he wished the Grenadian workers would emulate their Cuban colleagues a bit more! We also visited Cuban eye surgeons working in the St. Georges hospital, instructing Grenadian students and treating patients who could never have afforded treatment before the revolution.

This was no grey revolution, there was no suppression of the Caribbean carnival spirit. Calypso festivals flourished, where you could hear a whole number of political as well as non-political songs. In the evening the laughter and the sound of strumming guitars fluttered out of the open windows and from the roadsides; the new cultural centres organised dance and theatre groups, sewing and painting classes and at the open-air political rallies there was as much dancing, banter and singing as there was political speechifying. It really did seem like a dream revolution.

Almost prophetically Maurice Bishop warned of a possible US invasion at a rally we attended in the capital St. Georges, for the dead heroes of the revolution, and this was in 1981, two years before the invasion. The rally was followed by demonstrations in a number of places against CIA interference. This tiny country with hardly enough rifles for its militia and its main concern being to survive was, according to Ronald Reagan, a dire threat to the USA. It refused to recognise the Grenadian government because of 'its abuse of human rights' – there wasn't a political prisoner on the island and we certainly saw little sign of police or oppression. Maurice Bishop and other members of the government mixed freely on the streets with the people and their popularity was demonstrably obvious. The introduction of the first free health service, free schooling and scholarships abroad are not the sort of things I would understand as abuses of human rights.

On the roads there were big hoardings with slogans such as: 'Freedom means feeding ourselves' or 'If you can't teach, learn'. Of course even at that time there must have been differences among the leadership over the way forward, but we were unaware of it, despite meeting and talking with a number of government leaders. Perhaps we had simply been naive and not seen the political conflict taking place behind the beautiful scenery or perhaps it hadn't become so acute at that time, but we were all stunned and shocked when the conflict in the New Jewel leadership became so exacerbated that it gave the USA the opportunity it had been waiting for to invade. The USA had the invasion planned well before these differences within the leadership emerged. It had already carried out a mock invasion practice in 1981 near Puerto Rico – codenamed 'Amber and the Amberines'. It is of course an uncanny coincidence that Grenada's full national name is Grenada and the Grenadines.

The USA had installed a number of CIA agents among a group of US students in a hostel close to the new airport – it was to 'protect' the lives of these very students which became the pretext for the invasion – and had drummed up support from the surrounding Caribbean nations which feared the Grenadian example. It has been said that Maurice Bishop's personal bodyguard was also recruited by the CIA and was to some extent responsible for sowing distrust between Maurice Bishop and Bernard Coard. In any event the bloody end to the revolution with the assassination of many of the New Jewel leaders was a terrible and tragic event. The consequent farce of a trial against the surviving ones, the attempt to make them the scapegoats for the deaths is a travesty of justice and a burying of truth. These leaders – Bernard Coard, his wife Phyllis, Selwyn Strachan and others – are still languishing in Grenadian jails under sentence of death.

Since the USA 'freed' Grenada from the New Jewel government the promised change for the better has become a bitter fruit. During the 1979-83 revolution unemployment was cut from 49 to 14 percent; in less than a year the US-installed Blaize government has pushed it back up to 30 percent. From a comprehensive primary medical care system under the People's Revolutionary Government there is now only a patchy and expensive health service where essential medicines are unavailable and there is insufficient nursing and medical staff. Hard drugs and violence now flourish as in the other Caribbean islands dominated by North American tourism and finance.

CHAPTER 6 – THE OPEN VEINS OF HISPANIC AMERICA
El Salvador – without a saviour

My first assignment to Latin America is to El Salvador, in October 1979, where a military coup had overthrown the dictatorship and the country was in a state of chaos with the political vacuum being filled by popular organisations and right-wing death squads. Almost the only reports that Europe receives from Latin America are of mass killings and political assassinations. Our images of these countries, until very recently, had been formed almost exclusively by Hollywood characterisations of lazy, scruffy slant-eyed Indios with sombreros and speaking in broken English. The cliché has it that the Latin American countries have revolutions more often than we in Europe have football matches and are thus dismissed in the same way. The regularity of coups and counter-coups is, though, contrary to popular belief, not because the people are too immature to practise democracy, but because their countries have been permanent battlegrounds of conquering economic forces since the Spanish incursions of the 16th century.

Any attempt made to build democratic or independent states, as Simon Bolivar dreamt of or as Dr. Francia tried in Paraguay or Arbenz in Guatemala, was soon crushed by foreign intervention. The only reason the North American and European media descended on this tiny country in 1980 was to film the corpses. The background to the killings, the history of colonialism and US imperialism, the grinding poverty of the peasants were all irrelevant. It was a civil war between the extreme right and extreme left and no more questions were asked. My views, too, were also largely coloured by these images and the recent blood-curdling reports of daily assassinations, of brutal torture and mutilation in El Salvador had not calmed my feelings of trepidation as we set off on this assignment.

After the plane's engines had been shut down and the passenger door opened, we are hit by a wave of hot humid air, as if an oven door in a bakery had suddenly been opened. The dimly lit airport building beckoned a short walk away. There aren't many of us on the plane and we are apparently the only foreigners. The customs area is deserted apart from a few heavily armed soldiers in battle fatigues, looking dangerously bored. Our passports are examined with the utmost meticulousness, each page being studied as if it contained secret hieroglyphics (I'm pretty sure the official can't read English). He asks in Spanish where we will be staying and for how long, breathes heavily on his dry rubber stamp and bangs it down on an empty page in the passports; only customs now. They make us open every bag and carefully examine every item. The camera equipment doesn't seem to worry them once we say we are journalists and that our accreditation is waiting for us in San Salvador – a white lie. They seem more concerned about whether we have subversive literature or weapons, and my colleague's khaki trousers almost cost us the trip because an immigration official insists that they are army issue and "the wearing of uniforms is not allowed". Only after some vociferous and stubborn argumentation do they let us through in the end.

It is already dark when we emerge from the airport building, already sweating profusely in the oppressive humidity. We are immediately accosted by several unsavoury looking characters, unshaven with stained T-shirts and ragged trousers, grabbing at our suitcases and offering taxis to the capital – perhaps those Hollywood images are true after all? We are in danger of losing sight of our twelve pieces of luggage as the men begin running off in different directions. We only just manage to retrieve them and get them loaded into the first dilapidated taxi we can. The driver stows as much of our luggage in the boot as best he can and ties the lid with string to hold it down, threading it through the hole that used to be the lock. The tripod, camera and tape recorder we take into the car with us. I sit in the back trying to settle my backside between the protruding, rusty springs. The driver starts the engine with a throaty roar and heads for town. The car rattles and bumps, threatening to fly asunder at any moment.

As soon as we leave the dimly-lit airport the night spills over us like a sack of soot. Our car doesn't appear to possess lights and the road, too, is unlit and pitted with treacherous pot-holes, but our driver seems to know it by heart. It is a long haul into San Salvador – about 35 km – and the road is uncannily deserted apart from the odd jeep laden with soldiers, their helmeted heads and guns silhouetted against the starry sky. At one point we are waved down by a torch wielding sentry, who pokes his M-16 through the open window and demands our passports. There are a lot of ambushes along this road, our driver tells us, because it is used regularly by the army and that is why they are very jumpy. We are relieved to see San Salvador's twinkling lights appear on the horizon and even more relieved to flop down on our beds in the hotel and turn on the air-conditioning.

We have no time to orientate ourselves next day because a fellow journalist staying in the hotel tells us that it is the Day of the Dead and there will be a carnival procession with strong political overtones and we should definitely cover it, but there is likely to be trouble from the army. San Salvador is an archetypically Latin American city: Its centre resplendent with monumental white colonial buildings, like fossils from a once glorious past, the surrounding shops and office blocks are dilapidated and uncared for, its narrow side streets bustling with a myriad of craftsmen, street-sellers, beggars and shoppers; surrounding the commercial centre are the running sores of the "Barrios", the stinking hovels and makeshift abodes of the poor. In the hilly suburban areas, where the air is cooler and fresher, are the mansions and bungalows of the wealthy, protected by high walls, big iron gates with electronic locks and often a guard with a shot-gun or a ferocious dog. With their well-tended lawns, flowering bougainvillea hedges and hibiscus shrubs, half screening the shining Mercedes or Buicks in the driveways and the silence is only broken by bird song or the soft rain-sound of irrigation systems; they provide a stark contrast to the noisy and sweaty throng of the city centre below.

The central square is dominated by the cathedral, like some gigantic beached liner. On its steps colourful knots of people are already gathering. There are the mothers of the disappeared with placards hung around their necks carrying photos of their sons, husbands or daughters who had been kidnapped and never seen again; there are the students in death masks and carnival costumes or with monkey masks and top hats, the girls in gaudy make-up and big feathery hats aping the bourgeoisie. There is a sense of good humour and joviality. The only factor marring the jollity is the 'discreet' presence of heavily armed soldiers on the street corners and roof-tops of the surrounding buildings, perched like hungry vultures awaiting death. We start preparing our camera and tape recorder when there is a sudden, rapid firing. Everyone dashes for cover and we throw ourselves on the ground, but then just as suddenly people start laughing and the tension breaks: someone had let off firecrackers as a joke. Several thousand have now gathered in the cathedral square and the colourful procession starts off through the streets. There is singing and a chanting of revolutionary slogans, demands for human rights and an end to the death squads. We are in the centre of the march column. After walking for about half an hour the march comes to a sudden halt and we hear the sound of gun shots, this time the real thing. We aren't going to hang about because we know the Salvadorian army doesn't play games and certainly won't shirk at firing on unarmed men, women and children, something they are quite adept at. We run off down a side street, hail a taxi and drive to the central hospital and wait at the main entrance. If there are casualties this is where they will be brought and the numbers will provide a real indication to the extent of the confrontation.

We don't have to wait long. The afternoon light is beginning to wane when the first asthmatic tooting of ambulance sirens reaches our ears. Not long after, the entrance to the hospital resembles a front-line red cross station: white coated orderlies ferry the blood-stained casualties on metal stretchers into the operating theatre. They are several women, young girls, a cripple and then one or two young men, all dressed simply in thin, faded cottons, often barefoot, their limbs and clothing soaked in blood. This is the regime's answer to peaceful protest! The next morning in the tiny brick mortuary in the centre of the city cemetery a crowd of anxious relatives blocks the entrance. We make our way through the people and there, unceremoniously thrown on the floor in transparent plastic sacks, like meat carcasses, are half a dozen corpses. The bullet holes in faces and chests still clearly visible; they are all young, in their late teens or early twenties. They probably only went along for the fun and now they lie here as anonymous corpses and, as yet, unclaimed.

The Salvadorian Communist Party is of course banned, as in almost all other Latin American countries, but we are keen to meet and interview Shafik Handal, the General Secretary. We had been told that we can make contact with the party through one of the community houses in San Salvador: a derelict-looking place, not far from the city centre, where meetings are held, leaflets produced and banners painted. Here the brother of a recently assassinated left-wing deputy says he can arrange the interview with Shafik Handal for us. When we return at the appointed time the next evening he tells us to follow him in our car. After a half-hour's drive through the narrow suburban streets, criss-crossing the city until we are totally lost, he pulls into the side of the road and tells us to load our equipment into his car and leave our own there. "Don't worry", he assures us, "It will be watched". We then drive off and spend another half an hour motoring through the dark streets until we eventually turn into a driveway of a large house and are told we have arrived. Shafik Handal is waiting in the dining room.

He is a man in his late thirties, very Arab-looking (I believe he is of Lebanese extraction) and rather nervous and tense. He knows that if we have been followed or are not 'kosher' it can cost him his life – there is a high price on his head. We only want a short ten-minute interview, but this was incomprehensible to him. We've come all this way from Europe for a ten-minute interview! He had prepared a small speech on the history of El Salvador's struggle and despite our pleading for it to be short, is determined to deliver it. Although much too long for our half-hour report it is a fascinating and informative historical analysis. We drive back in a similar circuitous way, but by now it is midnight and there are no cars on the streets anymore; we have no idea where we are or where we had been. The party's security was efficient. Shafik was able to evade the death squads to the end, while many others were being picked off one by one, and resurfaced years later as one of the leaders of the guerrilla struggle in the hills.

The next day we meet a man of a similar mould to Shafik, but he would, in all probability, not have considered himself to be on the same side: Archbishop Romero, the courageous Catholic priest who spoke out against the killings. We are to meet him in the administrative offices behind the cathedral. There is no need of secrecy here, everyone knows him and as Archbishop of the capital city, San Salvador, he feels safe from terrorist attacks by the right. The lush vegetation in the courtyard and the damp quiet of the cloisters conveys an air of relaxation and calm, such a contrast to the square and streets only a few hundred yards away. We are led into an office to wait. On the walls are dozens of photos, mainly of young men, but a few women too. They are priests or lay members of the church who had been murdered by the 'security forces'; underneath each photo is a short biographical note and details of what had happened. Romero enters as we study the photos. He is dressed in his plain black cassock, his short grey hair and heavy-rimmed spectacles lending him an inoffensive academic air, his large, dark eyes expressing an intelligence and warmth. We shake hands and he says that he is at our disposal. We ask him about the present situation, about the role of the Catholic Church and what the international community can do to help. Like most representatives of the Catholic Church, he answers with care and circumspection, not wishing to be accused of political bias, but he is clear and unequivocal about where the blame for the killings lies: in the poverty and exploitation of ordinary people and the attempt by the oligarchy to keep it that way. He criticises the USA for giving arms rather than aid and appeals to the countries of the world to help restore democracy to his war-torn land. Little did we imagine that only a few months later he, too, would be lying on the cold floor of his own cathedral with an assassin's bullet in his chest.

The man generally acknowledged to be behind the death squads and Romero's murder was Major Robert d'Aubuisson, the former National Guardsman and now leader of ARENA, the neo-fascist party of Salvador. We had to wait another three years before returning to El Salvador in 1982 in order to capture him and his cohorts on film. ARENA's offices are in a quiet residential quarter of San Salvador. In the evenings it is the American and Japanese jeeps, with their darkened, bullet-proof glass windows which dominate the street scene. People don't walk to places anymore. While we are eating in a nearby restaurant one of these jeeps pulls up and two burly men with sunglasses jump out, the tell-tale bulges under their jackets. They take up sentry positions and then a couple descend quickly from the car and enter the restaurant. One of the bodyguards stays outside watching the jeep while the other takes a table near the entrance.

ARENA's office is also well guarded: a high, locked metal gate bars the entrance, in the driveway two jeeps with shotguns lying ready on the front seats and an armed guard who opens the gate for us. The small reception room also has heavy metal bars on the windows and even a steel door. The walls are decorated with ARENA posters and choice anti- Communist slogans. We feel distinctly welcome. If our cover were blown here It wouldn't require much imagination to work out our destiny. After a while we are led to Major Roberto d'Aubuisson's office. A youngish, trim man greets us from behind his desk. He is incredibly tense and obviously ill at ease with the press; his hands fiddle with his pen and his eyes are never still, but he agrees to answer our questions. Our aim is not to provoke him or force him into a corner but to allow him to tell us what his organisation stands for and what his vision of El Salvador is. We hope to win his confidence so that we can spend some time with his organisation. He relaxes visibly as he realises we have no nasty or awkward questions to put to him. Finally he invites us to go along with him to an election meeting in the countryside. A convoy of jeeps and big American cars is put together, a veritable armoury of shotguns, machine guns and rifles is loaded into the vehicles and all ARENA officials carry their own pistols. There certainly seems to be no restriction on carrying guns, unless ARENA is simply taboo for the authorities.

We are taken in a 'press car' and with us is a veteran *Time* reporter who is, perhaps sensibly, wearing a brand new bullet-proof jacket. He doesn't want to endanger his health, he says emphatically. We are ferried out of San Salvador and through the countryside, sending up clouds of red dust from the unmade roads as we speed past the squalid peasant shacks, sending chickens squawking and pigs squealing into the ditches. After an hour and a half we arrive at Nueva Concepcion, where the meeting is to take place. In the main square about a hundred or so locals have gathered around the makeshift platform. Not having been to any other election meetings we don't know how the people usually react, but here they stand with expressionless faces, revealing more a sense of duty than enthusiasm for the speakers who are desperately trying to warm them up for the big man. Only when scanning the crowd for interesting faces do I notice that the whole square is surrounded by men with shotguns, carried inconspicuously at the side of their bodies, while they lounge nonchalantly in doorways or at the street corners. No wonder the peasants aren't too enthusiastic! The platform tries unsuccessfully to get the people going with ARENA's anthem, crackling from makeshift speakers mounted on the platform:

*The Nationalist Republican Alliance of El Salvador
is present here for the fatherland.*

Liberty is written with blood

Work with sweat
Blood and sweat unites us...
When in our beloved fatherland
Foreign voices are heard
The nationalists rise up
Saying this: Fatherland yes, Communism no!
El Salvador is the tomb
Where the reds end up...
Criminal communists, Communist animals
Have murdered and raped
Have ruined our fatherland.
Tremble communists... etc.

D'Aubuisson then speaks, reiterating the primitive slogans of his party's hymn: "Good morning brothers of Nueva Concepcion, brothers from the province of Chalatenango and all Salvadorians who are listening to us. It cost us 30,000 fratricidal deaths during our civil war". (Here he is referring to the civil war in the early 1930s where mass killing of peasants by the army took place). "We killed each other because the international communists poisoned our minds. Fifty years have passed but we still have the same aggression. You can end this by voting for the Republicans..."etc.

When I return to the hotel that evening I spend a long time under the shower. I feel that I am not only removing the sweat and dust of the day, but also the filth, hatred and poison from the pores of my skin. When we later speak to the organisers of the Committee of Human Rights – in the main ordinary women from the barrios and countryside – and hear their harrowing tales of persecution, torture and the disappearance of their families at the hands of the right-wing death squads or the army, the full realisation that Major d'Aubuisson's words are not just empty rhetoric is forcibly brought home to us: a communist in this country is anyone who raises a voice against injustice and poverty.

Of course we want to talk to the guerrillas as well, to show what the other side is like and what their aspirations are. This is not easy because although, at this time, they control liberated areas of the country, access to them through the army lines is almost impossible. A Salvadorian journalist friend makes it possible for us. In our small hired car we set off early in the morning towards Chalatenango. We pass the heavily guarded military airport and a number of sandbagged sentry posts on the way, being careful to slow down and stop at each one. Patrols of soldiers on foot try to keep the arterial roads free. Most of these soldiers are only boys, often dressed like Rambo, with coloured kerchiefs tied around their heads, belts of cartridges slung Mexican-style over their chests and carrying heavy machine guns. We drive past pylon after pylon, twisted or lying contorted on their sides like collapsed giraffe skeletons. Even the bridges had been blown up by the guerrillas who operate virtually freely at night. We are not far from our destination, between Puerto de Oro and San Miguel, when we see a bus ahead of us, parked in the middle of the road, with its passengers lined up in front of it. A small man in checked shirt and trilby, an ancient shotgun slung over his back is lecturing them. We jump out of the car and ask if we can film. The guerrillas don't mind – there are a number of them standing guard in the bushes at the side of the road. The little man is telling the passengers to donate to the cause: "You see we are killed but we don't let that stop us. Our fight is a just one. We don't gain anything from it, we suffer hunger, we don't even earn 10 Colones a day, we live oppressed but we survive because we know that tomorrow the whole people will forge ahead, those who are today hungry, miserable, infected with parasites and by epidemics. This is a battle of the people..."

He isn't a good orator or particularly subtle and the bus passengers don't reveal their reactions, but his commitment is clear. After passing his hat around he tells the people to climb back into their bus and the car passengers too –in the meantime several cars had arrived– and he and his comrades melt back into the wilderness. Our Salvadorian friend says we should now drive off smartly because after such episodes the army often comes and starts indiscriminate bombing or shooting in the hope of eliminating a few guerrillas. We walk quickly back to the car and I feel in my pocket for the key, but can't find it. I begin a frantic search of all my pockets, then we all begin looking on the road – perhaps I'd dropped it. In the meantime all the other cars and the bus have disappeared, leaving us stranded alone and vulnerable in the middle of the road, only the eerie sounds of cicadas and birds in the bush punctuate the silence. My companions are becoming more and more exasperated. We try to force the boot with a stick, thinking I may have locked it in there. Again I search my pockets for the umpteenth time and then I find it! I had inadvertently slipped it into a tiny second pocket in my jeans which I never use. We are more than relieved and speed off with no more delay, thanking our lucky stars that the army hasn't turned up. That day our attempt to contact the guerrillas in the liberated area is unsuccessful. The army presence is too dangerous. But then in the following week we are offered an unexpected chance of entering a liberated area.

There is a national day of immunisation being undertaken by UNESCO and for this day the army has agreed to let teams of medical people into all areas. We simply tag along with a group of Swiss doctors and pretend we are part of the team. We head for a tiny village, called Tenancingo, not far from the capital. The army controls all access routes to this village and is even reluctant to let the medical team through, which they only do after much argument and threats of international repercussions. Beyond the army post the rutted, dirt track is deserted. We drive slowly and carefully to avoid an ambush – even clearly marked red or green cross vehicles have been attacked. After a few kilometres we are stopped by two young men in fatigues and red kerchiefs around their necks, but when they see who we are they smile and wave us on. Tenancingo itself, a village with one main street and the usual monumental church, has a semi-deserted atmosphere about it: only a few women stand, watching from doorways, mildly curious. A few cats and dogs roam lethargically on the road where grass tufts and weeds sprout between the stones. This village is one of those which alternate between being a 'liberated area' and being retaken by the army. Most people had had enough and had left, leaving a few hardened characters behind. The doctors park their jeep in the main square, set up a table with their equipment and wait for their patients. Women with small children soon begin queuing. While we are filming this columns of young guerrillas begin emerging from the surrounding scrub land and empty buildings. They are colourfully and individually clad and appeared to be well armed, most with American M-16s. Some stay and watch the immunisation process taking place, others melt back into the undergrowth.

We interview one section commander, who had been a student and even now would look more in place on a campus than out here with his pistol and grenades. His pimply face with its wisps of beard and his nervous hands, continuously toying with the red kerchief around his neck, make him appear very vulnerable. He is bursting with idealism and youthful optimism, gives us a long lecture on Latin

American history, the long years of colonial domination, oppression and misery which are now coming to an end as the liberation forces gain strength. I wish we could share his optimism. Not many months after we had left, the army with new weaponry and technical advice supplied by the Reagan administration, launched a new Phoenix-type offensive and drove the guerrillas out of the liberated areas. Any peasant caught in these areas was seen as a guerrilla or at best a supporter and dealt with accordingly; the army here took no prisoners of war! The third and last time we return to El Salvador is in 1986. Because of the increasing number of fatalities among journalists working in El Salvador we decide to have special T-shirts printed before we return there again. They have our firm logo on the front and in very large letters, TV and PRENSA on the back. We hope this will deter any soldier taking a pot shot at us with the excuse that he thought we were guerrillas! Ironically I have to give one of these shirts as a 'present' to a colonel in the army who takes a fancy to it.

During this trip we visit and talk to some of those peasants who have fled the slaughter and are now living in big camps set up by the church on the outskirts of San Salvador, as well as those in the UNESCO administered camps in Honduras. In one of these camps a small, 13 year- old boy, Jose, tells us a horrific story of how he fled with his parents from one such army raid on the liberated area of the Guazapa volcano and was cut off from the column of fleeing adults. He spent days hiding from the searching soldiers and saw them raping and murdering several women and killing an old man who was too old to flee with the rest. Jose had lived on wild fruit and berries and eventually found refuge in a deserted peasant hut. He is a lively, likeable youngster who tells his story as if it were about an every day experience in the local park. He has not yet found his parents and is being looked after by the church volunteers in the camp.

On our way back to San Salvador's airport we pass by the military hospital in San Salvador. Lounging along the wall outside is a long line of soldiers, young peasant boys, in their teens or early twenties, but each and every one is maimed: feet or legs are missing, some have only one arm or stumps in bandages, others hobble along the pavement on makeshift crutches, one or two stand chatting with girlfriends or family members. These are just a few of the victims, on the army side, of mines or grenade attacks. I dread to think how many there must be on the other side. Earlier we had spoken to ordinary government soldiers, mostly young peasant boys conscripted, often against their will, to kill their own people. One soldier we interviewed was so brutalised that he boasted to us of killing his own brothers and uncles. An indication of the brain-washing that they undergo was revealed to us when we asked who the people were that they were fighting and the answer came back promptly, "Russians and Cubans". We asked innocently whether they'd actually seen any of these Russians and Cubans and one of the soldiers said, "yes, he was big and black"! As we spoke a group of uniformed US 'advisers' arrived at the base in a helicopter, disappearing into the command office. We collar one of them, Colonel Steele, according to his identity tag, but he tells us he is on special assignment and can't talk in front of the camera.

Robert White, Carter's ambassador in El Salvador, had been fired by the incoming Reagan administration after he had made critical remarks about the futility and injustice of America's involvement there. He was replaced by a hard-line man, Oliver Tambs, who openly spoke of the "need to destroy the civilian support base of the guerrilla". The Phoenix Operation, planned and organised by the USA drove the guerrillas out of the liberated areas by making them free-fire zones, thus forcing the remaining peasant population out and into concentration camps or what they euphemistically called 'protected villages'. Settlements were bombed and burnt down, livestock destroyed so that the guerrilla would be starved out. There are now no more liberated zones as such but the army can still only operate freely during the day, is regularly attacked at night and the guerrilla still operates throughout the country. A decade on, tens of thousands of deaths registered, tens of thousands of refugees, hundreds of orphans, of maimed and tortured and the war is no nearer a conclusion than it was at the beginning. This is the cost of the war 'against world communism'.

During my time as foreign correspondent I went to El Salvador three times and each time the situation there was worse than during the previous visit. Each time we spent only a fortnight in El Salvador but the images, impressions and experiences were so concentrated that each trip felt like an eternity spent in a contemporary version of Dante's *Inferno*. This, the tiniest of Latin American countries had been turned into one hell-hole. What began as a modest movement of peasants for a modicum of land on which to grow crops to feed their families, had been transformed into a bloody crusade against communism.

The USA, with all its wealth and weaponry and in league with the small corrupt Salvadorian oligarchy was fighting a surrogate war against a small band of guerrillas who enjoyed widespread support among the poor and dispossessed. As in all wars it was the ordinary people, who bore the burden. The wealthy lived in well protected villas and anyway spent much of their time holidaying and shopping in Miami, sending their scions to study in the USA and thus avoid having to fight the dirty war themselves. Each of our three films had shown a different aspect of the reality in El Salvador, always with the backdrop of the war and the killing, but attempting to explain the processes taking place. The first had concentrated on the new democratic possibilities after the military coup and the return of civilian leaders to the country, the second had concentrated on the right wing death squads and their links to the oligarchy and the USA, and the third had brought out the progressive role of the lower echelons within the Catholic Church and the new sophistication of the Salvadorian Army with new and generous aid from the Reagan administration. Our second film was awarded the Egon Erwin Kisch prize at the Leipzig International Film Festival. The fact that the film was judged by our peers from the international film-making fraternity and that we were, in this way, associated with this pioneer of socialist journalism, gave us a sense of pride.

CHAPTER 6 – THE OPEN VEINS OF HISPANIC AMERICA
Guatemala – blood and volcanoes

From El Salvador we went on to Guatemala, the most Indian of all Latin American countries. It is a green, hilly, jungle country, a steamy and voluptuous hothouse. The dazzling, colourful fabrics woven by its women give vent to an inchoate craving for release from the drabness of their daily lives.

The bombastic white colonial churches tower like beached galleons over the huddled flotsam villages, their hulls ablaze inside with the gold of hundreds of flickering candles and the smoky, acrid aromas of incense. Here the weft of Catholicism intersects and intermingles with the warp of Mayan gods and the sheer desperation of those whose last pagan resort is to beg any of the gods to release them from penury and misery.

Symptomatic of the country's demise is the fate of that beautiful, mystical bird, the quetzal, whose iridescent plumage adorned the head-dresses of Indian priests and whose glorious flight represented the people's freedom. This bird, now almost extinct in the remnants of rain forest, is immortalised on the country's coinage. The quetzal is now no longer a symbol of national pride and independence, but of barter, of the cheapness of human labour, dishonesty and uncontrolled greed. Its shimmering viridian feathers have been dulled to a verdigris silver.

Its population of just over seven million is 52 percent pure Indian, speaking some 20 languages and a hundred separate dialects; over 50 percent of the population is illiterate and poverty perhaps the worst in the region. The country only enjoyed a very short lease of democracy in the fifties when the democratically elected Arbenz government began introducing reforms and curtailing the pillage of the big US fruit companies, which virtually ran the country till then. This government was soon toppled by the CIA and local oligarchy and since then it has experienced only uninterrupted dictatorship of the most brutal form and a protracted guerrilla war since 1964.

This country has the reputation of being even more arbitrarily despotic than El Salvador and has been largely ignored by the world's media because of the difficulties and dangers of working in it. This is the country, perhaps next to South Africa, I fear working in most of all. It is 1982 and the bitter war against the guerrillas is still being waged unabated. There have been several cases of tourists or journalists simply disappearing while travelling in the country. Two of my Guatemalan friends from Babelsberg, a young cameraman called Christian Johannson and one of Guatemala's best known poets, Otto René Castillo, had been shot and killed in the forested hills of Guatemala only a few years previously. I feel very queasy about coming here and feel even more vulnerable being British – it is the only Latin American country where we need a visa because of the long-running dispute with Britain over Belize sovereignty.

It is impossible to obtain a visa in Britain (because of the long-standing feud over the sovereignty of Belize, it has no ambassador in London) so we apply for it in Costa Rica and within a day we have it stamped in our passports. Our arrival at the airport of Guatemala City is uneventful; it is empty apart from the few arriving businessmen and diplomats, and the same faceless military is omnipresent as in El Salvador. The only differences are that here the soldiers have Israeli Galils instead of US M16s and they are shorter and stockier than their Salvadorian counterparts and their swarthy faces betray their strong Indian heritage.

We arrive in the afternoon, tired and sweaty, and after settling into our hotel, showering and unpacking the equipment, decide to go out for a meal. In the meantime it is already dark – near the Equator the sun drops like a heavy stone, dragging the curtain of night down before you realise the day is over. Our hotel is in the city centre and we decide to walk. We find it difficult to believe that this is the capital city: the expected bustle is missing and the colourful street sellers have disappeared, the streets are ill-lit and eerily deserted. Almost the only moving objects are the unlit jeeps packed with well-armed vigilantes or soldiers which roar through the streets at regular intervals, ignoring traffic lights, and the ambulances, their sirens screaming, on their way to pick up the first of the evening's toll of injured or corpses. We have the distinct feeling that perhaps we shouldn't be on the streets. We are not sure if there is not some sort of curfew in force.

Although we haven't gone very far, we decide to retire to the safety of one of the big hotels where we will have to put up with 'international cuisine' and the company of US businessmen rather than real Guatemalan fare in a local restaurant. Actually the meal is not only much better than we had expected, it is an obscene feast. We are served an enormous selection of roast meats from the charcoal brazier in the centre of the restaurant, much more than any of us can manage despite our enormous appetites. Even though well hidden by the thick walls and dangling forest flora we can't really enjoy the meal. It's too much like having a banquet in the midst of a famine; we are too close to the rickety, barefoot kids we saw on the streets earlier, when we arrived from the airport. Here is a superfluity of best beef, goat, pork and sausages, whereas many Guatemalans are unlikely to see more than a sliver of meat the whole year.

Our first priority in Guatemala City is to obtain press credentials. We have heard enough about this country not to be foolhardy and work without proper credentials. In addition, as British nationals, citizens of an 'enemy country' we can easily be accused of military espionage if we film army personnel. So we go immediately to General Garcia's presidential palace and are ushered up the marble staircase into the presidential secretary's enormous office. The palace itself is surrounded by soldiers of the elite regiment, newly equipped with Israeli Galil guns and smart uniforms. They stand, too, on every level of the staircase, in the corridors and on the balconies as if expecting an attack at any minute.

There are already three Italian journalists waiting in the office who are also keen to obtain press credentials. The secretary, a voluminous man with the face of a Mafia boss: simple, lugubrious and swarthy, sits behind an enormous oak desk which is 'decorated' with two red telephones, a red leather blotting pad and a pen stand, all of which look unused. He is slumped back in his throne-like chair and, after we tell him our purpose, gesticulates generously with his over-large hands: "But senores Guatemala is a free country, you can go anywhere you wish, you don't need press credentials, as long as you obey our laws and do nothing wrong". We told him that we fully understood that, but we would nevertheless be grateful if he would issue us with a document to say that we are journalists, just in case we are questioned or have problems. He simply reiterated: "It is really not necessary señores. If any problem arises just give me a ring and I will sort it out..." Our pleading was in vain. The presidential secretary is adamant. Now we know why no bona fide journalists are ever killed in Guatemala – there aren't any! He proceeds to lecture us for half an hour longer on what the government is doing for the poor, giving them land, carrying out illiteracy campaigns, and then tells us bluntly that the foreign press distorts reality and manipulates the reports. We take the point!

In contrast to El Salvador, where journalists have been able to give quite wide coverage to the war, even though, in the main, of a sensationalist nature, Guatemala is a relatively closed world. Here a war has been going on for 40 years, hundreds upon hundreds killed, others brutally tortured, including Catholic priests and lay workers, thousands of Indian peasants herded into 'strategic villages' where they vegetate in appalling conditions, but there has been virtually no coverage. The rest of the world doesn't seem interested. Any inquisitive journalist who decides to take a peep is clearly told what to expect, so they just stay away.

During the day the city comes alive and the brightly woven dresses and shirts of the rows of women selling their meagre produce on the pavements lend the streets a gaiety only contradicted in the sullenness of their faces. Pot-bellied babies crawl around in their skirts or in cardboard boxes at their side. Traffic clogs the central market area and the city appears, on the surface, almost like any other metropolis. A newspaper seller offers us a paper. We are surprised to see that it has no text, but only photo upon photo of grisly corpses and traffic accidents. This paper comes out daily and obviously has a morbid readership sufficient to keep it in business!

We decide to continue working without credentials, but testing the waters carefully. Our second official contact is with the army – the true power in the country. We know that without its support we can film nothing because it controls the whole country. After a number of attempts we are eventually offered an interview with Colonel Rabanales, the army officer responsible for public liaison. He is in his early thirties, a suave, athletic man with eyes like a bloodhound, making you feel transparent. On his desk is arrayed a small arsenal of toy canons pointing in our direction. After politely welcoming us and asking our purpose, he asks to see our passports

– we are three, my sound-man and a friend who is acting as interpreter for us. Col. Rabanales takes our passports, studies them, then returns them to us with a sardonic smile on his face. I suddenly realise that we have made a cardinal mistake: the photos in our passports show us all with thick beards, but when working in Latin America I and my colleagues always shave because a beard in the army's eyes is a sure sign of, at best, decadence and at worst, guerrilla sympathies. We carry on regardless and he doesn't let on that he has tumbled our primitive attempt at camouflage. He tells us that poverty and social deprivation are not the causes of unrest in the country, but are simply manipulated by international Communist forces. "No state", he says, "has evolved where there is no impoverished strata, there is no equitability in the distribution of wealth anywhere." The struggle for equality or for dignity is therefore, in his mind, one imported from outside. We ask whether we can film with the army on patrol or in action against the 'insurgents' and are promised that he will look into it. "But why are you journalists always only interested in violence?" he asks, as if we are the cause of it all. Needless to say, despite our pressing him daily, nothing ever materialises of his promise.

We decide to risk filming without army permission and drive out into the countryside north of Guatemala City. The countryside is beautifully lush, everywhere a rich green jungle of natural rain forest with picturesque Indian villages nestling among the trees on the hillsides; volcanoes dominate the skyline, some still smoking or spitting fire and exotic bird-song echoes from the tree canopy. What mars the idyll is the presence of army roadblocks, convoys of armoured trucks or foot patrols on seemingly every road. At one road block where we take our camera out to film we are immediately stopped and questioned by an arrogant lieutenant, who interrogates us with a strong Argentinean accent. We explain that the president's personal secretary told us we could film anywhere and that we are keen to show under what difficult circumstances the army has to work here. His expression softens and he begins to tell us of the invidious tricks the guerrillas use to attack the army. We manage to persuade him to let us film a patrol, but only on condition that we film no faces! We agree, but ignore his stipulation of course.

The Guatemalans, being almost pure Indian, are very short of stature and the soldiers in his platoon look like young school boys; they are certainly no more than 15 or 16, but have the height of twelve-year olds. The lieutenant takes us half a kilometre up the road and into some bushes at the roadside. He proceeds to remove a cover of woven grass and sticks to reveal a deep hole, lined at the bottom with a series of sharpened sticks pointing upwards. He explains to us that when the patrols walk up the road the guerrillas open fire, driving the soldiers to cover. They dive into the bushes and fall into such traps, landing on the sharpened sticks which are often smeared with excrement so that the wounds later become infected. He says the guerrillas have learned these tricks from the Vietnamese and that they also have underground hospitals and resting places like the Vietnamese. The Guatemalan army, for its part, has copied the brutal methods used by the US in Vietnam. They have herded much of the population into 'strategic villages', virtual concentration camps, where the people can hardly earn a living and are not allowed to move freely around the country. In this way they hope to starve the guerrilla of support and food.

The villagers we try to speak to in their fields or on the country roads are very reticent and monosyllabic. Opening one's mouth too wide here can cost you your life. We approach a leading journalist on Guatemala's national daily newspaper, Prensa Libre, for some background information. He won't talk to us in his office, but invites us out for lunch, where he indicates the sort of difficulties journalists have to work under. When we ask if he would be willing to talk on camera he refuses, saying matter-of-factly, "we have already had 4 journalists killed and even talking to foreign journalists as I am with you now could cost me my life." We don't press him after that. This story is to be repeated so often.

We contact a Protestant pastor, a middle-aged Texan from the USA, who is working in a purely religious capacity in Guatemala. We simply want him to tell us about his work but he is so frightened, saying, how he can be sure we are who we say we are. Eventually, after some persuasion and showing him our passports, he does talk to us, but not in front of the cameras. We sit on his bed in the little makeshift room at the mission, his hands are twitching, and alone the fact that we have contacted him at all makes him nervous. He tells us that his wife has already returned home because she couldn't take the strain any longer and he will be leaving shortly. In the past month he has lost two of his lay associates, Guatemalans, one of whom was helping peasants to learn to read and write and another, a lawyer, who was offering them advice on land ownership. They were found one morning with their throats slit open. Even teaching people to read here is considered a subversive or activity. He himself has already received several death threats. He is totally anti- communist with a firm belief in the 'Free World' and believes it was God's decision to send him to Guatemala. He tells us of the widespread corruption, the wholesale exploitation of the poor and the robbery of the peasants' land – if they are given any land by the authorities the former owners come back and drive them off it or simply kill them. He tells us all this, but still reiterates his faith in the 'Free Enterprise System'; he is non-political, he insists, and only "doing God's will".

We also speak to a different category of priest, a Canadian Mennonite, who professes not to know what we are talking about when we mention the killing or harassment of the Indians. He feels the government is doing all it can to help them. His sect has already translated the bible into several Quechuan (the main Indian language spoken in Guatemala) dialects, he tells us proudly, and the president is supporting their work. He lives in a comfortable apartment with a grand piano in the front room, a large garden surrounding the building, protected by a big fence. I am not unduly surprised that he has no criticism to make of life here. Such Protestant sects are making headway in Guatemala and attempting to oust the Catholic church which they see as susceptible to left-wing influence.

It is widely accepted in Guatemala that many of the death squad killings of trade unionists, social workers and progressive churchmen are carried out by *La Mano Blanca* (the White Hand), a para-military offshoot of the fascist party, MNL (Movimiento Nacional de Liberacion). We decide to pay them a visit and try to interview their leader, Alarcon Sandoval, one of those who was involved in the overthrow of the democratically elected Arbenz government in 1954.

Inside the courtyard of the ordinary looking building is a large wall with a badly executed painting on it of a ferocious Russian bear, blood dripping from its fangs. In front of it a wall is half-built and slogans on it appeal for you to buy bricks as a means of supporting the party and to brick-in the bear of 'atheistic communism'. In the reception area of the headquarters is a shrine with a facsimile of the Black Christ of Escipulas, the patron of the counter revolutionary forces. We arrange to meet Señor Alarcon, the leader, at his home in a leafy middle-class suburb of Guatemala City.

We arrive in front of the enormous steel gates, topped with barbed wire and a sentry tower above it. We are admitted by armed guards into the garden with its big trees and tropical palms; a gaudy macaw screams from the branches and a monkey on a chain jumps up and down with excitement. A whole armoury of guns is lined up against the wall by the gate, a polished white Mercedes stands in the garage and a gardener is hosing the flower beds. Inside the house it is refreshingly cool from the air conditioning. We are ushered into the large lounge, furnished in typical colonial style mock baroque furniture. A bronze bas-relief of the *Last Supper* hangs over the dining room table and, above the generous stairway, a kitsch oil-painting of a half naked girl being painted by the artist; on the other wall a silver crucifix.

Señor Alarcon descends the stairs to meet us. He is a stocky, olive-skinned man with a clipped moustache, dressed in a dark suit and tie, like an insignificant office clerk. It is a tragi-comic situation: he has had cancer of the throat and can only speak through an inserted voice box, reminding me of Arturo Ui, the evil, but pathetic figure in Brecht's eponymous play. He is almost impossible to understand and the sounds that come out of his voice box are disembodied like that of a computer. All the time he lovingly strokes his little white poodle lying next to him on the chair – and this is the man who boasts that he personally has killed hundreds of 'communists'. Sitting around us are several fat goons with bulging holsters and loose suits. He reiterates the old clichés about the dangers of Soviet imperialism and atheistic communism threatening the Christian way of life, but in his view trade unionists, liberation theologists are all just crypto-communists. In Europe we would simply laugh about such ravings but here they have to be taken seriously because this man has sufficient power to make his views felt.

The longer we stay in Guatemala the more surreal and threatening the place becomes, and we decide not to push our luck. The only thing we have not been able to document is the daily death toll of those assassinated by the death squads. We read the stories in the morning paper each day but have no first hand evidence. In Guatemala, as in a number of Latin American countries, the voluntary fire brigade or Red Cross are the first to be called out to the injured or dead rather than the police, who are not trusted. We manage to persuade the chief of a small fire station in one of the suburbs to let us spend a night with a team on the pretext of making a report on their diverse work as voluntary firemen. In this way we hope to get what we want without unnecessary risk to ourselves.

RED REPORTER
COVERT CORRESPONDENT FOR EAST GERMANY

We arrive at the station at nine in the evening and sit with the men, in their small office, waiting for the first calls. We sip tea and chat to them about the work they do, asking them what they get paid, how dangerous their work is, trying to gain their confidence and tell us something of their personal lives. We spend the first hours in this way until just before midnight when the first alarm rings and we all rush for the van. It is a battered old vehicle, rather like a stock-car, high off the ground and with very hard springs. We have to dive in the back within seconds, clutching our light, camera and tape recorder, because the driver won't wait. As we scramble inside, clinging to anything firm we can get hold of, it screeches around the corner and away. We are bounced up and down, banging heads, backs and arms on the metal sides as it careers suicidally down the narrow streets, like a berserk buffalo. We arrive at our destination in about five minutes, but are disappointed to find it is only a fire in a cafe, which is soon put out with a few pails of water. Most calls are of this sort, some are marital feuds, knifings or road accidents.

At two o'clock we are beginning to think we are wasting our time, when the telephone rings again and the officer answering it tells us it may be what we are interested in. Battered, bruised and tired we clamber once again into the back of the van and suffer another half an hour's torture before we reach the destination. We are surprised to find it is a big hospital. We are met by a group of grave-faced and tense nursing staff at the door who lead us along the corridors and into one of the operating theatres. Our footsteps resound echoingly off the greenish walls, dull neon tubes cast their cold aura; hardly anyone speaks, and then only in subdued whispers. In the operating theatre a surreal scene confronts us like something out of a horror film: A man is lying on the operating table, his brains splattered over the couch, and on the floor next to him are two white-coated hospital staff, also dead. We feel sick. Only later do we learn the full story. The man on the operating table had been the victim of an assassination attempt which had gone wrong. He had been brought to the hospital to be operated on, but his assassins had followed the ambulance, entered the hospital, finished the job off and killed the operating doctors too. Everyone is too frightened to speak to us, but one assistant is willing to show us the spent cartridges from the gun that was used: they are, he says, from an army issue revolver. This is the reality of Guatemala. The perpetrators are never found, it is just one more in the catalogue of daily killings of social workers, trade union leaders, journalists or just ordinary citizens who may have been overheard saying the wrong thing.

In Latin America as a whole, in the last two decades, it is reliably estimated that 90,000 people have been killed in civil warfare and in Guatemala alone 30,000 have disappeared. Guatemala did, for a short time in the late forties and fifties enjoy a democratic government and under Jacobo Arbenz Guzman it brought in some vitally needed reforms, but he had the temerity to challenge the big US multinational United Fruit Company and, with a little help from the CIA, was removed in a bloody coup in 1954. Dwight Eisenhower, testifying later before a House sub- committee in 1961 said, "We had to get rid of a Communist government which had taken over." The Arbenz' government was in fact a coalition of liberal and middle class intellectual forces with mild reformist aims. Since then this pitiable country has endured one bloody dictator after another and these regimes have enjoyed the tacit if not open support of the USA, which is so concerned about the abuses of human rights elsewhere in the world that it is apparently blind to those in its own back yard.

CHAPTER 6 – THE OPEN VEINS OF HISPANIC AMERICA
Chile – ghosts and fears

On 5 November 1970 Salvador Allende gave a victory speech to the jubilant thousands who filled the national stadium to hear him. He told them, "this is a triumph for our long-suffering people... at last we can say basta! enough is enough. No more economic exploitation. No more social inequality, no more political oppression". What hope and joy the mass of the people felt in those heady days and how no one at that time could imagine that only three years later those same forces which had oppressed the people for so long, in cahoots with the USA, would instigate a bloody coup and plunge Chile into another 15 years of darkness.

In the early eighties the resistance to Pinochet's regime was again on the increase and we felt it would be an ideal time to enter the country in order to expose the horrors of his tyranny and at the same time show the courage of the people and some of the problems they face in their struggle. Again, because Pinochet had saved Chile from communism the western media showed little inclination in exposing his regime. There were a few films made, but these were, in the main, made by progressive film makers on their own and not by the big TV companies.

In deciding to go to Chile we realised we were taking a big risk and that the consequences of being apprehended could be unpleasant. Heynowski and Scheumann had already hoodwinked the regime there and brought out a damning report. They were unlikely to be tolerant with someone who tried it again and also less trusting. However, we felt that if the Chileans were brave enough to do what they were doing, risking bullets, beatings and torture, then it was not asking too much of ourselves to risk making a film.

Again I go through the process of cutting my hair short and shaving my beard – it is amazing how appearance affects people's attitude to you. We agree to say we were making a travel report, looking at Chile from a tourist point of view and ignoring the political aspects. This will allow us to apply for press credentials in Santiago. We arrive in Chile in late April of 1983 and book into the Sheraton Hotel, a rather expensive, typically American luxury hotel, but a place where communists or left wing people would not be expected to stay. Once we have our credentials we will move out to somewhere cheaper and more pleasant. We meet our friend and interpreter at the hotel. He doesn't know yet what we have planned and we hope he has no qualms. He has come from Costa Rica and it is a lot cheaper for us all to meet straightaway in Chile, than elsewhere, because it would have meant taking another expensive flight to get here.

We, that is my German colleague Otto and I, arrive with an enormous baggage of preconceptions, images and fears. We have in our minds the hundreds of bestially tortured, the hundreds of 'disappeared', the imprisoned and assassinated. We imagine the DINA – the Chilean secret police to be very effective and efficient. Every minute of our time here we will be aware of the risks, particularly for those who work with us. We aren't even sure we will get in, let alone be able to film, but at the airport our baggage is only given a cursory check and our camera and tape recorder not even seen.

What is so surprising in Chile, particularly Santiago, is its European character, so different from the very Indian atmosphere of Central America. The buildings are neo-classical in style, the people in the main would not look amiss on a street in Paris, Rome or Berlin, the business men and government officials wear dark suits and ties, and sit over their lunches in spacious restaurants with bottles of wine. The whole city is much wealthier than its Central American equivalents, it has beautiful parks and the European influence is pervasive. Everything appears very civilised and ordered on the surface that it is hard to imagine what had taken place in the years since 1973.

We need to apply for press credentials in order to gain access to official functions and hope our names will not be on any list. It is a good thing I'd kept my nose clean at home because it is well known that the Chilean embassy spies on the exile organisations. We are given our press credentials with surprisingly little fuss, but the government press office doesn't do anything further to help us because the suspicious little bureaucrat who hands them to us has heard my colleague incautiously speaking German – this must have reminded him of the last time the GDR penetrated their security – and expresses his surprise at such a polyglot team of a Briton, Costa Rican and German. On our return to London after filming we discover that the Chilean embassy has been ringing our office to check if we have any connections with East Germany and what our team is doing in Chile! While in Chile we are very careful of our movements and work very fast so that by the time they catch up with us we will be out of the country. We ask the press secretary to arrange a number of things for us, amongst them a visit to a copper mine, none of which he manages to do. The only thing he does arrange is for us to attend the official May 1st event where Pinochet will meet representatives of "workers organisations" and junta officials. On this day, however, we have other plans: we have been informed by comrades that a group of workers and students are going to try holding a proper May Day rally in the Plaza de los Artesanos, despite the bans. We later tell him that our car broke down in the countryside and we were delayed and were unable to make the official event. Unbeknown to us we have been filmed by Chile's TV people on 1 May and can only trust to providence that he hasn't watched the news that night.

The May Day demonstration is to be the first public May Day demonstration for a decade and an open act of defiance against the junta. There is no precise time given us but we are told to be there by 10 o'clock in the morning. We go there earlier to reconnoitre and find where the best camera positions will be. The streets are still seemingly deserted, only the odd street cleaner or shift worker can be seen going about their business. We park in a side street not far from the square and go there on foot. Whether it is my subjective feelings or not I can't be sure, but as we approach the empty square I can sense a strange tension, of impending violence. A few shopkeepers peer nervously out of their doorways and at each entrance to the square silent groups of grey-uniformed riot police stand watching the area, their truncheons and guns prominently displayed.

In the dark, narrow streets off the square grey buses are parked, packed with more waiting police and in the shadows of doorways others stand, their plastic visors glistening on their helmets, clutching their machine guns. As we walk around the square, trying to look like innocent passers-by, I feel as if I were captive in an arena, waiting for the lions to be let in and all my escape routes are blocked. I can't imagine how our friends are going to organise a demonstration under these conditions. We stroll in front of a group of riot police, their black leather gloves clasping their long truncheons nervously. They look at us with vacant, impenetrable expressions, like programmed machines waiting for the signal. Even with our press credentials I don't feel confident that we can rely on their co-operation.

We retire from the immediate area and go for a coffee, to hang about and wait will only make us more suspicious-looking. We return to the square just before 10 o'clock and see that there is already a tiny knot of people sitting under the central monument, but other smaller groups of twos or threes are wandering around or near the square, obviously waiting for a signal. We take our equipment from the car and wander over, feeling the tension mounting. We are still the only press people around and thus feel even more vulnerable.

As the small group under the monument begins to grow we recognise a few faces, but no one betrays that they know us or we them; the clusters of riot police around the square also increase. Very suddenly a comrade we know well, a building workers' leader, shouts "Long live the first of May!" and raises his clenched fist. He is rapidly surrounded and followed by others, men and women, who then start marching around the monument. While we film we notice that a handful of other press photographers and press people have arrived. Concentrating on the demonstration we hadn't noticed the police pouring out of the buses and lining up for battle, their shields held tight, visors down and truncheons ready. A friend whispers to us to be ready to flee and points out what is happening: the para-military police are descending from the buses and lining up in full gear.

Suddenly the grey figures break loose, like a rogue wave, rolling towards the small group of vulnerable figures chanting their resistance. As it draws closer, the marchers run too, in all directions, closely followed by the truncheon swinging police. We dodge to the side, still filming. While we wait to see what will happen next an unmarked van draws up and a small group of lumpen-looking characters get out and come towards us. As they come they draw thin black pipes from their jacket pockets – these we were told afterwards are rubber pipes with lead core and can do a lot of damage – and start attacking the press people. These civilian hirelings of the secret police, lumpen elements, recruited in the slums, are used to intimidate opponents of the dictatorship, have no uniform or identification marks so the authorities can deny any knowledge of them. One video cameraman is knocked to the ground, another has his camera snatched and smashed and then one of the thugs tries to grab mine. I tear it from him, losing my radio transmitter microphone in the process, turn and run. Another tries to trip me over, but I manage to jump over his leg and just flee as if there are lions behind me. I am acutely aware of the uniformed police, still standing in the shadows, holding their machine guns and half expect to hear shots, but miraculously they ignore me. Eventually, after dodging down several side streets, I manage to hail a taxi and dive inside. The driver, without asking, appears to know what I've been doing and indicates to me that I should hide my valuable film cassette and camera under the seat.

Although I feel a deep sense of relief at having escaped I can't help still being perturbed about what could have happened to my colleagues left behind in the square. I quickly deposit the camera in the hotel room and return to the square. I find them both, somewhat shaken but in one piece, sheltering in a cafe nearby. Otto had had his microphone ripped out of the tape recorder and didn't know what had happened to it, and had taken a few blows of a truncheon, but is otherwise unscathed, as is our interpreter Daniel. Others had fared less well: the next day we were taken to visit a professor from the university who had merely been standing at the side of the square, watching. He was a man in his sixties, but we found him in bed with concussion, his shirt drenched in blood from a head wound and his glasses smashed to smithereens. Others, too, had been hurt and several arrests had been made, but no one seriously injured.

Primarily out of curiosity we return to the square the following day and ask the cafe owner, where my colleagues had taken refuge, about what happened after we'd left and if anyone by any chance has seen what happened to our equipment that the police had snatched. He tells us to wait a minute and disappears into the back, returning with our microphone in his hand. He explains that the policeman had thrown it onto a roof and a young boy retrieved it and they had kept it for us in case we returned!

We manage to get General Pinochet in front of our lens a few days later when he attends the passing out parade of police cadets. There I get within feet of the little man and obtain some good 'mug shots', his neatly trimmed moustache over his tight lips and his arrogant eyes – I almost wish I had a gun rather than a useless camera. Nevertheless the images, I hope, reflect the realities: the goose-stepping, jack-booted cadets, stamping around the sports ground, Pinochet and his posse of white jacketed and uniformed junta officers, resplendent with medals, dark sun glasses and corpulent wives. It is disconcerting, though, to see alongside those from other South American regimes, the USA and Britain, military attaches from China.

On the pretext of wishing to show Santiago's sporting facilities we gain access to the huge football stadium which Pinochet converted into a horrific concentration camp shortly after the coup. Here thousands were herded together, starved, beaten up, tortured and killed. It was here that Victor Jara had his hands smashed and was then killed. Filming in that empty stadium and wandering the cool, underground corridors, past changing rooms and toilets, I can feel the blows and the boots, hear the screams and moans, see the faces of fear, disbelief and brutality. I am relieved when we are outside again and can erase those images. I was later disgusted to learn that the GDR and the Soviet Union had agreed to play in this self same stadium during the Pinochet dictatorship as part of the world cup series.

A young comrade who helps us considerably in Santiago is an organiser in the barrio (suburban slum area) of Santa Victoria. He takes us to meet the women who had organised themselves into a cooking team, obtaining cheap vegetables and scraps from the shops and cooking a big pot of soup, the 'olla commun', for the very poor and hungry. He himself lives in semi-clandestinity, in a wooden shack in the barrio. When we ask him how he copes with the daily fear of arrest and probable torture, he shows us a small, dog-eared book – the Spanish version of Julius Fucik's *Message from the Gallows*. He says that the courage expressed by this Czech patriot gives him strength too and prepares him mentally for possible ordeals. We hope and trust he may never fall into the hands of the secret police.

He takes us to see the graves of Victor Jara and Pablo Neruda in Santiago's enormous central cemetery – just two simple plaques on the wall, but adorned with bunches of fresh flowers. We, too, pay our respects to these giants of Chilean culture, both in different ways broken and killed by Pinochet and his henchmen. Many others who were murdered by the junta have no marked grave, have simply disappeared, leaving relatives still clinging to vain hopes that they may still be alive somewhere. Salvador Allende's grave is not far from Valparaiso, in Viña del Mar and for many years was guarded by the police to prevent visitors bringing flowers and turning it into a shrine of resistance. Even when we are taken there we are told to be quick because if we linger we risk being arrested.

Valparaiso is Chile's largest port, built on the narrow coastal strip and the surrounding hills, looking out over the enormous breakers of the not so Pacific Sea. The city spreads upwards and over the hills like an octopus clambering out of the sea; the higher one climbs the more flimsy and poor the houses become; the roads mere dirt tracks and the people trying to eke an existence in some way or other. Only the magnificent view over the bay offers a richness otherwise missing. Pablo Neruda had his house up there on one of those hills, a modest building, now maintained by close friends as a museum.

The rooms are just as he left them when he died, simple furniture, a few books on the bookshelf, and a collection of the shells he collected from the beach and so loved that he wrote poems about them. The friend of his who showed us around told us about how nervous Neruda used to be before a poetry reading, whether to a small group of workers or a large audience of intellectuals, he would be like a small boy, embarrassed to go on stage, his friend said, and would hide away beforehand, not wanting to see anyone. I could see why he loved living up here, among ordinary Chileans, close to their daily worries and preoccupations, but also close to the sea with its wide free expanse and its constant movement and change.

As I expected, the government press officer failed to obtain permission for us to film in the copper mines, probably already too suspicious about what we were doing, so we went to a mining area ourselves, to Rancagua, south of Santiago. There the miners put on a cultural evening for us, singing songs made famous by Inti Illimani and Victor Jara, to the twanging the strings of the charango and haunting notes of pan pipes. We speak to Rodolfo Seguel, the Christian Democrat leader of the copper workers who tells us that the US embassy had put pressure on him to call off a forthcoming strike and of threats to his life by anonymous individuals. He was later arrested by the junta, but released again shortly afterwards due to international protest.

We moved hotels a number of times while were in Chile in order to avoid attracting too much attention – it is difficult to hide that fact that one is filming, leaving the hotel each day with big bags, and charging batteries in the rooms. We had been able to make contact with comrades in Santiago without much difficulty and Volodia Teitelboim's brother, a lawyer, organised for us to leave our exposed material at his daughter's flat where it was relatively safe and let us use this flat for clandestine meetings. Anyway we managed to avoid being caught by the police and were able to smuggle out all our material without a problem. On leaving, too, the checks were minimal and no one even saw our cameras or film.

CHAPTER 7 – USA: LAND OF POSSIBLE IMPOSSIBILITIES
Fascination and irritation

Over the two decades of filming I and my colleagues shot 16 documentaries in the USA. I have been over there perhaps twenty times in that period and although there are many parts of it I still don't know –it would take a life-time to know what is virtually a continent – I have been able to explore large areas to the east and west, north and south. I have spent time in the big cities of New York, Los Angeles, San Francisco, Chicago, Dallas and Houston amongst others, but have also stayed in numerous small towns and villages in a number of states. I've motored through the wild prairies of Wyoming, the coastal desert and agricultural heartlands of California, the German-looking farmlands of Minnesota and the scrublands of Texas. The landscapes in the United States range from the extremes of the vast cornfields of the Mid-West to the arid, awe- inspiring mountain ranges of Arizona, from the European-like quaintness of New England to the brashness of Florida. While its countryside is impressive and the strength, tenacity and pioneering spirit of its people can only command my respect, its dominating materialistic conservatism and cultural philistinism is something which repels me.

The USA – I dislike the term America, because it implies ignoring the whole of Canada and Hispanic America – is a complex country full of contradictions, probably more so than any other country in the world. Coming from Europe you realise what a relatively modern creation the country is in its present form, and because it unites within its borders almost all nations and races it is nevertheless, at the same time, a collection of mini-nations, each with its own different identity and aspirations. Of course, we need to remind ourselves that this vast land was, before the coming of the white man, occupied by a number of Indian tribes which roamed its wild landscapes in complete freedom. They have now been reduced to little pockets, in reservations where the majority vegetates, lost and confused by the disappearance of its culture and the rapidity of change.

I had never been to the United States before I was given my first filming assignment and my picture of it was formed, I suppose, like that of anyone else who hadn't been there, from the Hollywood cowboy and gangster films, or the few books I'd read, by authors like Upton Sinclair, Jack London, Theodor Dreiser and Irving Stone and maybe a few modern ones like Saul Bellow, Kurt Vonnegut or Howard Fast. Over and above this my picture of it had been largely formed by my political environment. As Communists my family saw the USA as the incarnation of all the evils of capitalism, the arch-enemy of socialism.

So for me it meant, in the first instance, the harassment, beating up and assassination of trade union leaders like Joe Hill and the anarchists Sacco and Vanzetti; it meant the Joe McCarthy witch-hunts of the fifties when Communists, trade unionists and other progressives were hounded out of society. People like Arthur Miller, Charlie Chaplin and Lillian Hellman were blacklisted and prevented from working, thousands of others, lost their jobs, their lives ruined, and several committed suicide. Internationally known figures like Bertolt Brecht and Hanns Eisler were ordered to testify before the Committee on Un-American Activities, and artists like Picasso, Diego Rivera and David Alfaro Siquieros were denied entry visas. Hysteria and paranoia gripped the country then. In the tow of this inquisitorial climate, where politicians like Richard Nixon and Ronald Reagan won their right wing spurs as denunciants and stool-pigeons, two Jewish Communists, Ethel and Julius Rosenberg were framed and put on trial as atomic spies and died in the electric chair, despite world-wide appeals for clemency, including one from the pope.

I recall vividly the persecution of one of its greatest singers, Paul Robeson and the withdrawal of his passport, refusing him permission to travel, and the hounding of a young black woman, Angela Davis for defending her people from racist abuse. She was put on the most-dangerous criminal wanted list and framed on a murder charge. In this instance world-wide protest prevented another judicial murder. I remember the young civil rights workers murdered in Alabama and the killings of Martin Luther King and Stokely Carmichael. One could go on, these are only the most well- known cases. These things actually happened, they were all true, but it did give me a very biased and one-sided picture of the country. Even hearing the North American accent on the streets was enough to raise my hackles, although, as a child I had met some marvellous people from the United State who visited my mother in Coventry, who were involved in the peace movement. It took several trips to the United States, however, and the meeting of many hospitable, sincere and courageous people before I lost this prejudice altogether.

The new colonialists who landed on that bleak east coast in 1623 on their small ship The Mayflower would have starved to death if they had not been offered the hospitality of the indigenous 'Red Indians'. This generous 'act of god', as it later became known, is celebrated by North Americans each year as Thanksgiving. The thanks the Indians got was to be virtually wiped out within two centuries as the white man stole their lands and butchered their people.

In those early days one didn't have to go through visa application procedures which are necessary today for anyone wishing to visit the States. The application form which can be obtained from the US Embassy includes a question, which asks the applicant to "please state whether you have suffered from any mental illness, have been convicted of any criminal or drug-related offences and whether you have been a member of the communist party or any of its front organisations". An answer in the positive would mean automatic denial. No other country in the world demands to know such political affiliations before allowing you in. Even if the visa is issued, it is still up to the discrimination of immigration officials in the USA whether they let you in or not. I, of course, lied and hoped that my name was not included on some list or other.

On arrival in the States there is always a long queue at immigration and the would-be entrant is often grilled as to their purpose in visiting the USA, their planned length of stay, whether they have a return ticket and where they intend staying. The immigration officer meanwhile leafs through a large book full of names, checking whether yours is included. That was always the moment when I held my breath, thinking my name would be there, but it never was and I never had any difficulty entering the United States. For us it was a double risk because the US has regulations forbidding filming without special dispensation, in order to protect its own film industry. So each time, when asked, we had to pretend we were tourists.

For the overwhelming majority of immigrants who came to the States over the decades it represented everything they'd dreamt of. From the first Puritans fleeing the religious oppression of the Catholic Charles I, to the Jews fleeing the pogroms of Eastern Europe, German peasants released from the tutelage of the landed gentry to the newcomers today from Palestine, the Lebanon or Central America, fleeing civil wars, poverty and discrimination. For the more recent generations of immigrants their first view of the Statue of Liberty standing proudly holding her torch of freedom over the grey waters of the Hudson River, against the impressive backdrop of New York's skyline, it was a welcome they hadn't dared imagine. The vitality and colour, the pace of life and the wealth on the streets of New York must have been an enormous culture shock for most of them. The pioneering spirit, the strong tradition of tolerance, democracy and free enterprise, where laws governed human relationships, all this must have seemed like a paradise to the starving, poor and oppressed who arrived on this nation's doorstep to be taken in and given a chance to make something of their lives. Many did, of course, do well, were able to buy a place to live, open a small business or find a steady job. Because of this, irrespective of where they came from, the loyalty of most immigrants is first and foremost to this country which gave them back their human dignity and a new found freedom.

In cities like New York or Los Angeles over 80 different languages can be heard on the streets. A New York cab driver is just as likely to be a recent Jewish immigrant from Yalta, a Lebanese Christian or a genuine third generation New Yorker. On 5th Avenue big Cadillacs with dark-tinted windows glide by regularly; blonde women wearing immaculate make-up and the most exquisite fur coats sweep into Macy's or Tiffany's; in Central Park dog-walkers are tugged along by groups of expensive pedigree animals, taking them for their daily exercise on behalf of their too-busy owners; around the Bowery or on 42nd street the homeless and rootless hang around the shabby corners or run-down apartment blocks; on Broadway the porno cinemas vie with the latest big musicals and hit plays. Downtown hotels have security locks on the doors with notices warning you to keep them locked at all times and not to open them to unauthorised personnel. Life is colourful, extreme and fascinating, crammed beneath the vertiginous skyscrapers and the narrow strips of visible sky.

Where in New York you feel claustrophobic, outside in the country you feel the sense of unlimited space: enormous stretches of farmland, often so mechanised that you hardly see a single example of that almost extinct species, the farm labourer. In the agricultural heartlands the fields stretch to the horizon, empty of life, and with a monotonous perfection, the roads often as straight and empty as the fields. Then without warning you enter a small town or village where the simplicity and meagreness hits you smack in the face. Their inhabitants, though, are often so cut off from the nation at large that they are oblivious of their situation.

Sweetwater is such a place. A cemetery quiet and dull little town, located on Interstate 20 west of Dallas, in the flat and dry scrubland of Texas. Here we came to film the annual Rattlesnake Round-up. Thousands of rattlesnakes are brought in by the local farmers and then milked for their venom, skinned to make handbags or belts and their meat roasted as a snack. Writhing masses of these serpents are kept in big containers and provide a creepy excitement for the visitors. There is even a rattlesnake queen, chosen from among the local farmers' daughters. She has the privilege of skinning a snake for the press cameras. The farmer who catches the biggest snake gets first prize. The town is made up of two or three main streets with the basic shops, their window decoration reminding me of the GDR in the fifties – dowdy, half-empty and old-fashioned – and the bank, fire brigade house and sheriff's office. Most days it is virtually deserted.

In centres of born-again Christianity like Jerry Falwell's Lynchburg, Virginia, the atmosphere is one of affluent white middle-class suburbia. Jerry Falwell is a nationally famous evangelist with his own nation-wide religious TV programme, is extremely right-wing and very wealthy. He was a founder of the Moral Majority movement which helped bring Reagan to power in the early eighties. Here you find a professed morality not very different from that brought over by the Puritans three centuries earlier. At his Baptist University, where the theories of Darwin are banned as the Devil's work and Genesis is the only acceptable explanation for the world's existence, the students are severely reprimanded for showing physical affection for the opposite sex in public and dating has to be officially sanctioned. Anyone indulging in illicit sexual relations is immediately expelled.

Because the USA has such a short history and because a large number of its citizens are first or second generation only, there is little sense of permanence or unifying culture apart from that imposed by commercial interests. So often when travelling through the country, coming into small towns or suburban housing estates I have the feeling it is all a film set or theatre scenery. The houses are usually in a mock-European baroque or neo-classical style or mixture of several styles, built rapidly of chip-board and enclosed in a coating of plaster or thin brick with artificial roof tiles. Doorways are often surmounted with neo-classical architraves and columns or adorned with '18th century' coach lamps. There is a continuous attempt at recreating history, but without a sense of what that entails. Motels have the outline of castles or half-timbered medieval mansions, but it's all just board and paint, fading and peeling after a few years.

Many visitors miss the small towns and villages of Middle America. They either speed through in cars on the big Interstates, or fly from one big city to the next. However, like most other countries, but even more so here, the big cities do not reflect the realities of the nation as a whole. New York with its concrete and glass monuments to capitalist accumulation, its frenetic life-style, the myriad of images, events and happenings, its museums, theatres and art galleries, restaurants and discos is as far removed from the rest of the States as the moon is from earth. Washington DC is the centre of government, generously laid out in Napoleonic fashion with wide boulevards, nestling picturesquely on the banks of the Potomac River. It is a quiet, unhurried city, a contrast to New York and as different again from most other cities.

Because capital has a completely free reign here and market forces are the only valid ones, factories and industries are not built where communities need them, people have to move to where the factories are. As soon as workers organise themselves and create unions to defend their rights the owners often just close down and move elsewhere. The former industrial heartlands of Detroit, Chicago, Philadelphia or Minneapolis are now graveyards, the former factories rusting skeletons from a past era. Often the city centres, once bustling with shoppers and traders are now boarded up, run down and left to the flotsam of the old society, the drug pushers, alcoholics, mentally ill, the poor blacks and recent Hispanic immigrants. Most of those with money have either dispersed to the leafy suburbs or followed the industries south to the Sunbelt. New shopping centres have been built up in the suburbs: enormous palaces to consumerism. You enter an artificial world of make-believe. There is no natural lighting, it is all bright neon. Silent escalators transport you through glass-domed atria, decorated with plastic trees, past dozens of glamorous shops and fast food outlets. Some have skating rinks and you can sit having lunch watching pretty little girls taking skating lessons on the ice below. A separate world is created where the jeans shops are made to look like old frontier stores, the cafes like French bistros or Mexican bars, but it is all about buying and everything is arranged, designed and planned to that end. These centres are usually safe from the asocial, indigent elements because you can only reach them by car and they are usually well away from the old city centres.

The impermanence, the inability to build up and consolidate real living communities has formed the North American character and culture. Everyone is on the move. So many of the houses are hastily erected as if for short tenures or are made to be transported like the caravan mobile homes. There is a permanent fear of losing one's job or falling seriously ill, both of which can plunge families into dire poverty overnight. There is no developed welfare system in the States and no free health care. Everything is left to the individual – you insure against ill health if you can afford to do so and you try to save money for the hard times.

In Detroit we talked with some unemployed workers doing community work, cleaning up the parks – here you are only given food and clothing coupons if you work for it. They arrived for the day's work in big cars and vans, not how we would think of the unemployed. They explain that you can't exist in the States without a vehicle of some sort. If you don't have one you are like someone without legs, you can't get anywhere, you can't look for a job, go shopping or go to the cinema. Distances are enormous and public transport almost non-existent. So the car is the last thing you hang on to. Nobody walks anyway and there are few pathways or pavements for pedestrians outside the big cities. If you try and walk you are likely to be picked up by the police and charged with vagrancy; at any rate people will view you as a weird character. One US citizen who enjoyed walking was arrested so many times while doing so that he went to the Supreme Court to have his right, as an American citizen to walk in his own country, confirmed.

North Americans are, on the whole exceedingly friendly,

approachable and conversational, but this is, in non-intellectual circles, invariably of a shallow, superficial nature. The friendliness, like the other ephemera of their lives, is something easily discarded and forgotten. There is a fear of deep relationships because they will probably have to be broken when one party moves somewhere else. The prime aim in life is to make money because this is the only thing which can guarantee security, and social status. It is the only measure of success according to the media. Society as a body doesn't exist and has no responsibility for its members, there is only a collection of individuals. These individuals compete with each other out there in the open market and there will be winners and losers. There is no concept of a dialectical relationship between society and the individuals which make it up, that there can't be healthy individuals if there is no healthy society and vice versa.

When making our film about Texas we met two millionaires, one who had made his money from oil and the other from commercial television. Both were self-made millionaires, had worked hard, had good luck and become wealthy. They prove the point that it is possible and, of course, for them the system works even though they readily admit that for many it doesn't. They were both very hospitable and, if you met them in a local bar you wouldn't feel they were any different from any of the others sitting there. One of them had a reputation for being an eccentric. He had surrounded his big house with enormous pop-sculptures, one of which has become a famous tourist attraction: it consists of twelve Cadillac cars, standing upright in a row, their bonnets buried in the earth. Seeing it from the road you think at first that it is a hallucination. It is, of course, a very apt metaphor for the 'throw-away society'.

Coming from Britain with its class-ridden system I find it like a breath of fresh air in the States that although there are enormous economic differences between individuals and sections, there are no clearly defined cultural class distinctions. There is a strong sense of egalitarianism: you may have money, but you are still looked upon as a simple US citizen like everyone else.

Almost everywhere in the States I feel, alongside a still existing pioneering spirit, a sense of degeneracy and an underlying social chaos beneath the polished exterior. Drugs are the biggest destabilising factor, followed by armed violence. Most citizens live in fear, locked safely behind multi-locked doors or in their cars. To walk the streets of any big city after dark is to tempt providence.

One film we made was about a shooting 'academy' in Columbia, Missouri where, according to its publicity, it "offers training in shooting to anyone from the free world". Here, people can learn to shoot and handle guns of almost any description. Such 'academies' have become profitable institutions in the present climate. There we met old men frightened of race riots, determined to defend their homes from the hordes of have-nots, small shopkeepers who have been robbed so many times they have lost count and who were now determined to shoot first. There were young women frightened of rapists and the usual collection of nutters who just loved weapons. At Ray Chapman's shooting Academy Ray, a former US combat pistol champion, instructed his motley collection of students in the art of weaponry. His assistant, Andy Langley, a former mercenary with the Selous Scouts in Rhodesia, taught small groups the basis of guerrilla warfare, how to use machine guns and shot guns. Shortly before our arrival there the US mercenary magazine *Soldier of Fortune* had held its convention and its editor Bob Poos was on the course we filmed.

In the USA the cult of violence is all-pervasive. The early pioneers conquered the land with the gun and this was turned into an entertaining mythology for generations ever since in the form of cowboy films (although the real cowboys don't wear guns!). The cinema and TV fare is largely gangster and police films, horror or war. Go into any children's toy store and see the mountainous stacks of guns, weaponry and war games. It is scarce wonder that new generations see the gun as a means of overcoming frustration and solving problems. To examine this phenomenon we went to Dallas, notorious for the assassination of President Kennedy and the TV soap opera of the same name. Here a new indoor game for young people had been developed and pioneered, called Photon.

Inside a large empty warehouse a mock space-age labyrinth had been built. In the semi darkness teams of space-age warriors fought battles with laser guns. The winner was the team with the most hits or highest body count. One little boy I overheard yelling excitedly, "Papa I shot you! I got 70 points, I tried to shoot you Papa." Outside youngsters queued to don the helmets, the battery packs and guns and enter this fantasy world. They enjoyed it, they said, because it got the adrenalin going, it was exciting. They didn't see that it had anything to do with war or killing it was just a game. Perhaps they are right?

A few hundred kilometres south of Dallas in a few acres of rough woodland groups of grown men spend weekends working off the week's built up frustration by donning combat uniforms, charging through the undergrowth and shooting each other with coloured paint pellets, playing the Survival Game. This, too, is a rapidly expanding and popular game. One of the organisers explains its attraction: "Some of our biggest companies come down here to play, 60 or 70 at a time, office types and management. There is a permanent conflict in many factories between the worker bees and the bee-keepers so-to-speak. Here you can play out the situation that exists in the factory or office – there where you are full of frustration – here the worker bees have a chance to beat the beekeepers, can work off their anger, frustration and envy by shooting their superiors."

At local festivals there are often gun stalls which are extremely popular, selling wide selections of guns, knives and other assorted weaponry which would not look amiss at a NATO exercise. Gun shops are found in every little town, gun magazines abound and there is even a very vociferous National Rifle Association which is one of the chief lobbying groups campaigning to maintain the American citizen's right to carry arms.

We raised the question of violence in the USA in a number of our films and in a variety of different ways, because it is so symptomatic for the country as a whole and has, I must admit, a certain fascination for me because I would like to understand the psychology behind it. In this connection I thought it might be an interesting idea to make a sort of psychogram of typical American GIs, what their dreams, hopes and worries were, how they saw the enemy, their own country and their views on war and peace.

I knew it would be no good writing to the Pentagon from London because all such requests have to go through the embassy and would be automatically checked with Scotland Yard and vetoed. As we happened to be in Washington on other business I thought I'd try approaching the Pentagon directly. As I indicated earlier the USA is a confusing contradiction between amazing openness and democracy on the one hand and the dictatorial power of capitalist interests on the other. In no other country of the world could you just walk into the front door of the armed forces headquarters as I did in the Pentagon. I told the officer in reception of my request and he directed me to the film and press office. By myself I wandered along the corridors, past doors with various generals' and colonels' names on them, past dreary oil paintings of various Chiefs of Staff, until I arrived at colonel B's office. I knocked and the door was opened by a crew-cut, athletic-looking officer who welcomed me warmly and seemed impressed with my idea of a portrait of 'the modern soldier'. His office was adorned with stills form Hollywood films and he told me how he had worked with John Wayne, Clint Eastwood and a whole string of other big stars, until I began to feel very small. However, I don't think he was trying to intimidate me, but to boost his own standing in my eyes – so many North Americans suffer from an acute inferiority complex vis a vis Europeans. He told me I should have gone through the US Embassy in London, but promised his full help nevertheless, as I was here. I was amazed when I received a letter on my return to London telling us that we had been granted permission to film in Fort Bragg. An officer had been detailed to liaise with us on arrival at the base. We replied immediately to arrange a date, but were greeted with silence. Despite follow-up letters we received not another communication. Obviously, even though the wheels of Pentagon bureaucracy turn slowly they get there eventually – they had obviously double-checked with their London embassy and been told to have nothing to do with us. Well it was a good idea even if it didn't come off!

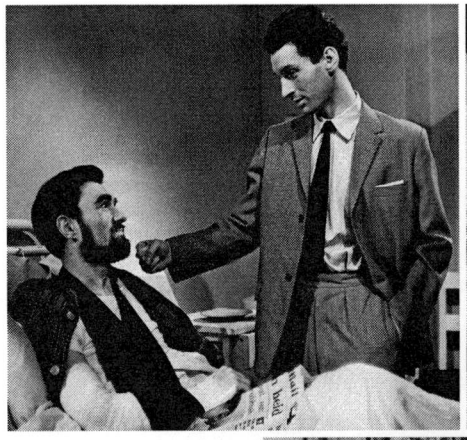

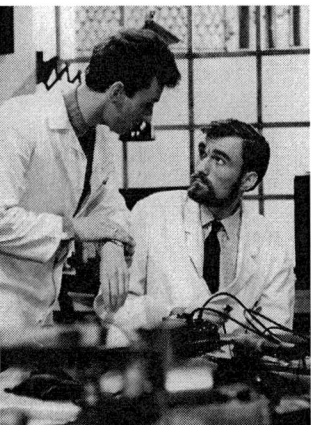

1964-65 *Above left and right:* as actor in the GDR television language series, *English for You*;
1965 *Right:* Filming exercise with the Arri 35mm at the national film school, Babelsberg;
1966 *Below:* the foreign students in my year

I

RED REPORTER
COVERT CORRESPONDENT FOR EAST GERMANY

1966 *Above:* Relaxing in a boat on one of Berlin's many lakes;
1967 *Left and above:* playing an English gentleman in a fellow student's production, Babelsberg

1968 *Right:* Venezuelan student colleague, Alfredo Lugo, directing Death of the Uncle; *Below:* on location in Potsdam for the film

RED REPORTER
COVERT CORRESPONDENT FOR EAST GERMANY

1972 *Above:* Audience with Archbishop Makarios, President of Cyprus; **1974** *Left:* future president of Portugal, Mario Soares, at a rally; *Below:* German war memorial in Namibia

1974 *Above:* with SWAPO National Organiser, Aaron Mushimba; *Left:* With Kent miners after being taken underground; *Below left:* in Portugal with Klaus Weigle; *Below right:* in Portugal with Gina Kalla

RED REPORTER
COVERT CORRESPONDENT FOR EAST GERMANY

1974 *Left:* with young Portuguese officers who led the Carnation Revolution;
1975 *Above:* May Day demonstration in Lisbon, Portugal; *Below left:* with GDR producer, Sabine Katins; *Below:* Dias Lourenço, editor of Avante, explaining his escape from the notorious prison of Peniche

1978 *Left:* Aladdin's lamp country, Tehran; *Above:* Street scene in Tehran; *Below:* at home in London with my daughter Siski 'helping' with editing

RED REPORTER
COVERT CORRESPONDENT FOR EAST GERMANY

1979 *Above:* demonstrators in the capital, Salvador, El Salvador, just before a massacre by the army; *Left:* corpses of shot demonstrators; *Below:* making tortillas in a refugee camp

1979 Rhodesia soon to become Zimbabwe. *Above:* with a ZAPU Commander; *Left:* with the most trusted and formidable automatic assault rifle of the 20th century – the Kalashnikov AK47

Red Reporter
Covert correspondent for East Germany

1982 *Top and above:* Rambo clones – regime soldiers are ever present and menacing; *Left:* with colleague and interpreter, Michal Boñcza on the road, Guatemala

1982 *Top:* Guatemalan millionaire coffee plantation owner showing us his sun dried beans; *Above:* rubbish tip scavengers in Guatemala City; *Right:* regime soldier

RED REPORTER
COVERT CORRESPONDENT FOR EAST GERMANY

1982 *Above:* the notorious 'Escuela de las Americas' US training facility for Latin American military personnel in Panama; *Left:* back-breaking toil for banana workers in the snake-infested plantations

1982 *Left:* young guerrilla mounting road check, El Salvador; *Above:* Salvadoran boy refugee in Honduras; *Top:* Salvadoran family with their meagre maize harvest

Red Reporter
Covert correspondent for East Germany

1983 *Top:* Archbishop of Santiago, Raúl Silva Henríquez, at May Day rally, Chile; *Above:* with young comrades in front of Victor Jara's tomb, Santiago; **1984** *Above Right:* a meal of whale meat with Inuit family, Greenland; right: an old seal hunter in traditional kayak

1985 *Top:* Frente Amplio activist putting up posters during the first elections after the overthrow of the military junta, Uruguay; *Above:* with Young Pioneers, at Marx's grave, Highgate Cemetery; **1986** *Right:* FMLN guerrillas in Tenancingo, El Salvador; *Insert:* Press credential issued by El Salvador's Ministry of Defence

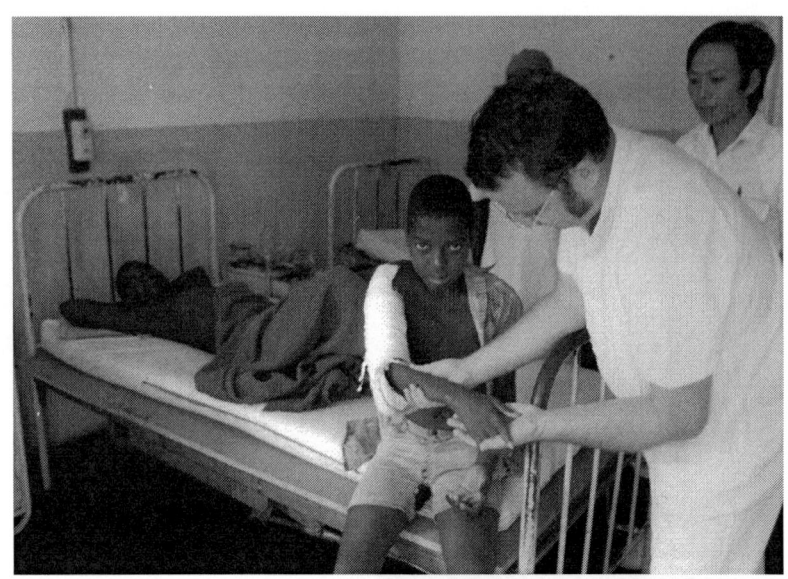

Red Reporter
Covert correspondent for East Germany

1987 *Top:* GDR and Vietnamese doctors treating victims of Renamo terrorists in Chimoio, Beira Corridor, Mozambique; *Right:* Graham Greene's favourite hotel, the Polana, Lourenco Marques, (now Maputo); *Below:* having a laugh with our government guide playing cameraman

1987 I find 'my own' star on Hollywood's Walk of Fame;
1989 *Left:* Presidential guard in Asuncion, Paraguay; above: filming Iguazu falls on border between Argentina, Paraguay and Brazil with my colleague, Liesbeth.

RED REPORTER
COVERT CORRESPONDENT FOR EAST GERMANY

1988 *Right:* rattlesnake 'roundup' in Sweetwater, Texas;
1989 *Far right:* the great peace demonstration in Washington DC;
1989 *Bottom:* World Anti-Communist League conference, Brisbane, Australia;
1990 *Below:* with Maibritt Illner, the popular TV anchor woman, in Markgrafenland, Germany.

Über das Markgräflerland als Urlaubsziel und vor allen Dingen über das kostbarste Gut dieser Region, den Wein, informierte sich ein DDR-Fernsehteam. Die Journalistin Maybrit Illner interviewte dabei auch den Geschäftsführer der Müllheimer Winzergenossenschaft, Peter Gries. Bild: Vigl

CHAPTER 7 – USA: LAND OF POSSIBLE IMPOSSIBILITIES
Welcome to California

All of Hispanic America is flooded with a certain type of US culture, the cheapest and most commercialised kind. This culture portrays life in the USA as the pinnacle of civilisation, something to be admired, aspired to and dreamt about: glamour, luxury, affluence and power. This, combined with US economic exploitation of these countries, increasing the poverty, the misery and the suffering at the hands of US-supported oligarchies, has led to a steady stream of would-be immigrants to the USA. This has become a big headache for the US government which appears to be quite happy if people admire and envy its image as the world's No. 1 paradise, but not if these people come and want to taste of its fruits.

The USA, in the past, had always had a liberal and open policy towards immigrants and not many genuine refugees were refused visas, but in recent years this policy changed. There were now double standards. If you came from Europe or particularly if you were categorised as a 'victim of Communist oppression' you were given a residence permit with few formalities. Those fleeing right-wing dictatorships and/or poverty, particularly those from the USA's own 'backyard' – Hispanic America – were treated very differently and for the first time in its history the USA began mounting strict border controls on its southern frontier to Mexico in order to keep these refugees out. The result of this attitude is that those desperate individuals escaping the tyranny and poverty of their own countries in the south try to gain access to the USA by illegally crossing the border.

It is largely due to US economic policies and support for the military dictatorships and powerful oligarchies in Latin America, with the resultant civil wars and lack of basic human rights which has produced the flood of would-be refugees. Yet the USA is not willing to take responsibility for this state of affairs, and it is denying these desperate individuals and families the sanctuary they seek. We wanted to examine this border situation and expose the duplicity of US policy. We viewed this as an integral aspect and extension of the problems we had been examining in Central America.

The typical immigrants have walked, hitched or bussed their way up through the mountains and forests of Central America and Mexico until they arrive, virtually penniless, on the Mexican side of the border in small towns like Tijuana. Here they encounter the 'coyotes' who, for a sum of money or other services, ferry them across the border into the USA. If they can't pay they have to find their own way across, swimming the Alamo Canal and then dodging US Immigration police (this is how illegal immigrants acquired the term 'wetbacks'). The US Immigration Police have only 300 men to patrol 2,000 miles of border so it is not too difficult for those who are determined to get through.

The Californian Immigration Service is very co-operative and let us spend a day and a night with their border patrol. The US-Mexican border, because of its length, is virtually impossible to seal or patrol properly. The section between San Ysidro and Tijuana is marked by a high wire-mesh fence, which regularly has gaping holes cut by refugees entering illegally. It is patrolled continuously by immigration police in four-wheel drive trucks. We ride along in one of these vehicles, kicking up a spiral of white dust behind us, keeping an eye open for the more 'cheeky' ones who attempt to cross in broad daylight and to check the fence which looks more like a piece of bad knitting with its ragged holes. We stop to look through binoculars at the other side of the canal where a whole string of would-be immigrants sit, like swallows on a telegraph wire, in the sun, next to their small bundles of clothing, waiting for night to fall, when they will make their dash over. The officer tells us that things are usually quiet until just after sunset when most will make their bid.

We return to the central office which is very much like a police traffic control centre with TV monitors, two-way radios and a constant influx of calls from patrol vehicles. The car park is full of impounded vehicles which had been used to smuggle immigrants across the border. One successful smugglers ring, we were told, had been a group of US marine wives who had used navy vehicles for the job, making good money to supplement their husbands' salaries!

At the communications centre another officer explains how the system works and how they co-ordinate their action. He tells us that they have benefited from the Vietnam War experience and now use sensors mounted in the earth in places where the refugees are likely to cross. These send out radio signals when touched. The Service also has image- intensifying binoculars and helicopters with searchlights. Captain Oliveira takes us out to a spot where there are usually incursions. We bump along the rocky track, through the scrub, our headlamps creating an eerie halo of light as they sweep the bushes. The warm air is vibrating with the incessant chirp of the cicadas, but it is an otherwise still and clear night.

We park our truck behind some large bushes, turn the lights off and wait. Meanwhile Captain Oliveira scans the horizon with his night binoculars. After about an hour he grunts, "here take a look, close to that large bush on the horizon there". I look through and after a while can make out a dark blob moving up and down behind the vegetation, then several more. Captain Oliveira gets on his radio telephone, giving details of the sighting. Within minutes we can hear the drone of a helicopter approaching and then see its mosquito shape appear on the horizon and its searchlight beam suddenly shoots from its belly, fluttering over the low scrub. The engine of our truck roars into life and we bump off rapidly in the direction of our sighting. From a different direction we can see the twin beams of a second truck bobbing towards us. The helicopter is now hovering low over a group of bushes and in its broad beam we can make out a small group of figures scurrying rabbit-like, first in one direction then another, trying to escape its hold. We close in on them like hunters preparing for the kill. The officers jump out of their trucks and hold the pathetic group of six, lightly clad figures in the strong beams of their torches and order them in Spanish to raise their hands. They are then stood against the side of the trucks and individually frisked before being handcuffed and bundled into the back and driven back to the centre.

At the centre there are already other captured individuals sitting there, dejected and awaiting their fate: their worn cotton shirts over their skinny torsos, in their faces expressions of haggard resignation. Each one is fingerprinted, their name and address taken -they usually give fictitious ones – and their belongings confiscated. Each empties his pocket on the counter revealing perhaps a handkerchief and a few coins or crumpled notes from a South American country. After completing the formalities they are then returned to the arrest cells to be held until morning when they will be driven back to the border crossing and pushed back into Mexico, only to try again a day or so later and perhaps be successful next time. The border police capture a hundred or so each night.

The whole exercise is a game, at least for the immigration officers, and they admit as much, knowing that they can't stop the border crossings and that their presence is merely symbolic, a slight hindrance. The group caught the previous night are lucky, they are still alive, but regularly individuals or groups die while trying to enter the USA, some of asphyxiation, locked in lorry containers or car boots, others in the swirling waters of the Rio Grande. Those that do get through work as undocumented labourers (i.e. without the necessary permits and papers) on the farms or in the clothing sweatshops of Los Angeles, each day fearing that the police will come and escort them back over the border.

Some land labourers we spoke to, living under plastic tents, hidden in a small wooded valley, had come from the south of Mexico and were only staying until they had earned enough money to buy seed-corn for the next sowing in their home villages. Without the conscious connivance of employers illegal immigration would cease, of course. For them the cheap labour for which they have to pay no insurance is a boon. As one big farmer says, "The class of labour we want is the kind we can send home when we get through with them". Although the employers deduct social security payments from the illegal immigrants this money goes into their own pockets. The workers have no entitlement to health care or unemployment benefits. Some unscrupulous employers call the Immigration Police when they want to get rid of their workers – before pay day of course, so that they can save a week's wages. Even if this doesn't happen, for the immigrants there is the continuous fear of being caught and also the danger that if they are taken ill or have an accident they have no protection and can get no medical attention.

What is interesting about the whole area of the southern USA, which was annexed after the Mexican War in 1848, is that it is now being re-colonised by Hispanic Americans. In Los Angeles, Houston, Miami and the border towns you hear more Spanish spoken than English today. Many of these people came legally in the years before the US began closing its borders, others are first or even second generation illegals. A recent amnesty for those already resident for several years and who were willing to apply for citizenship was an attempt to formalise an increasingly impossible situation. Many Hispanics are now legalised immigrants but a substantial number are still illegals.

Our film was called sarcastically *Welcome to California*, because this is the first road sign that greets you as you cross the border from Mexico.

CHAPTER 7 – USA: LAND OF POSSIBLE IMPOSSIBILITIES
Appalachian interlude

Our first assignment to the USA was to cover a long running strike of the coal miners in the Appalachians in 1978. This ridge of mountains once formed an insurmountable barrier to the early pilgrims, trying to find a way through to the rich plains of central USA. The ridge runs through the states of Kentucky, Virginia and Tennessee. It is an area which has been by-passed by the consumer advance seen elsewhere. Before coal was discovered it was an area of subsistence farming. It is said, that because of its isolation, you still hear some of the purest English spoken here. It is also where the hill-billy music originates. It is certainly a different USA to that seen by most tourists. It is as if time and progress has passed by and missed the place.

We drive down by car. It is November and the stately beech trees on the hillsides stand stark against the clear blue sky and the sun is bright but snow is already clinging stubbornly to the hillsides and clusters of icicles, like enormous fangs, hang down from the banks at the side of the small, winding roads. We pass by isolated small, decrepit weather-board houses between the trees. Occasionally a pale face peers from behind the faded curtains or a static figure stands like a sentinel in the yard, staring at our car as we pass. Once we need to ask directions and approach a house near the roadside, but are confronted by a silent figure in the doorway brandishing a shot-gun. We beat a cautious retreat without the information we need. People here, because of their isolation, are very suspicious of outsiders. The only compromise with the modern era appears to be the large limousines, invariably parked in the yards in front of the houses, surrounded by discarded junk, the odd chicken or mangy dog and unkempt children playing. The few people we catch glimpses of appear rather wild-looking, shabbily dressed and with that empty, transparent expression of the inbred and mentally retarded. What could have been picturesque rivers cascading through the valleys are awash with discarded fridges and other household items, like nostrils clogged with mucous from a bad cold. At the foot of the valleys are the large trailer parks where the victims of recent floods and the less well-off live in their euphemistically called 'mobile homes', large caravans which can be easily towed away to another site.

Our goal is Harlan County or 'Bloody Harlan' as it is affectionately known, because of the battles waged over the years between miners and coal owners. Coal mining is now virtually the only occupation here. When it was discovered, lying in rich seams close to the surface, the robber barons moved in, bought up the land from the small farmers who were glad to get a good price for it, and began their plunder. The magnificent Oscar- winning documentary, *Harlan County* by Barbara Koppel and Hazel Dickinson reflects the bitter and bloody struggle of the Appalachian miners.

In the USA the history of trade union organisation is one of brutal and violent battles, often ending in murder. The employers have used every means at their disposal to make union organisation unworkable, resorting to the law when possible, but any other means where it was not. Still today there are a whole number of organisations dedicated to smashing the unions. One of them, the cynically named 'Right to Work Institute' run by Reed Larson helps employers and administrators draft anti-union legislation and undertake union-busting operations. When we spoke to him he readily told us how he works internationally and not just in the USA. One of his friends and heroines was Margaret Thatcher who was shortly to implement his policies very successfully.

The US miners union, the UMWA, was no exception to the other unions and when the employers couldn't break it from outside they infiltrated it and bought off corrupt union bosses. In the early seventies when the progressives in the UMWA managed to win the presidential election with Joe Yablonski, the right wing had him murdered. In Harlan County the union is still largely in the hands of the right wing mafia.

When we arrive at the union local to meet the area president, we are ushered into the office to wait. He arrives shortly afterwards, dressed in high-heeled cowboy boots, a white sports jacket, his hands adorned with expensive rings. Before he speaks to us he bangs down his pearl-handled pistol on the desk and proceeds to fire off orders like a general to his troops and only after he's done this does he pay us any attention at all. We are dismissed in a few seconds and given a 'minder' to look after and help us in our work. Brad, our guide, is obviously a trusted lieutenant of the president. He doesn't appear to have any real union responsibility despite the fact that the union has been on strike for a month already. He ferries us about in his gleaming, sporty Oldsmobile with its white-leather upholstery, showing us the union halls and the pits in the area. He is a small bullet-headed man with a slow southern drawl and sharp eyes.

We kerb-crawl around, feeling like petty-criminals on the prowl. Occasionally he stops and chats to old cronies at the roadside. On some of the trips we are accompanied by Molly, his girl-friend and a voluntary police officer who carries a dainty little silver pistol in her handbag. On other occasions his brother-in-law, Gerry, a former teacher turned miner for the pay, comes with us. Gerry loves telling us sadistic little stories of his exploits, like slowing his car down for hitch-hiking hobos, then accelerating away just as they reach him, afterwards taking out his pistol and shooting up the ground around their feet until they flee in terror. He takes us to the birthday party of his nephew, where he amuses himself by taunting the poor kid. He is just ten and, like so many North American kids, grossly overweight. Gerry keeps on asking him how many girl-friends he has, making his face go bright red and then forces him to do press-ups on the floor, which he finds impossible because of his bulk, eventually collapsing in a quivering mass of flab and tears. The other adults just look on, apparently amused too.

We are accommodated in the only motel in the little town of Cumberland. It looks deserted and unlived in, a single two-storey block flung unlovingly against a scrape in the hillside. When we arrived the first day we parked our car before what appeared to be the entrance and rang the bell. After a short wait a middle-aged woman hobbled to the door and unlocked it. "We booked a room", I said. Without a word she shuffled behind the counter and produced a key and a form. "Fill in your details here, it's on the first floor", she said, pushing the key across the counter towards us. Our motel has no restaurant; it probably isn't worth it for the few guests who occasionally pass through. We take breakfast in the centre of town, in the Tri-City Cafe where truckers and a few locals sit sucking on their hot mugs of coffee and tucking into their bacon and eggs. The only other eating places are three fast food restaurants and by the end of our stay I can't face another 'finger lickin' chicken at Colonel Sanders' Kentucky Fried, another deep-fried frozen scampi at the Captain's Table or a cartwheel-sized, cardboard pizza at the Pizza Hut. Evenings are hell because there is no entertainment of any sort apart from the in-house video in our hotel rooms. The only place we can go for a drink, and to which Brad immediately takes us, is the US Veterans Club. In this dingy hall with its bar and pool table, a few brawny, tattooed ex-Vietnam veterans sit around drinking US-Budweiser out of cans. There are no women and no blacks. After a short while listening to the flow of blue and sick jokes we feign exhaustion and retire to our motel.

We ask Brad if he's seen the famous *Harlan County* film, made about the miners' strike two years previously. We would like to see it if we could, we say. He tells us that a local miner has a copy but he would advise us not to visit him because he is a 'Commie'. Gerry says that they will bump him off one of these days." We don't like reds in Harlan County", he adds. We manage to shake Brad off on a later evening, saying we are driving out of town, but in fact pay these 'reds' a visit. Anyone called a red must be interesting we think. We have managed to find out where he lives from one of the miners on the picket line. Making sure no one is following us, we park our car some way from the house and walk there. We go around to the back door so that no one will see us standing at the front. We knock and the door is opened by a woman in her thirties who immediately welcomes us inside. "I guess you've come to see Charlie," she asks. She ushers us through the small kitchen dominated by the enormous fridge and into the living room where Charlie 'Chuck' Parker is sitting playing with his small daughter. He rises, shakes our hands warmly and tells us to sit down. He is tall, with curly blond hair and a typical North American face: clean-cut and open with a ready smile.

We tell him of our convoluted journey to reach him. He laughs with a trace of bitterness, "yes the local mafia aren't too keen on democrats here. They've controlled the local (trade union branch) for such a long time and aren't going to give up easily," he tells us. We ask him why he is called a red. "Because I've been in the forefront of the battle to democratise this union", he says, "and probably because my wife has

RED REPORTER
COVERT CORRESPONDENT FOR EAST GERMANY

been on a study tour to the Soviet Union on behalf of the miners' wives organisation". Charlie is able to give us useful background for our film. He explains that because the mines are all owned nominally by different owners it makes it extremely difficult to fight them. Safety conditions are atrocious he says, injuries and even deaths being a commonplace, particularly in the non-union pits which use unskilled labour. During the strikes the local police and the National Guard are simply instruments of the owners and the intimidation and clubbing of pickets on the gates is usual. 'Accidents' or shootings of union militants has become accepted as part of the scene.

At the union hall there is always a flurry of activity. Here the wives and retired union members gather and help distribute relief. One grizzled old man stands in front of the hall every day with his UMW cap stuck jauntily on his head. His breathing is heavy and noisy as the air is forced in and out of his petrified lungs. He has made his own placard with Jack London's famous definition of a scab written on it:

> *"After God had finished with the rattlesnake, the toad,*
> *the vampire, he had some awful substance left with which he made the scab.*
> *A scab is a two-legged animal with a corkscrew soul, a waterlogged brain, a combination backbone of jelly and glue.*
> *Where others have hearts he carries a tumour of rotten principles.*
> *When a scab comes down the street men turn their backs*
> *and angels weep in heaven and the devil shuts the gates to keep him out.*
> *No man has the right to scab as long as there is a pool of water to drown his carcass in or a rope long enough to hang his body with.*
> *Judas Iscariot was a gentleman compared with a scab.*
> *For betraying his master he had character enough to hang himself. A scab has not.*
> *Esau sold his birthright for a mess of potage.*
> *Judas Iscariot sold his saviour for thirty pieces of silver.*
> *Benedict Arnold sold his country for the promise of a commission in the British Army.*
> *The modern strike-breaker sells his birthright, his country, his wife, his children and his fellowmen for an unfulfilled promise from his employer, trust or corporation.*
> *Esau was a traitor to himself,*
> *Judas Iscariot was a traitor to his God,*

*Benedict Arnold was a traitor to his country.
A strike-breaker is a traitor to his God, his country, his wife, his
family and his class."*

The feelings expressed in these words are also expressed in the fiery eyes of the old man carrying them. The use of scabs by the employers has always been a favourite method of breaking a strike and the feelings against them are not kindly.

Truckloads of food and clothing arrive regularly from the workers in the steel works or the car factories of the north and are delivered to the union hall. Today there is a union meeting to keep the miners up to date with what is happening. It is difficult to imagine how such small places are cut off from the outside world. You can't find a *New York Times* or *Washington Post* down here, only the local rag which is full of adverts and local gossip, but no real news. The hall is tightly packed. A gaunt, old miner is on the platform and although bent and frail looking his voice has the force of a kettle drum. He calls the meeting to order, removes his cap, focuses his eyes on the roof beams and begins to intone a prayer thanking the Lord for being on the miners' side in their just struggle. He commands the attention Moses must have done when he addressed the Israelites. It is a long rambling prayer, punctuated at intervals by Amens and Hallelujas.

The majority in the hall are men, some young and brawny, but most have obviously spent their lives in the mines; their faces pitted with coal dust, their cheeks hollow and their eyes deep-sunk like the pit-shafts themselves. Their expressions betray a longing for justice, a weariness of physical struggle and also an iron stubbornness forged by the inhospitability of the region. Their sallow skin, stretched over jutting jaw-bones gives their faces that same rugged quality as the surrounding hills. There is a sprinkling of women, some wives and others working miners – something unknown to us in Europe, but down here quite usual.

The meeting is more like a Baptist revivalist service than any union gathering I've been to before. There are some interjections from the floor, but mostly requests for information or about food distribution and strike pay. During strikes it is not only the miners who get no pay, but the retired miners who lose their pensions, and this is why so many of them are active on the picket lines. None of the strikers or retired miners are medically covered during the strike and the local doctors and hospitals are without work because no one pays them a visit for fear of running up huge medical bills.

With one of the truck loads of food from the north a group of young, idealistic Trotskyists come and start giving out their leaflets in front of the union hall, explaining the 'class struggle aspects of the strike'. They are given short shrift by the red-hating locals who slash the tyres on their cars and drive them out of the town. This doesn't do anything to bolster our feelings of security, and the fact that Brad has heard on the grapevine that we have actually visited Chuck Parker, make us feel that it is perhaps time for us to retreat too, before our tyres are slashed or worse. We have shot virtually all we need so we say a quick goodbye to the Parkers and drive off as speedily as we can towards Washington without taking our leave of Brad or the other union officials. We only relax again when we have put a few miles behind us and Harlan County.

This strike, like so many beforehand, ended in partial victory and partial defeat after more than a hundred days: some owners caved-in and granted better conditions and pay, but others remained adamantly stubborn, preferring to use scab labour or even to close down rather than grant concessions. It wasn't as bloody or violent as many have been, but there were shootings and injuries. In the end most of the miners returned to work, driven by mounting debts and exhaustion, gathering strength for the next round of battle in maybe a year or two.

CHAPTER 7 – USA: LAND OF POSSIBLE IMPOSSIBILITIES
Ben Chavis – man of Christ and revolution

Perhaps the most rewarding of our trips to the States and the one to result in one of our best films was a portrait of Ben Chavis. His became a household name in the late seventies when he, and 9 others were convicted of burning down a white grocery store and given a total of 282 years! They became known as the Wilmington Ten, after the town where their case was heard.

Ben Chavis was a young preacher with the Church of Christ and lived where his family has lived for several generations in North Carolina. He was co-chairperson of the National Alliance against Racism and Political Oppression, alongside Angela Davis and was one of the leaders of the struggle for human rights and economic justice in the United States.

As a student at North Carolina University he, along with other conscious blacks, led a successful campaign against the draft and the Vietnam War to bring it to an end and stop more young boys being sent out to fight. He also organised demonstrations and protest meetings on the campus which led to the establishment of a department of African and Afro-American studies where black North Americans could learn about their own history. These activities had shown him to be a capable and effective leader. The FBI and ruling circles in North Carolina had him marked as a dangerous radical and were determined to 'get him'.

North Carolina belongs to the Deep South and is very different to the northern United States. Here it is more reminiscent of South Africa and racism runs very deep, as does violence. The black population lives in the poorer ghetto areas clearly separated from the generally more affluent white population. If each section sticks to its own patch nothing untoward is likely to happen, but if social mixing or inter-racial marriage takes place then violence is not too long following. The ruling conservative elements here, while reluctantly accepting Federal integration laws are determined to make sure things down here stay pretty much as they always have done. Violence is never far below the surface; according to the local police statistics North Carolina has a serious crime every two minutes 34 seconds and a murder every 15 hours. These figures, though, are not higher than in many similar states.

In Charlotte, the capital, lives Dorothy Scroggins who made history back in 1957 when, as a small, neatly dressed school girl she tried to enter Harding High School as the first black child to do so. Her picture went around the world. "That was the most terrifying day of my life", she says, "the streets were lined with people jeering at me, 'nigger go back to Africa' and throwing ice and milk at me. But I still went forward". Now she is happily married with children of her own " but," she says, "People haven't changed that much, they don't show their racism so crudely today, but it is still there". North Carolina is also significant for having the largest concentration of military bases and personnel in the whole USA and this probably adds to its conservatism.

When we arrive in North Carolina in 1979, three years after the Wilmington 10 first entered prison, Ben is still serving his 28 year jail sentence, but under relatively liberal conditions since Amnesty International adopted him as a genuine political prisoner. The charge against him had been made worse by the state prosecutor including a concocted charge of 'accessory after the fact of a murder' which had taken place nine months earlier. He had already made seven fruitless appeals against the sentence through the US courts. Despite the fact that the only prosecution witnesses – all convicted felons – withdrew their evidence after admitting perjury and taking bribes from the prosecution, the governor still refused to pardon the 10. Ben, the only one not now on parole is permitted out on study release and once a month to preach in the local church. He has been continually harassed by the police in order to frighten him. He had an incendiary device placed under his car, but he was able to leap out before the car exploded, and there have been attempts on his life in prison, but he refuses to be deterred. One of his co-prisoners, the Black Panther leader Joe Waddell was beaten up by the guards and died. Even in prison Ben has become a leader, campaigning for improvements in the rat and cockroach infested quarters.

It is not very usual to find a politically militant Christian preacher and we ask Ben how it happened. "Well I know", he begins, "the church has been described as the opium of the people and this is true. The church can be used to put people to sleep, but I believe the church can be used as a liberating force – I am interested in liberation theology." He explains the role Christianity has played in holding his people together, giving them hope in times of despair, offering them succour. His grandfather, himself a slave and a lay-preacher, had taught other slaves to read and write clandestinely in the night after the day's work.

To hear Ben Chavis's sermon in the packed, mainly black Russell Memorial Church in Durham is to feel lightning sizzle through the still air. This young, slim, gentle person has his congregation listening intently to every word. Otherwise quiet and soft-spoken, he becomes a volatile evangelist, reminiscent of his hero Martin Luther King, but with a new political consciousness. He talks about the most recent rejection of his appeal: "I learned a long time ago not to put my trust in the courts of this nation that not only oppresses and exploits millions of people abroad, but which oppresses and exploits its own citizens because of the colour of their skin. I learned a long time ago not to put faith in a system that places more value on property than human life"... His sermon is interrupted by shouts of 'Right on' and 'Amen'. Ben becomes more excited, waves his outstretched arms like wings, then leaps over our camera and tape recorder into the congregation, ecstatically embracing members of his audience, appealing to them to give themselves to God. This form of service, so different from our European, low-key ones, is typical of the USA, with its strong evangelical tradition, but particularly so in the black churches. Everyone then holds hands and sings hymns together, rocking and swaying in unison. There is an intense feeling of togetherness and fraternity.

That same evening the church plays host to a meeting of cleaning workers from Duke University and the Rev. Chavis is there to talk to them. It becomes very clear why the ruling establishment so hates him. "Duke is the largest employer in Durham County," he says, "and yet somehow manages to pay the lowest wages. We all know who gets those lowest wages, some members of this church who are also members of the union. Some people might say, what does the

Christian church have to do with people organising for their labour rights? My answer is that at any time, any place where a child of God is being mistreated or exploited then the Christian church should be there!"

Although Ben is banned from talking to the press his sermons release all the ideas and thoughts dammed up by his incarceration and give them an added poignancy. Everyone who has had anything to do with Ben Chavis is influenced by his courage, his total commitment to liberation, but also by his love, gentleness and humanity. He is far removed from the picture his enemies paint of him – a man of violence. Only his words are violent, against oppression and injustice.

The case of the Wilmington 10 is just one example of racist justice in the USA. Only a few miles away in Charlotte, the Charlotte 3 received draconian jail sentences for allegedly burning down a stable. "One of the most heinous crimes I've come across", said the judge at the trial. Is it a coincidence that these three young black men were also political activists? There is a long tradition here of persecuting blacks. One of Ben's friends took us to Wilmington, where there are still alligators swimming languidly in the muddy waters of the aptly named Cape Fear. "Here, towards the end of the last century", he points to the estuary, "the Ku Klux Klan drove hundreds of revolting slaves into the river to be eaten by the alligators." This same Klan is alive and well today. Driving along Interstate 82 to China Grove there is still a big Ku Klux Klan sign with the words, 'Help fight integration and Communism'.

In the small town of China Grove a small group of demonstrating Maoists had been shot upon by members of the Klan and one was killed. The local church and black progressive organisations in the town call a rally to protest about their activities and are going to march to the Klan headquarters. We arrive there first in order to film the whole sequence of events. The Sheriff's car is already there and he is having an apparently friendly chat with the Klan leader, the Grand Dragon, a small, pompous local businessman with trimmed moustache and an air of self importance, called Gorrell Pierce. The Grand Dragon talks to us in a semi-articulate rhetoric: "I want to remind you that it wasn't me who burnt down Chicago, Los Angeles or Rhodesia, it was the niggers. Niggers tainted with communism is the biggest threat to this country. I am a racist and proud of it, I am a Christian too and I believe it is the biggest crime against the

Christian religion and God's plan to mix the races. That's why we need segregation". The KKK is of course a marginal organisation even though its following is not insignificant but it is only one of over 1000 registered fascist-type organisations in the United States.

The KKK building itself is surrounded by a motley collection of massive guys with tattooed arms, dressed in army fatigues, their faces expressing an empty, stupid, but dangerous animality. They are bristling with weapons: baseball bats, chains, bars, shotguns and pistols. As the demonstration approaches they goad it with racist remarks. Luckily the demonstrators refuse to be provoked. The police stand by and will intervene only if a breach of the peace occurs. I think there will be a full scale war, but it passes off without incident. The Klan prefers to carry out its dirty deeds under cover of darkness where there are no witnesses, and our camera probably helped to keep the peace. When the police do intervene it is usually on the side of the racists and it is the black victims who are arrested, to be locked up out of the way. As Ben himself says, "To be a political prisoner in the USA is perhaps worse than in most countries because here they make you look like a criminal. They charge you with some violent criminal act, railroad you through the courts and sentence you away from life and people really think you've done something wrong, when in actual fact you've only tried to speak out for the freedom of your people." We ask him if he is not afraid sometimes about what might happen to him. "If you are involved in struggle", he replies," you lose your fear". This became the title of our film portrait: 'Through struggle you lose your fear'.

Every evening Ben Chavis returns to his prison in Hillsborough where he sleeps along with 80 other inmates in an overcrowded block with hardly space to slide between the rows of metal bunk beds to the two open toilets, where not even a wall or door give privacy. Once a month he is allowed to visit his family.

A year after our film was completed Ben Chavis's last appeal was successful and although he wasn't declared innocent he was released and the last time I met him, at a big peace rally in New York's Central Park, he was preaching in a small church in a suburb of New York, but still active in the peace and liberation movements. He had been one of the lucky ones. His case had received national and international prominence, but others, like the Puerto Rican nationalists, the Christian direct-action people and dozens of other less well-known prisoners are still rotting in jail.

CHAPTER 7 – USA: LAND OF POSSIBLE IMPOSSIBILITIES
Missiles in the Prairies

Under President Reagan the big subject was Star Wars, that crazy idea for conducting war in space, as if we hadn't enough weapons here on earth. In 1983 we decided to take a look at the background to this development, talking to its promoters as well as its opponents. We spoke to some of the powerful lobbyists on Capitol Hill, those organisations backed by big dollars from the arms industries to win over the peoples' representatives, the senators and congressmen to support increased weapons development. General Daniel O. Graham of High Frontier, one of Reagan's close advisers on the so-called Strategic Defence Initiative explained his project to us, trying to sell it as the best possible guarantee of peace. His organisation, High Frontier, was set up with the express purpose of forcing through the Star Wars project because it would mean a virtually unlimited flow of government dollars for the big weapons manufacturers, to be used for research and development. High Frontier had produced a number of sophisticated videos and glossy publicity material to promote its ideas among congressmen and senators.

The American Security Council has its spacious suite of offices only a stone's throw from Capitol Hill and there we spoke to General Singlaub, one of the chief backers of the Nicaraguan Contras and a cold war warrior in the old mould. His organisation, with close links to the World Anti-Communist League is one of the most sinister, and effective in organising and promoting intervention against progressive regimes around the world. But there are also effective opponents of such plans in the USA, people like Ret. Admiral Gene LaRoque of the Centre for Defence Studies, an articulate and untiring campaigner for peace or Daniel Ellsberg, the former Defence Department official who revealed the lie behind the so-called North Vietnamese attack on US boats in Tonkin Bay, which was then used as an excuse to begin the mass bombing of North Vietnam; he too has been an activist protesting against new missile development and deployment. Meeting such men gives one a confidence in the ability and courage of progressive people to change US policies and they are not alone.

One of our attempts to deal with the war-peace issue was to organise a meeting between the European based Generals for Peace and Disarmament and those Catholic bishops in the USA who had been instrumental in drafting a new and revolutionary pastoral letter on peace. The publication of this letter had rocked the US establishment in the early eighties. Catholics in the USA have always been traditionally very conservative and only two decades earlier leading bishops had blessed troops going off to Vietnam with the words, "Every Communist killed is a service to God." Now, in this letter, they had come to the conclusion that the possession of and threat to use nuclear weapons was intrinsically immoral and against the teachings of Christ.

We accompanied General Gerd Bastian from West Germany and Brigadier General Michael Harbottle from London, both members of Generals for Peace, and recorded their meetings with Bishop Gumbleton of Detroit and Bishop Hart of Wyoming, as well as lay Christian activists. The generals, although in tune with and sympathetic to the views of these Catholic bishops had been motivated primarily by their experiences as army men. Harbottle, the former Commander in Chief of UN forces in Cyprus had experienced first hand how soldiers and armies could be used as a force for peace. Bastian had become disillusioned with the Bundeswehr after joining it as an idealistic young volunteer shortly after the war. He had been keen to contribute to a new, democratic anti-fascist army, but had seen how old nazis still held powerful positions, were not seriously interested in detente and were poisoning the minds of young recruits.

Bishop Gumbleton was one of the leading drafters of the breakthrough pastoral letter. He is a youngish, vigorous man, and an intellectual of recognised integrity. He allowed us to film a lecture he gave to students at the General Eisenhower High School in Detroit. His audience listened intently as he told them that, "500 million people, one eighth of the world's population destroyed, incinerated in a matter of minutes made me realise that we are in fact facing the most dangerous moral issue in the public domain we have ever faced. Dangerous because we are talking about the destruction of human lives on a scale exceeding anything the world has known. Even the intention to use these weapons – as we have in the USA today – is in itself a terrible evil. Every warship launched, every rocket fired signifies in the final sense a theft from those who hunger and are not fed, those who are cold and are not clothed. At the moment in the world there are 800 million people who live in absolute poverty, a condition of life that is totally degrading; they do not have even the basic things to sustain human life. 15 children are dying every minute yet the world is spending 600 billion dollars a year on arms and arsenals of destruction and death..."

His talk left his audience stunned. This was not the sort of talk they were used to hearing from leading churchmen. Gumbleton is not alone. The bishop of Seattle compared the Trident submarine base with Auschwitz because there they daily process megaton death. Bishop Hart in Wyoming, too, has a diocese stacked full with weaponry of mass destruction. We go with Bastian and Harbottle to visit him in Cheyenne, the seat of his expansive diocese of farmers and wide open grasslands, listen to mass in his cathedral, talk to some of his congregation before getting down to an exchange of ideas over coffee in his comfortable house nearby.

In the rolling prairie country of Wyoming, not more than a few miles from Cheyenne is the farm of the Kirkbride family. Driving through the rich grasslands, interrupted only by the odd sculptural red, rocky outcrop, from behind which I half expect an Indian to spring out and shoot his arrows at us, I take in the quiet air of rural calm. In the distance cattle are grazing and a cowboy, silhouetted on the horizon trots behind the herd.

The Kirkbrides farm is situated in a shallow valley at the end of a long unmetalled road. The generous low farmhouse comes into view as we round the top of the hill. The children are playing happily with their toys on the lawn in the front. Lindi, their mother, is cooking in the kitchen. The over-sized red ball of the setting sun sends a warm glow over the gently flowing acres of grass. No one seeing this farming idyll could imagine the terror lurking beneath its calm exterior. She welcomes us with tea and home-baked cake and tells us something about life out here in the prairie. "Our ranch is a good size", she explains, "it is about 60 acres. We have cattle and horses and our family has lived here and worked this land for four generations and that may not sound impressive to you, but it is for us out here!"

Lindi, against the wishes of her husband – who is worried about what his fellow farmers might think – has become very involved in the local Tri-State Peace Movement. This is a very conservative area with a large air force base nearby and is close to NORAD, the US Air Defence Headquarters on the other side of the Rocky Mountains. On the Kirkbride's farm are missile silos, containing missiles aimed at the Soviet Union. Now the government is talking of siting the MX-missiles here too – an enormous underground tunnel system, where the rockets can be continuously shunted around so that the enemy doesn't know where they are.

Lindi is an active member of her church, where two nuns had talked to her about the dangers of nuclear war and of the need to build a peaceful, safer world for future generations. Suddenly it had all been brought home to her that she and her family were sitting literally on a time bomb, that underneath the earth where her children played everyday and her husband tended the cattle there lurked megaton death and she had no control whatsoever over its use.

She takes us out to see the silos, a few minutes drive from her house. A high security fence surrounds the site with warning notices attached announcing that it is a forbidden area and trespassers may be shot. Inside the fence are what look like large concrete manhole covers and underneath these innocuous looking covers are the missiles primed and ready in their silos.

Lindi has already been on a delegation to the Soviet Union and has come back convinced that the people there want peace too and that the cold-war confrontational policies are outdated. She and the other activists in her committee have already organised demonstrations and protest actions against the siting of missiles here. Some Christians went even further and actually entered missile bases and damaged them and are now serving long prison sentences for their courage. Not only the local Catholic bishop has taken a stance against the arms race, Bishop Jones, the head of the Episcopal Church has also been won over to an anti-nuclear position and is even more forthright in his attitude: "I don't think this administration wants an arms freeze, I don't think they want to negotiate. I don't think Mr. Reagan is willing to do anything constructive in arms limitation", he says bitterly.

The views exchanged between two ex-soldiers from Europe and

leading US churchmen had been invaluable not only in offering different regional perspectives on disarmament but also in bringing together two very different approaches to the struggle for peace.

CHAPTER 7 – USA: LAND OF POSSIBLE IMPOSSIBILITIES
An FBI man opts out

My last job in the States is to make a portrait of an interesting and courageous man who lives in the small town of Peoria, south of Chicago. I picked up the story in a small-circulation Catholic magazine and instinctively felt that it would make a good programme.

Jack Ryan worked as an FBI officer for 20 years and at 49 years of age was ten months before retiring when he was summarily sacked, losing all his pension rights. We meet him at his small, modest apartment in a quiet suburb of the town. His stand of conscience has cost him dearly, not only has he no pension, but he and his wife were forced to sell their house, their small sailing boat and their car. He looks the epitome of a US law-enforcement officer – tall, well-built and athletic with a rugged, determined expression on his handsome face.

We are really curious to understand how a long-serving FBI man comes to take such an unusual stand. Jack tells us about his life, how he was brought up in a strict Catholic family, the all American boy whose sole interests were baseball and American football. His boyhood heroes were people like Joe McCarthy, the Communist witch-hunter of the fifties and John Wayne, the macho film star. After finishing school he went into a seminary and hoped to become a priest, but was recruited by the FBI at college. He had all the right ideological credentials, he says. He believed Communism to be supremely evil and anyone who appeared to criticise the United States or threaten its stability was a de facto Communist. People like Martin Luther King, for instance, or Cesar Chavez, the Hispanic union leader. "My world was black and white", he admits ruefully, "just good and evil, goodies and baddies and I was on the side of the goodies. "He believed in God and implicitly in the intrinsic virtue of the American way of life.

His superiors had asked him to spy on some peace activists, saying they were terrorists. Some of these people had been accused of squirting super-glue into army recruitment office door locks to draw attention to the Veterans Fast for Life on the steps of the Capitol in Washington DC. These army veterans went without food for 50 days in order to draw attention to US military involvement in Central America. "It was absurd calling these four veterans terrorists", he says, "they were pacifists." One of them was Brian Wilson – the anti-war protester who lost both his legs when a nuclear train, carrying Trident warheads to Seattle, deliberately ran over him. Jack had met some of them personally through his local church and knew them as convinced pacifists, openly anti-war and he could not accept the FBI accusation as having any foundation.

He tried to convince his superiors of this but had no success. His sacking made him a local cause celebre and he found widespread support in his battle for the reinstatement of his rights. "Under J Edgar Hoover investigating peace groups was a way of quelling dissent", Jack tells us, "I didn't believe that it was happening again now, but it was. The FBI's approach to the Communist Party was similar. It was seen as something totally detrimental to the government and had to be stopped at any cost. Quite often no laws were being violated yet a great deal of effort was spent 'investigating' the party with the aim of disrupting its work, causing chaos and discouraging people from wanting to join."

He now looks back on his work in a more critical way. He admits that he loved police work, but says, "working for the FBI should have something to do with justice, but that sometimes takes second seat in favour of winning at all costs and in order to win you become the 'good' guy and the other person the 'bad' guy and it is easy to lose sight of why you are an investigator."

It was at his local church, after he moved to Peoria, that he began to hear for the first time about the theology of liberation, about US economic exploitation of the Third World. To begin with he rejected it all, eventually though he began to understand the connection between US wealth and privilege and increasing Third World poverty. This new understanding led him to take a stand against spying on fellow US citizens who had done nothing to contravene the law or the constitution.

His wife is now the only bread-winner for the family and Jack is not finding it easy to be at home all day with little to do, after being a man of action for over 20 years. He is devoting himself to setting up a peace library in his town, giving lectures and doing voluntary work in the local church mission for the homeless – a very different life to his previous one, chasing the Mafia on the streets of New York. Although he misses the comradeship of his fellow officers he has made new friends, people like Phil Rettinger, the former CIA officer who helped overthrow the legally elected Arbenz government in Guatemala or Vern Lyon a CIA operative in Cuba who was involved in the introduction of a very infectious pig disease into Cuba, decimating the country's pig population and who was also asked to do a similar thing, introducing a virulent flu virus into Cuba's kindergartens.

Jack had been a staunch upholder of the system, a loyal servant of the state all his working life, with a comfortable retirement awaiting him and he had thrown it all away simply because his conscience and his sense of human dignity told him to. We felt that this example could be an inspiration to others in a similar position and that it would reveal that even in a democratic western system the state not only spies on its own citizens, but considers dissidents, in this case peace activists, as a threat and it can be vindictive with whistle blowers like Jack.

This item was shot just before the revolutionary upheaval in the GDR during October/November but was shelved by Adlershof. We felt it would have had even more relevance after the disbandment of the Stasi and the consequent disclosures, but it remained on the shelf where it is still gathering dust.

This last item contained within it that strange contradiction of the United States I mentioned earlier: on the one hand it is a democracy which allows dissidents to protest, demonstrate and propagate their views and also allows those who defect from the system to say why and to survive, but it still views those same people with intense suspicion and attempts to silence them, branding them as terrorists or subversives. It did it with the Communist Party in the fifties, with the Black Panthers and Civil Rights Movement in the seventies and the peace movement of the eighties. Even in the States with its strong libertarian tradition and guarantee of individual rights true democracy is a fragile seedling needing constant vigilance and protection if it is to flourish and survive. At present these freedoms survive largely on the basis of denying them to those in other countries which supply much of the United States' wealth. It is only the lack of basic human and trade union rights, the lack of work safety and low pay in the Third World countries which makes them lucrative sources of investment and profit for US capital, as Jack Ryan began to realise in the last years of his work for the FBI.

CHAPTER 8 – BEHIND OUR OWN LINES
Afghanistan – falcons and minarets

Franz was always keen to respond to events as rapidly as possible so that our TV could bring the news as fast as, if not faster than the others. In this he was always battling the bureaucrats in GDR television who wanted to check everything with the party hierarchy first and be told what line to take. When in May 1978 King Daoud is assassinated in Afghanistan and a new progressive government installed he telephones, telling us to fly there immediately. He realises that such events in a key country on the border with the Soviet Union are of enormous significance. Probably to boost his own image or to give us a sense of the importance of our assignment he tells us that it has been given the go ahead by Joachim Herrmann personally – Herrmann is head of agitation and propaganda in the Central Committee. This gives us big headaches later.

We arrive in Kabul, flying in over the snow-capped mountains which ring the dusty city in the valley below, and into the seemingly chaotic airport where we have to queue for two hours while the huge bundles of carpets, radios, food-stuffs and clothing of each and every Afghani passenger is carefully unpacked and meticulously examined. Our equipment is viewed with some suspicion and confiscated by customs – the first time this has ever happened to us. They tell us we can collect it when we have permission to film from the ministry. No problem we think, we'll soon sort that out. Kabul is a fascinating conglomeration of mud and brick, mainly small, one-storey buildings; everything, even the people are mud-brown from the dust and sun. Here you feel the orient: the turbaned, grizzled and wrinkled Asiatic faces and the chador-clad women, their heads and bodies covered from head to toe and with only a small mesh for the eyes. The poverty is worse than any I have seen in Europe. Many people have footwear made from old rubber car tyres and there is hardly a donkey or mule to be seen; enormous loads are pulled and manoeuvred by men or boys, sweating and grunting in the heat. The streets are heavily laden with the scents and smoke of small bakeries and kebab houses which seem to be baking and cooking all day.

Our first visit to the Ministry for Internal Affairs the next day is unproductive. We are told we need an official letter from our embassy to establish who we are. They give us, however, a personal 'guide' from the ministry who will attend to our needs (and make sure we do nothing we shouldn't do!). There is no way we can get this official letter from the British embassy which will be more than curious to know what we are doing here and for whom we are working, and there is no GDR embassy, so we have a dilemma. We try to obtain help from the Soviet embassy, where the staff are very friendly, but say they can do nothing, suggesting we contact the GDR embassy in Teheran. Of course Afghanistan has long been virtually cut off and ignored by the outside world and modern technology is very basic to say the least and to telephone involves registering the call and then waiting perhaps hours for it to come through. We eventually get Teheran on the line and pass on the message for them to tell Berlin to send a telegram to Kabul, establishing who we are. We wait impatiently for an answer. In the meantime we decide to look around, find our bearings and ferret out what is happening.

Big Soviet-made tanks stand on the street corners, garlanded with flowers, their guns protruding like big elephant trunks hung with necklaces of flowers. The soldiers sit or lounge near their vehicles, some adorned with flowers too and chat to passers-by and are embraced by ordinary people from the street. The atmosphere, despite the presence of soldiers and tanks, is relaxed. We are taken by our 'guide' to the King's palace, now thrown open to a curious populace for the first time. In the main drawing room a crowd of men, women and children stand around a patch on the big, richly woven carpet, one or two have falcons on their hands as if they'd come from hunting. There on the carpet is a dark red patch and, it is explained to us, this is Daoud's blood from the wound which killed him. People are fascinated by the carved furniture, the rich ornamentation and big brass and copper vessels in the rooms, staring with naive amazement at such luxury. We are itchy to start filming, but without our equipment we are impotent. There are still very few journalists in the country and we are among the first to be here and will have a real scoop, if we are allowed to film. We spend the following days traipsing to the ministry each day, pushing them on the permission, asking whether Berlin has been in touch, then telephoning Teheran again and again. In the end, after a week's wait, we are becoming so exasperated that we threaten the embassy that if nothing is done there will be repercussions because, we emphasise, "the film has been commissioned by Joachim Herrmann personally". Little are we to know that this, as it appears later, has been made up by Franz. Apparently Herrmann is livid that his name is being used in this way and he reads Franz the riot act. He, together with the Director General of GDR television, Heinz Adamek, and the hierarchy at Adlershof decide to teach Franz a lesson and let us stew in Kabul – rather than being thrilled at the opportunity of getting 'hot news', they prefer to punish Franz for 'individualistic behaviour' and not adhering to party norms, using us as ammunition.

We only find all this out on our return. In the meantime we wait and wait. Each morning awoken by the wail of the Mullahs from the minarets of the mosques which dominate Kabul's skyline, like bayonets. The big red eye of the sun rises slowly over the distant mountains, tingeing their snow-capped peaks a soft pink, and the first aromas of baking flat-bread tickle our nostrils. Another beautiful, but fruitless day awaits us. We would have taken the risk of shooting without permission if only we had our camera and tape recorder.

After wasting a fortnight like this, we decide to pack up and go home. On the day of our planned departure a telegram arrives to say a GDR journalist will be coming out to work with us the next day. It arrives in the hotel as we are on our way to the airport. A combination of Afghani intransigence and bureaucracy, together with pettiness and infighting in the GDR had meant the loss of an important historical record, because as far as we know no one else filmed during those early days immediately after the coup. The long and circuitous flight back in a small Soviet YAK aircraft, wedged between cargo containers and piloted by a young Afghani, was not an experience I would like to repeat again and nor was the fortnight's 'holiday' in Kabul sitting around all day waiting for telephone calls, feeling useless and frustrated, while history was being made on the streets before our very eyes.

CHAPTER 8 – BEHIND OUR OWN LINES
Solidarnosc and the problem of truth

Our brief had always been to work in those countries where it was impossible or difficult for GDR citizens to operate. That situation had now, in the late seventies, changed. As I have already indicated our prime function now seemed to have shifted and more and more became that of apologists for GDR policies i.e. our reporting was to become an adjunct of foreign policy, a justification of and propaganda for it.

The birth and rapid rise of Solidarnosc in Poland caught the socialist world by surprise, and frightened the leaders. They found it impossible to believe that such a strong movement could have grown up by itself, unaided. It must be a creation of outside forces and be fuelled by them. The GDR obviously, because of its geographical position, felt very threatened and perturbed by the rise of Solidarnosc in Poland. Apart from the fact that a non-communist Poland could cut it off from the Soviet Union by land, there was also the uncomfortable example of workers taking control of their own factories: the disease could be catching. We were given the task of exposing the foreign connections of Solidarnosc and its essentially anti- socialist character. We were to go to Gdansk as tourists and film with Solidarnosc there, and also follow up its links in Britain and the USA.

This is an unusual assignment in the sense that we have never been asked to film in a socialist country before – this was something they could adequately do themselves under normal circumstances. But this was a delicate matter: inter-state relationships within the socialist bloc did not permit critical reporting, which would be considered as interference in the internal affairs of a fraternal nation.

As an independent company we could probe where official GDR teams couldn't. The situation was already farcical because viewers could watch West German TV each night with in-depth reports on the activities of Solidarnosc and the general situation in Poland, but on their own station there was a painful silence. Because of this delicate situation we could be given no help from GDR reporters inside the country nor could we approach the Polish party for help either, so we were on our own with little knowledge of the actual situation and not a word of Polish between us.

Again I travel with Klaus, my colleague from Spain and various other assignments. We take his car and drive via Szczecin to Gdansk. It is December and there is thick snow everywhere. The northern Baltic landscape is bare and windswept. The odd peasant cart, drawn by horse, clattering along the road and the neglected houses by the roadside gives Poland a deserted atmosphere, as if time has somehow passed it by.

Gdansk, too, although large and industrialised is grey and desolate. We stay in the only three star hotel in the city, an anonymous modern, single storey building on the outskirts. The food is plain and monotonous, and the service sullen. Prostitutes sit around at the tables, bored, waiting for custom.

Our first task is to locate the offices of Solidarnosc – in December 1980 and Solidarnosc is still an illegal organisation. To begin with we have no interpreter and, as I said, neither of us speaks a word of Polish, despite the fact that Klaus had spent his boyhood in Danzig, as it was called before the war. The old town centre has been largely rebuilt in the original Hanseatic style. In the past it had been an important focus of trade and commerce here on the Baltic coast. The tall facades with their Dutch and Gothic gables look out over the wind-swept central square; on the waterfront the old wooden warehouses loom darkly but the ships which had once supplied them are sadly missing. As we wander about, looking at the shops, trying to engage people in conversation, either in German or English, in order to pick up some useful information, we happen to see a notice in a cafe window about a meeting of KOR the same evening. KOR was the political midwife of Solidarnosc, and consisted of a small group of dissident intellectuals which led the opposition.

The meeting is held in the basement of a church, not too far from the town centre, and no one questions our being there. Of course we understand virtually nothing of what is said but we do manage to locate a student from the local university, who is studying physics but speaks broken English, and offers his services to us. Through him we make contact with the KOR leadership, the 'Movement of Independent Students' and to Solidarnosc itself. Solidarnosc headquarters are in Hotel Morski in Wrzeszcz, a suburb of Gdansk. It occupies a couple of tiny rooms on the first floor, and the atmosphere is one of hectic bustle. It is impossible to talk to anyone for more than a few minutes before someone else takes them away on urgent business. After forceful argument, however, we do manage to arrange interviews with Anna Walentynowicz, former crane driver in the Lenin Shipyards and close friend of Lech Wałesa, Bogdan Boruszewicz, a KOR member and leader of Solidarnosc and Andrzej Gwiazda, also in the Solidarnosc leadership. We also interview a number of members from the student movement. What comes across in all these interviews and in our chance conversations with other Poles, is the deep-seated hatred of the Russians and of Communism. The Soviet Union is blamed for all their ills. They speak with passion about past struggles for Poland's independence, reliving battles from past centuries as if they had happened yesterday. This intense sense of history, their almost fanatical nationalism and strict Catholicism remind us both of Ireland, where oppression and colonialism has engendered very similar attitudes.

They admit that they are being helped by their exile organisations abroad but are not willing to reveal to what extent. They stress that they belong to an organisation which has taken root and grown within the country itself, and our limited contacts confirm this assessment. What is very obvious, though, is that Solidarnosc is not a simple trade union, that is only its legitimisation. It is clearly a political opposition party in every sense of the word.

We are also interested in the peasant branch of Solidarnosc, simply in order to obtain the non-industrial angle, the feelings in the countryside. Eventually, after much pressure, it is arranged for us to meet a leading peasant farmer. We set out early in the morning by car, driving through the drab suburbs, past smoking factories and deserted warehouses, out into the open countryside. The snow-covered fields are separated into tiny strips and the odd wooden farm house stands black against the white emptiness, grey smoke curling up from the chimneys; only a few people are to be seen, encoiled in thick coats and scarves, their broad, Slav faces ruddy from the cold.

I feel as if I am travelling through a Tolstoy novel. After two hours' journey on the ice-packed roads we come to a small complex of farm buildings. They look deserted but, on knocking, the door is opened by a tall, rugged-looking man who bids us enter. Inside the spacious room thick woollen rugs decorate the floor, the furniture is crudely rustic and a tiled stove in the corner radiates a dry heat throughout the room. This farmer owns 40 acres of land and is considered to be a large landowner in these parts. He tells us that he comes from landed aristocratic stock and that his family have lived here for several generations. His chief complaint is the lack of state funding for the independent peasant farmers, the lack of mechanisation and the way the state gives preferential treatment to the co-operatives and state farms. He can tell us little about the Solidarnosc organisation in the countryside and we have the distinct feeling that it is more an urban phenomenon and is probably made up of only a few individual and vociferous peasants in the countryside. Although he is obviously one of the wealthier farmers his farmstead conveys a strong impression of decay, neglect and backwardness. A few scrawny chickens poke about in the snow, an emaciated and cowed dog prowls in the distance and a timorous, mooing echoes from the rickety barn. We wonder how he manages to make a living at all.

On our way back we pass a school where the children are being shepherded out by their teacher, across the road and straight into church for evening confession. How tragic, I think, they reject one form of dogma but willingly submit their children to another. Communism has failed to take root in Poland, primarily because it has always been seen as an alien, imposed ideology but the Polish strand of fundamental Catholicism was not exactly designed to lever the country into the twentieth century either, I feel.

We had originally planned to go on to Warsaw after Gdansk but we soon realise that to fully grasp the Polish situation and the significance of Solidarnosc it is virtually impossible without a first class interpreter, and anyway the idea of 'exposing' Solidarnosc as an arm of outside forces is an impossibility simply because it doesn't accord with the facts. It is blatantly obvious to us that, irrespective of what one might think of Solidarnosc politically, it is a genuinely popular movement, and to cast it simply as an implanted organisation is sheer political cretinism.

Some of the people we spoke to openly expressed distrust or reticence towards journalists of any description, one, they tell us, turned up as an Argentinean photographer and reporter but could speak no Spanish! Writing journalists, though, always have an easier job, they can quote unnamed sources, piece together fragments of conversations and overheard comments, describe atmospheres and draw conclusions, even if false ones. This time, particularly, we are dependent on direct, first hand visual and sound evidence. We decide to call it a day and head home directly so that at least we will spend Christmas with our families and not with a posse of prostitutes and odd travellers, over a plate of pork chops and sauerkraut, in a gloomy hotel.

Our only remaining headache is whether we will be able to smuggle our film and cameras out of the country without the customs discovering them. We needn't have worried. We arrive at the border late that afternoon and are almost the only car on the road. There aren't many tourists travelling the Baltic coast in late December in any year but no doubt the precarious economic situation and political instability of the country has put off even those who may have considered it. Two guards come reluctantly out of their warm office, their breath steaming in the sub-zero temperature, and examine our passports. One of them then asks Klaus to accompany him into the building. My heart is beating nervously. Klaus first goes to the boot and takes out his briefcase. After several anxious minutes he comes back to the car, smiling. "Well", I ask, "what's happening?" "Nothing, we can go," he replies, turning the ignition key. Back on the other side of the border we feel relieved that all has gone well. "What did they want to know?" I ask Klaus. "They wanted to know if we had any cigarettes or booze," he says, "so I gave them the bottle of Johnny Walker I had in my briefcase and they were more than happy!" We could have smuggled out the Kraków city gallery's Leonardo and they wouldn't have cared a damn. No wonder Solidarnosc has no problems bringing in its equipment.

Our Polish assignment is not the last attempt to nail Solidarnosc. Early the following year, in 1981, we are in New York and are told to find the Solidarnosc representatives there and interview them. We go through the motions out of duty and also our own curiosity.

The office is run by young people, the children of Polish exiles, and their commitment and virulent anti-Communism is no different from that of their compatriots in Gdansk, but lacks the latter's understanding of Polish realities. Theirs is a Reaganite view suffused with a nationalism handed down by their parents. They express their political views freely in front of the camera but can tell us little about what concrete help they are able to send Solidarnosc, although they mention office equipment and photocopiers, which they also admit are not difficult to get into the country.

We speak to the leader of the Polish exile government here in London, President Raczynski. He is a large, imposing man with silver-grey hair and broad Slav face. He ushers us into the drawing room of his spacious official residence, in Eaton Place, Belgravia, its walls hung with portraits of the Polish aristocracy in gilt frames, and the windows draped with red satin curtains. Here again, in the centre of London, is the atmosphere of a feudal past, a way of life and a mentality maintained with obstinacy but refusing to acknowledge the changes that have taken place in Europe since 1945. As he speaks we feel that we are listening to a voice from the graveyard of history, bemoaning the tragedies, the lost opportunities, the treachery of the so-called allies who'd let Poland down, but with the absolute conviction that his exile government will shortly be back in power leading the Sejm in Warsaw.

Our material, we are relieved to know, is never actually shown and as far as we know is still gathering dust on the shelves in Adlershof.

CHAPTER 9
A new name but old politics

In the late seventies Franz was becoming increasingly frustrated by his protracted battles with the party bureaucracy and the clay-footed approach of Adlershof to every project. The Deputy Director of GDR Television, with whom Franz was on good terms, had always been sympathetic towards us, but was weak and obviously unwilling to fight on our behalf. He appeared to have no power or be capable of influencing decisions in any way. Like many other individuals in senior managerial positions he had been placed there by the party, as a reliable comrade, and as long as he toed the party line his position was safe. On those occasions when our group met in Berlin he would often join us for an evening, but like so many others in 'leading' positions he would avoid any real discussion of problems and, helped by alcohol, would tell a string of the latest political jokes.

Franz saw that programming could not be changed without a change in the leadership of television itself. Adameck, the director general, was glued firmly to his seat and had surrounded himself with party apparatchiks who were unwilling to take any decisions involving risk, but who prevented anyone else from doing so. In desperation Franz even drafted a letter to Honecker himself, which we all signed, pointing out the inadequacy of television coverage of world processes and events and the necessity of reacting rapidly, reporting informatively and honestly if we were to compete with West German television. There was no response, and Franz then chose to go it alone, but the repercussions were soon to follow.

Franz had a complicated character. He was a mixture of innovative potential, unbureaucratic in his way of working, but at the same time anarchistic and often dictatorial. He had, together with Sabine Katins, brought the Katins Group into being and been largely responsible for many of our successful projects, but his undemocratic way of working, the unpredictability of his decision-making made it increasingly difficult to work with him.

In the final months before the Katins Group was killed off he was making increasingly adventurous and unrealisable decisions, destined to bring down the ire of Adameck and his coterie on his head. He began setting up a new editing centre outside Adlershof. The Berlin party secretary, an old friend of his, had given him the use of a large villa in Pankow.

He brought me and other colleagues over to Berlin to film a series of short *Alltag in der DDR* (Everyday life in the GDR) films, "to show them that we can produce good films on home ground", not just in the west, as some colleagues maliciously asserted. He had ideas of expanding into the multi-media area, using film and slides and we spent days filming in many of Berlin's theatres. None of these ideas worked and those involved soon realised that they were ill thought out and doomed from the start. Franz felt he could prove to the party hierarchy that he was capable of doing everything, and in this way win the autonomy he so desired, but he exaggerated the group's potential. We felt increasingly that we were being drawn into and used in a personal struggle between himself and Adameck.

Our job wasn't in Berlin making light-entertainment films. We felt we were being manoeuvred into an impossible position and that Franz was becoming increasingly obsessed by this struggle. He felt so certain that his connections and reputation would pull him through and that in the end he would be able to establish the Katins Group in a separate studio, like the well known GDR team of Heynowski and Scheumann or perhaps even taking over TV chief Adameck's job himself, but his star had long since reached its zenith. The old boys at the top decided that he had gone too far and had to be taught a lesson. His services were no longer as vital as they had been: the GDR was now recognised throughout the world, had embassies, trade delegations and reporters. Franz was now expendable, as was the Katins Group. We were in a cleft stick. We wished to continue making the sort of films we'd always made, but in a better climate. We were far from satisfied with television policies and the attitude to news and information, but felt strongly that Franz' response was misguided and motivated as much for personal reasons as for altruistic ones. We also felt (with hindsight wrongly, that there was hope for change in the GDR media). We saw clearly that we would be committing collective suicide if we followed Franz and Sabine down the road they had taken. I tried at the time to discuss what I saw as the increasingly obvious mental aberration of Franz and the consequences for all of us, but Sabine and her close associates would hear nothing of it and in the end viewed us as traitors to the group when we felt we could remain accomplices no longer.

Neither Joachim Herrmann nor Heinz Adameck were keen to keep this gadfly around any longer, were determined to stamp him out. Franz lost the battle, but couldn't cope with the humiliation and suffered a serious nervous breakdown. Adlershof assumed we were all involved in Franz' escapade and decided to have nothing more to do with us.

He was a tragic figure: warm-hearted and generous with a strong sense of international solidarity, but suffering, like many short men, from a misplaced sense of inferiority, driving him to seek domination. His need for power and his short-fused choleric temper often made him a difficult person to work for. I was very lucky, for some unknown reason I was spared his anger and his sometimes petty vindictiveness and always enjoyed a special relationship with him, probably because he never saw me in any way as a threat. To give Franz his due, he did have a very good sense of what was news and what was good TV material and was continuously frustrated by the weak-willed obsequiousness of so many employees at Adlershof. He just wasn't the right person to successfully combat it.

After Franz's nervous breakdown in 1979, Adlershof severed its relationship with the Swedish firm of Nordreporter AB. The firm had never made serious efforts to expand its list of customers and had relied almost entirely on the GDR. When this source of income dried up the firm was wound up shortly afterwards. This left all of us "on the other side" with a serious dilemma: we wanted to continue working for the GDR, but weren't sure how to make that clear. All negotiations and contractual matters had been dealt with by Franz or our Swedish director; we had no useful connections to the top, no names of those who were informed of our existence and about the work we did. The director-general didn't want to have anything more to do with us, we were practically cut off; we were dropped like a hot potato. Suffice to say that eventually, by means of a chance contact, we were able to restore a line of communication to Adlershof and reassure those responsible for foreign reporting that we were prepared to continue working should they still require our services.

The leading political commentator and former correspondent in the Federal Republic, Günther Herlt, was given the task of liaising with us and put in charge of *Alltag im Westen*. We all felt a sense of relief that we had emerged from what seemed like a nightmare and managed to stave off a total collapse of our group. We now hoped to be able to continue our work in a saner and more stable atmosphere. A new company was established in Copenhagen, with a Danish director and Danish shareholders and we hoped with this new company we would be able to continue supplying the GDR and perhaps expand our sales, to reach a wider audience than before. Unfortunately for a combination of reasons this was made impossible.

To begin with Günther Herlt made a good impression on us. We knew nothing about him and were willing to take him at face value. He praised our past work, expressed his determination to continue in a similar vein and we felt optimistic. He probably meant what he said, I can't judge that, but unfortunately the promises were not to be fulfilled. Herlt was very much an apparatchik who followed the party line with unswerving loyalty. He commented disdainfully on the artistic claims of Katins' films and on our "Hunting and collecting" method of working, as he called it. His idea of television was illustrated political commentaries – propaganda rather than information – and while he stressed the fact that our programmes had to be entertaining, his whole approach contradicted this idea. He was very fond of pithy or witty sayings and seemed to think that a catchy title in itself was already a film.

Under Katins we were expected to produce our own ideas and filmic concepts. This gave us the freedom to search for interesting subject matter and develop our own projects. Under Herlt this was severely curtailed – we were expected more and more simply to interpret or realise projects put forward by the party ideologues. Not all of these were pedestrian, but the overwhelming majority of them were in the form of illustrated *Neues Deutschland* (the party paper) editorials, completely ignoring what the audience wanted. If the present campaign happened to be unemployment or homelessness then that was what we were required to bring. If Honecker had read that morning in the *Bildzeitung* (West German equivalent of *The Sun*) that police had shot a worker climbing over the fence to enter a factory, then the suggestion came down the line, became an order, and someone had to go out immediately and film an item on 'police brutality' (this actually happened).

We couldn't face making yet another portrait of an unemployed worker or a homeless family. Not that these weren't real problems, but if this were the only aspect of reality being shown then our audience would not believe us and they were, in any case, over-sated with such stories in all the media. Under capitalism inter-media competition for audiences and thus profits from the resultant advertising automatically involves repetition and parasitism, but in a socialist society the media should, ideally, complement each other. The total centralised control, though, meant that if *Neues Deutschland* had a campaign on Berufsverbot (the blacklisting of left-wing individuals in West Germany), then so did television, radio and every magazine. People felt attacked from all sides and, understandably rejected this form of persuasion altogether.

Many of our own suggestions at departmental meetings were either swept aside or if made would, in quite a number of cases, lie on the shelves until they had gathered too much dust to be shown. A good example of one suggestion we raised a number of times without success was a programme or series on the rising tide of racism and growth of neo-fascist parties in western Europe – the National Front in Britain, its equivalent in France, Le Pen's Front Nacional and the various others in West Germany and elsewhere. There were increasing attacks on minority races coupled with a fervent nationalism. The suggestion was dismissed by Herlt and his colleagues, who said, "we have no problem of racism in the GDR and it wouldn't be relevant". Recent events have tragically revealed that the banning of the public expression of racism and fascism doesn't eliminate it and that valuable educational work on such issues was neglected. There are many examples where GDR foreign policy, diplomatic sensitivities or simply the blinkeredness of the SED leadership led to a petty censorship. Certain words or expressions would be eliminated in the editing process if they were deemed dangerous. The mention of actual wage levels in West Germany, for instance, was taboo. Images, too, if they didn't conform to the picture painted by the party paper would be censored. A working class living room, for instance, would not be shown with video recorder, Hi-If and big colour TV or if the family had an Opel or Mercedes in the garage.

The fact that the SED leadership insisted on television being a state institution, thus making it a mouthpiece of the party and government left journalists hamstrung and unable to comment or inform as they wished to. Iraq and virtually the whole Arab world was, in the eighties, out of bounds as far as criticism was concerned. The fact that Iraq was employing chemical weapons in its war of genocide against the Kurds, was utilising the most inhuman forms of torture against its own citizens and was murdering Communists made no difference. GDR trade links determined the information policies of this period and led not only to mis-information and distortion, but also, in the last instance, to the creation of a cynical public. Slowly but surely under Herlt the reputation of the Katins group was lost, the quality of the programmes was now too erratic to keep a faithful audience and many were clearly seen as 'party contract' films.

Not long after Herlt had taken over as departmental head the name *Alltag im Westen* was dropped and the department became simply Aussenpolitik (Foreign Affairs). As was the norm in the GDR at that time, when important decisions were taken or when individuals were removed from leading positions there was no attempt to inform the people, they were simply confronted with the new reality. It was the same with the Katins Group: it simply disappeared and no one was told why. I was often asked by people in the GDR to tell them what had happened to Sabine Katins, "because her films were so good and worth watching".

By the mid-eighties we not only began to feel frustrated in our own work, but were alarmed at the waste of money and resources on programmes which were never shown. We made a pre-Olympic report from Los Angeles, exposing the hype and largely undemocratic nature of the Games' organisation in L.A. It was not shown for political reasons, after the Communist countries' withdrew their participation in the Games.

Our film about Solidarnosc, dealt with elsewhere, was never used; films on the role of the media in the USA, on the neo-fascists in Britain and a number of others were never edited and completed. Then there were the 'prestige' films costing, in GDR terms, large sums and consuming much creative energy. One was *The Lie of the Century*, a favourite project of Günther Herlt's, about the continuous calumny and slandering of the Soviet Union. It was based on a book written by the West German peace researcher and historian, Prof. Kade. The premise of the programme was to take a historical look at the way western countries had, since 1917, attempted to isolate and destroy the Soviet Union by the use of lies and distortion. It involved filming in England, USA, BRD, France and the Soviet Union and took many weeks. In the end the planned two-part programme was reduced to one and never fulfilled its promise.

Another was a projected film to commemorate the 100th anniversary of Marx' death. The idea was laudable: to show how, in different parts of the world, Marx's ideas are still very much alive and relevant. To do this through the words and actions of ordinary people, not the speeches of party leaders. We managed to film some marvellous material: In Nicaragua we talked with young Sandinistas defending their country, with a shoemaker who described in graphic detail how a small group of workers had studied Marx in a darkened back room during the Somoza dictatorship, risking persecution, imprisonment and possible death. Only one of their number was literate and could read, the others listened and then discussed together. In Mexico we were very lucky to obtain permission to film the awe-inspiring murals of Rivera and Siqueiros, the two great Mexican Communist painters. We filmed in the libraries where Marx had studied, in London, Paris and Brussels. We amassed a mountain of superb material most of which was never used. The project became a 'party affair' and was made into a paean to the SED leadership as the true inheritors of the Karl Marx legacy. Again a valuable opportunity to brush the dust off Marx's works and bring him alive for people, had been crushed.

In the last year before the resignation of the GDR government in November we were sent to Australia to cover the conference of the World Anti-Communist League and to Paraguay to make a film about the legendary Communist leader Antonio Maidana who had been kidnapped and had disappeared. We also completed the shooting of a film about the grandmothers of the Plaza de Mayo in Buenos Aires, still searching for their grandchildren who had been sequestrated by the military dictatorship.

None of these films was ever completed and shown. During the eighties Joachim Herrmann, the head of agitation and propaganda in the central committee, was the man controlling GDR media. It was he who laid down the guide lines, the taboos and instructions. He was clearly not concerned with creating a genuinely popular information service. He kept all the old cadres in their positions and stifled innovation. He was one of those products of the "nomenclatura", a workaholic – he would often work until late at night before being chauffeured back to Pankow in his limousine. He lived and worked entirely in his party cocoon, isolated from the life of ordinary citizens. Once, when he went to visit one of his children in his newly acquired Prenzlauer Berg flat, he saw some of Berlin's dilapidated house fronts, apparently for the first time, and told his staff how surprised he was to see that Berlin still had some old, unrenovated streets. He had never strayed from the 'Protokollstrecke' before and this peek into real Berlin had been a revelation (the Protokollstrecke is the main road designated as the route for government and party officials to take from their work to the ghetto in Pankow where they all lived). This simply illustrates the degree of isolation of such leading figures.

Sometime during the early eighties Joachim Herrmann installed a new 'consultant-cum-party censor' in the department Aussenpolitik. I think I only met him once, he was otherwise a shadowy figure in the background, but with a lot of power to veto or permit projects to go ahead. He was obviously there to make sure the department toed the leadership line and didn't stray from the straight and narrow. He was involved in no discussions with us, never spoke to us about our work, but controlled what was done in the department. This was symptomatic of the Kafkaesque situation we were in, not knowing exactly where the power lay or how to approach those with decision-making powers; everything was nebulous.

The increasing narrowness of themes and subject matter during the Herlt period and the obvious attempt to use our films more and more to bolster policies which were becoming obviously untenable. One or two of us began to be more openly critical, to fight for our ideas and against the manipulation from above in our twice yearly meetings and to question the basic structures and aims of the television medium in the GDR.

The audience we had gained under Katins had been dissipated. We knew that our programmes were being watched by less and less people, so that the waste of money, resources and our own energies became a continual preoccupation. As journalists, each time we confronted a new problem, we now found ourselves asking whether we could justify our filming in each instance, whether it would be misused or even used at all. The vagaries and zigzag path of policy, particularly in the foreign affairs field made a mine-field of our work.

The USA became taboo when Honecker speculated on travelling

there, Colombia was also taboo because it exported coffee to the GDR; a film on Jamaica was not completed because the consul didn't want his trade negotiations jeopardised; England had to be treated with kid gloves because its embassy was, apparently, super critical of any programmes about the United Kingdom, and so on. Any attempt at balanced or informative reporting was impossible; our brief was to make pretty travel films about those countries Honecker was about to visit or stick to the well-worn and 'safe' subjects of unemployment, homelessness and Berufsverbot.

Our strength as a group lay in our experience of the western world. Our first-hand knowledge of the conflicts and arguments which have grown out of the debilities of the 'market economy' and the consequences for those not 'marketable' – primarily the so-called Third World. Our specific experience was less and less in demand during the Herlt period. A critical approach to different social systems came to play a secondary role to that of diplomacy. While we welcomed the gradual breakdown of the cold war legacy the positive changes which we thought this would bring to the GDR didn't materialise, neither for the people in general nor for the media in particular.

Of course trade and diplomacy are important for any country, but to make your information media dependent on such factors is a disaster. Even the foreign relations of a country are not dependent on diplomatic niceties; a foreign trade agreement will not depend on whether a critical film on that country is shown or not. States and capital follow clear interests and not the rules of diplomacy. Information must be free of such restrictions if it is to be of use to those watching and listening. Our views, though, were never a real determining factor and sadly we increasingly felt that. We were made to feel outsiders and that it was our job simply to carry out our assignments and not involve ourselves with internal policies. This change in orientation did, though, have its consequences. We produced less than before. The projects were often selected on the basis of a false assessment of the realities. Disappointments were common and a number of projects were aborted.

The department lost its trade mark and its firm place in the programming schedules. We could no longer claim to bring fast reports from any part of the western or Third World and at a competitive price. The increasing amount of material which remained unused and the failed projects of course increased the costs per minute of those items that were used. We pushed for closer cooperation between ourselves and the editors of our films. The demand for increased quality, which we made on ourselves and which came from our audience could only be achieved by closer cooperation. We had continuous debates throughout the Katins and Herlt periods about improving our work. With the *Alltag im Westen* series we were very concerned about avoiding black and white imagery. In practice there was always a conflict because the SED leadership wanted a picture which reflected its own propaganda, but we had reality to deal with. Despite agreement between us, the producers and the editors in Adlershof, many of our good intentions and goals were never realised because we always came up against the barriers erected by Joachim Herrmann, the SED propaganda chief.

No wonder that under Herlt's leadership our optimism soured. The late seventies and eighties brought with them the realisation that the Honecker regime had little interest in a real expansion of democracy and even on the economic level a stagnation was seen and felt by everyone. Only the vague, but increasingly unreal hope of a change in the wake of Gorbachov's Perestroika and Glasnost kept us going. Yet Gorbachov's election to the general secretaryship in the Soviet Union and the introduction of Perestroika and Glasnost had the effect that the atmosphere in Adlershof became even more oppressive and paranoid. A film we made about the South African lawyer, Albie Sachs, who was blown up by the South Africans using a car bomb, had to be re-edited because of a single word he used. In discussing his joy at still being alive, even though badly maimed, Albie speaks of the ferment of new ideas and fruitful debate taking place in the progressive movement throughout the world and mentions Perestroika as an example. This one word had to be cut out! Are words really this powerful, this subversive? Günther Herlt made it clear to us that the GDR had no need of Perestroika and Glasnost, it was far more advanced than the USSR. His view was clearly the view of most of the leadership within Adlershof and further discussion was pointless.

We were increasingly being asked to make films simply to provide an alibi for GDR internal or foreign policy: All stops were pulled out to cover Reagan's visit to West Berlin and the demonstrations occasioned by the meeting of the IMF and World Bank in West Berlin in 1988. There was no interest in the actual reasons or background to the demonstrations, we were told that only police attacks on demonstrators was of interest because it would counteract the bad press the GDR administration had received over its own police attacks on 'dissident' demonstrators during the annual Liebknecht and Luxemburg rally in Berlin.

Also in 1988 we were asked to go immediately to the US border and show it as a defensive barrier. We knew the idea was to use it as an alibi for the Berlin Wall – a silly idea anyway – and refused to go along with it. When one of our teams was asked to return to Grenada after the US invasion in 1983, we were horrified to hear that the fate of the revolutionaries there was of minor interest, the invasion was useful because "it will take the heat off us over Afghanistan". Whereas with Sabine Katins we were able to express a genuine international solidarity in our films, now we were being asked to exploit the predicament or misfortune of others to bolster up an increasingly unpopular and shaky GDR administration. Whereas before we felt we were part of an international brother- and sisterhood, working for progress and solidarity with all struggling peoples in the world, we now felt we were being used, our work prostituted for dubious narrow national and sectarian reasons. The original reasons for our working for GDR television were becoming increasingly irrelevant. Then it was a question of GDR citizens being unable to do the work we were doing, because they were denied entry visas by the countries concerned, but now it was more a question of them not being allowed by their own government to travel.

With Erich Honecker's increasing urge to travel the world as a top diplomat our teams were being used to make so-called 'Dialogue Films', film reports on the countries he was to visit, work that could have been done just as well by the GDR's own film teams. Luckily I was spared much of this, but I was given one assignment which epitomised the ridiculous state the 'court reporting' had reached. I was to be part of a back-up team to accompany Honecker on his state visit to the Federal Republic in 1987. We were to follow his every move and film incidents or happenings on the margins. Whereas Honecker travelled in special government convoys or by plane we had to follow as best we could in our car. We hired a very fast and powerful Ford – costs played no role on a job like this – in which we could hit 160km/h on the Autobahn. We spent every day and much of the night, too, travelling between towns in order to reach destinations before the dignitaries arrived. After a solid week's work only one shot of mine was used by the Aktuelle Kamera (the regular evening news programme) and that was a shot of the West German parliament building which the official cameraman had forgotten to shoot!

At the close of the visit to Dachau near Munich our trials and tribulations had a tragi-comic ending: we arrived at the site well in advance of the Honecker delegation which was being flown in by helicopter, so we decided to look over the site before taking our equipment. We left our GDR colleague and driver in the car. When we returned to collect our gear we found that our car had disappeared. After searching the surrounding streets we gave up – Honecker came and went without us shooting an inch of tape. About an hour later our car arrived back and our colleagues asked us nonchalantly if the filming had gone well. We replied angrily that we couldn't shoot very much while they had our equipment sitting prettily on the back seat of the car! They thought we had our equipment with us and hadn't even noticed that it was with them in the car all the time. Luckily no one seemed to notice our missing material so there were no repercussions. That was the one and only state visit I was involved in.

CHAPTER 10
And the Wall came tumbling down

At the beginning of October in 1889, we received a phone call from Berlin informing us that we would be having a meeting there with the Foreign Affairs (Aussenpolitik) Department on 8 November. Although the situation in the GDR was hotting up and we instinctively felt that it was only a matter of time before Honecker retired, we couldn't have imagined the speed of collapse after he went, or the momentous impact of that totally unexpected decision on 9 November to open up The Wall. It is a day I will never forget, because it was also my birthday, but I didn't have time to celebrate; we had an important meeting.

We were keen to meet and reassess our filming programme in the light of the rapid changes now taking place internally and internationally, and only under pressure did the meeting come about. We felt increasingly unhappy and worried about the deteriorating situation in the GDR during August and September. GDR citizens, largely young people, were fleeing the country in increasing numbers, the demands for Perestroika were increasing and the Monday demonstrations in Leipzig were attracting more support, yet the leadership was obviously paralysed. We, of course, wanted change too. We wanted a more democratic and truly socialist GDR and a more vigorous and independent media, but we knew that the more Honecker resisted, the more explosive and uncontrollable the change would be.

When we arrived in Berlin we imagined Günther Herlt would give us an up-to-the-minute report and analysis of the situation and how it affected our work, but to our surprise the attitude seemed to be: carry on as before. The usual palette of suggestions was proposed by the department. Herlt seemed indifferent to it all, as if he wasn't bothered what was agreed because he knew it would be irrelevant anyway, almost as if he divined what was to come.

All of us were somewhat paralysed by the situation: we knew that at the present time our potential audience was concerned only with its own immediate problems and the situation in the country, but at the same time we were expected to come up with suggestions of topics from the outside world, when the rest of the world was reporting almost exclusively about the ferment in the socialist countries and Germany.

I had already despaired long ago, either of expecting innovation or adventurous ideas from Herlt and of the relevance of our work. In the past I had always seen my task as investigating, reporting on and reflecting the struggle for human dignity, for peace, justice and enlightenment, peering into the closed cupboards and illuminating those dark corners and shadowy places behind the glitzy facades of the leading Western countries. This, of course, sounds simplistic and exaggerated, and I think we were all very much aware that black and white pictures of the world, primitive contrasts between slum dwellers and millionaires was not the way to deal with the complexities of the relationship between the south and the north, between the producers of raw materials and those who process them, between the granting of big bank loans to developing countries and the rise in infant mortality and disease. It was certainly not the way to deal with the problem of an increasingly distorted malfunctioning socialism confronted by an adaptable and economically efficient, if ruthless capitalism. Also, the more people became aware of the malfunctioning of the socialist system and the hollowness of its internationalist rhetoric, the less relevance and impact our films would have. We also felt that it was hypocritical to show genuine problems outside the GDR if these same or similar problems were being ignored inside.

However, we found ourselves trapped because, irrespective of how much we attempted to introduce the complexities, the half-tones into our films, they became converted back into black and white during the final montage process. We were very much aware that our potential audience was no longer interested in the sort of films our department was making; their trust had been lost long ago. A few years back we had felt that given the chance we could have perhaps recaptured our audience, but only if we had been given the opportunity of being less didactic and narrowly selective in our reflection of reality.

Unfortunately the SED leadership didn't seem interested in really convincing or informing GDR citizens, it was happy to rely on coercion.

We were in a cleft stick: we were not given the go ahead to make the films we wanted to and which we felt the audience would find interesting and rewarding, but at the same time it was demanded of us that we come up with new filmic solutions for old topics or shoot those subjects put forward or deemed important by the SED leadership. The lethargy, lack of imagination and opportunism had become endemic in the department. Years of struggling to make certain films or to avoid censorship, to maintain a journalistic dignity in the face of the browbeating, the petty restrictions, the party dictates and character assassination had all left their mark. It was clear to e more than ever that the department had no real function anymore and neither did we as a group of foreign journalists working on behalf of the GDR.

On 9 November Günther Herlt came to my hotel room and wished me a happy birthday, pushing into my hands a 'Goldener Lorbeer'(a sort of GDR 'Emmy' equivalent) and a certificate thanking me for my twenty two years of work for Adlershof. He commented wryly that the signature on the certificate would have historic value as it was that of Adameck, the man who had headed GDR TV since its inception. I thanked him unenthusiastically and mused on the irony of his giving it me now, when everything was collapsing. The years beforehand, I would have been proud to accept it, now I was ashamed, as he clearly was too, handing it over to me in the privacy of my room instead of in front of my colleagues.

Little did I realise that by the end of the day the ninth of November would be celebrated by millions of others! When we heard on the news what Günther Schabowski had unexpected, we couldn't believe our ears. Only the sight that evening of people streaming towards the border crossing points and the drunks in West Berlin, sitting astride the Wall, waving their beer cans and singing, convinced us that it was all really happening. I couldn't join in the celebrations because from my perspective, despite all misgivings, this was a defeat not a victory. I saw it as a defeat because it wasn't just the Honeckers who had been pushed aside, but the many genuine people who'd sacrificed much of their lives to build a new society and it was this, too, which had been lost. They had failed, we'd all failed. I could share people's joy at now being free to cross the border, the joy that a senile, intransigent and arrogant leadership had been swept away, but I was too much aware of the resulting world-wide consequences to feel euphoric.

Those courageous people who had fought for a democratic GDR, for a more humane society, for a truly popular socialism were not the victors. Those who had fought the war were robbed of the glory of victory that belonged to Kohl, Thatcher and Bush, to NATO and big business. I knew from first-hand experience what capitalism meant, not just its showcase version in the BRD, but also the jackboot version in many other countries and I felt sad at the widespread naivety of so many GDR citizens who appeared blind to the true character of West Germany. I realised that these attitudes had come about largely as a result of the people not being allowed to travel to the West and being subjected to a media even more distorted than that in the West, and which supplied only selected information. I felt sad and angry that the stupidity and narrow-mindedness of a few old men (and most were men) could destroy 40 years of effort and sacrifice and shatter the dream of a socialist Germany. I knew that the Berlin and the Germany I had grown to love despite its warts, its ulcers, scars and awkwardness, were now lost. It would now be bought, like Judas for a few pieces of silver, by the arrogant politicians in the West and would slowly come to accept their values of greed, affluence and hedonism.

The next morning while we sat and listlessly discussed our programme in a room on the Wilhelm Pieckstrasse we could see out of the window queues of Trabis and Wartburgs heading relentlessly towards the border. I had the distinct feeling of being irrelevant and impotent while out on the streets history was being made. There we were, journalists who over the last two and a half decades had rushed all over the world to capture such moments, had felt the pulse of history in so many countries, sitting there, making decisions that would be meaningless the minute we had made them. It was outside where we should have been with cameras and microphones, capturing the moment, the chipping away of a system that had refused to adapt.

We finished our deliberations and then we all left for our journeys home, knowing Europe was now a new place and our lives within it would be very different. I was filled with relief and melancholy at the same time. I knew, we all knew, that something just had to give, otherwise it would have exploded with catastrophic results; but we knew, too, that neither the GDR as a country nor its positive achievements would be able to survive for long; it would be swallowed up by its bigger brother.

I still carried on working, knowing that by the end of 1990 our services would 'no longer be required,' but I had already lost the urge to continue working for television, especially since, in the end, the opportunity of creating a lively, entertaining and informative socialist alternative to the largely commercialised and manipulative Western models of television had been thrown away by the interim CDU-SPD government.

The demise of the old SED regime in October had brought with it a new breath of freedom, not only on the streets, but also in the media. Now, suddenly and for the first time there was no censorship. Individual journalists took responsibility for their own stories. This period was more democratic and free than in any western country where journalistic freedom exists in varying degrees but in practice is severely restricted by powerful commercial forces and a concentrated private ownership. In the GDR during this short period thee were no business interests or government to dictate; the only limits were self-imposed ones. In this situation there were those who wee totally confused and non-plussed, lost without orders or clear ideological instructions; others grasped the opportunities immediately to reflect and interpret reality as they themselves saw it, to criticize, investigate and expose.

Our partner, the department 'Aussenpolitik', was no exception; these attitudes were found there too. Unfortunately, though, the general trend was an opportunist one, to appease the emerging dominant political forces by proposing such projects as portraits of Margaret Thatcher, Lech Wałesa, the British Commander of West Berlin and the Vatican to be neutral and largely uncritical. The other strand of programming undertaken by the department was a clear recipe for success: a series of travel films for a travel-hungry population, under the evocative title of *Azur*.

Adlershof did, of course, also produce excellent individual examples of what socialist television should have been about and some of these were seen during those first euphoric weeks in November and December when people were glued to their screens, many watching GDR TV with keen interest for the first time. Many journalists and technicians showed what they were capable of, but there was not a proper democratic concept for television as a whole.

After the Wall came down I had opportunities of being involved in the making of two programmes in the new atmosphere of freedom, a short item for 'Elf 99' on the question of German unity and a portrait of the ecological activist organisation, Greenpeace Germany, but these were exceptions.

Shortly before my last actual filming assignment, I was asked to go to Turkey with a youth tourist group to make a report for *Azur* on the tourist attractions there. I had been in Turkey only two years earlier to report on the trial of the leaders of the Communist Party, who had been badly tortured and could have been given the death penalty. I had spoken to so many Turks, young and old, students, workers and lawyers who'd been imprisoned and tortured. I saw and felt the oppression. I have close Kurdish friends who had told me graphically of the way the Turkish regime is practising genocide against their people. All this was still fresh in my memory and now I was being asked to make a film showing what an attractive tourist destination it was, where you could relax and sunbathe and forget your worries! For the first time, I actually refused to go and explained clearly why.

My last assignment was in London, shooting some footage of the Salvation Army. At its rally in the Royal Albert Hall I had the dubious honour of filming the welcome given to the GDR delegation, attending such a rally for the first time. The victory over atheism and communism was, for them, a cause for jubilation. I filmed a group of US American Salvationists paying homage at the grave of William Booth, founder and first General of the organisation, in Newington Green cemetery.

The irony was that I began my career as a correspondent for a non-existent GDR by filming regularly the commemorative events at Marx's tomb in Highgate cemetery and I conclude it by filming a Salvation Army grave in a cemetery nearby, still working for the same country that will again have ceased to exist by the end of the year.

For me it was very clear that an era had come to an end. The attempt to build socialist societies had, for the foreseeable future, failed. It had failed for a combination of reasons. It was not only the Stalinist structures and the corruption that had made this possible, but also the vicious Cold War waged by the West, the boycotts, blockades and sabotage, ensuring that socialism wouldn't and couldn't work. What was particularly tragic was that it wasn't only the bad that had been swept away in the wake of the popular uprisings in October, but the fact that many people were now being convinced that everything had been bad, and even the real achievements were denigrated. In television, a unique opportunity to make programmes unfettered by commercial or ideological constraints had been given up so easily, with little protest.

Of course, we all have to ask ourselves – we who were somehow involved in this now defunct system – how much responsibility we must accept for the abuses, inhumanity and downright incompetence of the GDR regime. One colleague in Adlershof put it to me quite bluntly, that I had, through my work 'supported the shooting of people on the Wall and kept the Honecker regime alive'. It is an accusation not to be lightly dismissed. I have myself reflected deeply, questioned my motives, my attitudes and my work, asking myself how far we did in fact contribute to the shoring up of an unjust system. It is certainly not an easy question to answer. I would, though, argue as the GDR writer Stefan Hermlin did when he was asked recently why he and many other left-wing intellectuals had written poems or articles in praise of Stalin. He answered that during the thirties Stalin had symbolised the only real opposition to Hitler fascism. We, of course, were also largely ignorant of the many injustices in the GDR, but ignorance is no excuse before the law or before humanity. For me, growing up in a capitalist society in which my own parents had been black-listed and sacked for being communists, where trade unionists are jailed for defending their rights, where there is no right to work, housing or to economic justice, a socialist society was a wonderful and exciting concept and I felt at the time that the GDR came nearest to a realisation of that goal.

In my work I had witnessed so much horror, misery, poverty, injustice and corruption, all of it caused, directly or indirectly, by the capitalist system. And much of it could easily have been overcome by a rationalisation of resources for social need rather than for the profit of a few very rich and privileged individuals and corporations. When I returned from places like El Salvador, South Africa, Colombia and Guatemala with the hungry, begging faces of pot-bellied children engraved on my memory, the stories of torture and brutality in Chile, Argentina and Paraguay still echoing in my ears, or from the streets of the Bronx in New York and central Los Angeles where the brutalised and marginalised individuals of the richest nation on earth kill each other with drugs or guns, where women are scared stiff to leave their houses after nightfall for fear of being raped, where crime is the most flourishing business, then the GDR did seem like a haven of rationality, humanity and freedom.

I had no fears travelling in the Underground late at night as I do in London or New York; my daughters could wander alone on the streets of Berlin without my having to fear that they would be kidnapped or raped. It was a country where Communists were not harassed, tortured, killed or blacklisted, but where in fact people fleeing from oppressive regimes could find refuge and help, as many Palestinians, Chileans and other Latin Americans did. I know this was simplified and not a very accurate picture (those of other persuasions or conviction were also often harassed in the GDR), but were not these aspects of GDR society nevertheless basically true?

In all my work I'd been concerned to reflect reality as honestly as I could. I was, of course, biased; I made choices about what to film or not to film. I did not pretend to be neutral. In today's world, neutrality in a journalist is, in my view, an abrogation of journalistic responsibility. Can one afford to be neutral about torture or starvation, acid rain, the pollution of the sea or the destruction of the rain forests? I was a socialist journalist committed to exposing the iniquities, injustice and basic inhumanity of capitalism. If I had lived and worked in the GDR, I would, no doubt, have seen my task somewhat differently.

In a sense our work could have been used or misused by the regime as an alibi for its own shortcomings, to mask inequalities, injustice or incompetence, but this was, I felt, an unavoidable by-product. Should I have therefore refused to film injustice in one country simply because there was injustice in the GDR? Should I not have attacked capitalism because socialism in the GDR was flawed? I am unable to give adequate answers to such questions, but I would like to feel that our work over the years has touched the sensibilities of some of our audience. I hope it has helped them feel more compassion, increased their notion of solidarity, and their sense of living in a world which doesn't end at the German border, has given them a feeling and understanding for the problems of others and a tolerance for those living in different nations and cultures. If our films achieved something of that in just a handful of people, I would feel it had been worthwhile.

I was happy to leave it to a new generation of TV journalists to confront the challenges and problems of a metamorphosed world and would like to feel that there will be sufficient individuals to carry on the tradition of enquiry and exposure of injustice and take up unpopular issues on behalf of the under-represented, ignored or oppressed. This tradition is essential to any society if democracy in any of its forms is to have meaning. As Lenin said, a true democracy can only be an informed one. Without ready access to information democracy becomes a hollow concept. All journalists have a decisive and highly responsible role to play in that process.

2009 Addendum

In the two decades that have passed since this book was first written, little has happened that has persuaded me to consider making significant changes or qualifications in the text. The reports of my filming assignments, written then, have been, in any case, left unaltered, as to change anything with hindsight would destroy their sense of immediacy and render them no longer historical documents of events witnessed first hand. The shock-waves of the global economic crisis that began to unfold in 2008, tragically, serve to underline even more forcibly my understanding of capitalism and its destructive capacity as witnessed in the many countries from which I reported.

The glowing paradise that German Chancellor Kohl promised his East German compatriots at unification in 1990 has hardly materialised; on the contrary, the social and economic problems in the East have continued to fester. The Berlin-Brandenburg Institute for Social Sciences (reported in the Guardian 28 November 2008) found that 62% of East Germans "still don't feel like citizens of the Federal Republic".

It is little wonder, and it is to the consternation and anger of West German politicians, that many in the East still feel a nostalgia for many aspects of life in the former GDR. They reject the idea that their post war experience in the GDR was simply one of living under a tyranny and that their lives were, by implication, wasted and misused. That is why many of them still vote for 'Die Linke', the alliance of the Left, which includes the PDS, because the hope of a democratic form of socialism is still alive, much to the chagrin of the right wing parties.

The demonisation of the GDR and the poor outlook for young people in east Germany since unification has, sadly but predictably, also propelled a number into the hands of the neo-fascists who scapegoat immigrants for their own contemporary problems. Young people feel ideologically confused, cheated and abandoned.

In terms of the film and television industry, what has saddened me particularly is that although hard-hitting documentaries are still being made, there are fewer of them and they have certainly been marginalised in mainstream television and in cinemas. The brutal wars that have characterised the last two decades have been and are being fought with the utmost disregard for civilians and distrust of journalists. The latter are no longer seen as legitimate observers, to be respected and left out of the conflict. The huge rise in the numbers of murdered journalists and their 'embedding' by the leading western armies, whether in the Malvinas, Yugoslavia, Iraq or Afghanistan, has also led to the emasculation of journalistic integrity and hindered journalists' ability of reporting neutrally or objectively from the various sides.

Television itself – and this includes the public broadcasters - has devolved into mere entertainment; its role of educating, informing, of promoting a humanitarian and social outlook, has been irrevocably undermined. Programmes are now often made by scarcely trained and inexperienced professionals on shoe-string budgets and resemble more and more a Roman 'bread and circuses' format, with so-called 'reality' shows, 'celebrity' fawning and voyeuristic banality. Big ideas and concepts are trivialised, history is made into candyfloss and news has become synonymous with sensation, the morbid and the apocalyptic. Our world is depicted as a frightening place, out of joint, ungovernable, chaotic and impenetrable in which we, as individuals, are impotent, and can only sit on the sidelines as passive onlookers.

For me, everything mentioned above only reinforces the idea that a different form of social organisation and global governance is necessary if humanity is to survive into the 22nd century. It doesn't have to be called socialism, but it has to take on board the urgency of environmental protection, of a more equitable social integration and based on relations of mutual respect and co-operation, not domination, exploitation and profit-based rapacity. A world ruled solely by so-called market forces and in which competition is lauded over co-operation and in which racial, religious and ideological intolerance leads only to bloodshed can no longer be tolerated if we and our children and our children's children are to inhabit a world worth living in.

Chronolgy of world events 1960-1990

1960
- Military coup in Turkey – democratic government overthrown

1961
- US-instigated Bay of Pigs invasion of Cuba
- FSLN liberation army launched in Nicaragua
- Berlin Wall built

1964
- Military coup in Brazil

1965
- Military coup in Indonesia – massacre of over one million communists and progressives; direct CIA involvement
- US marines invade Dominican Republic

1967
- Military coup in Greece
- Operation Phoenix in Vietnam – civilian population treated as the enemy
- Six Day War between Israel and Egypt

1968
- Martin Luther King assassinated
- Tonkin Gulf affair – followed by bombing of North Vietnam
- Czechoslovakia invaded by Warsaw Pact troops

1969
- Renewed flare-up in colonial war in Ireland
- Covert bombing of Cambodia

1970
- Allende elected first socialist president of Chile
- Military coup overthrows Prince Sihanouk in Cambodia – direct CIA involvement

1971
- Erich Honecker takes over as General Secretary of SED from Ulbricht

1972
- British troops kill Irish demonstrators on Bloody Sunday
- Military coup in Uruguay – direct CIA involvement
- Massacre of Israeli Olympic participants in Munich
- UNO recognises GDR as an independent state

1973
- Military coup in Chile, Allende murdered – CIA involvement
- Arab attack on Israel – Yom Kippur War

1974
- Strike by British miners brings down Heath government
- Portuguese revolution of 25th April ends 40 years of fascism
- Liberation of Portuguese colonies of Angola, Mozambique, Guinea Bissau, Cape Verde etc.
- Military dictatorship in Greece collapses – return to democracy
- Attempted military coup in Cyprus leads to Turkish invasion
- Military coup in Argentina
- Revolution in Ethiopia – Haile Selassie overthrown

1975
- Vietnam War ends – US troops withdraw
- Indonesia invades East Timor
- Spanish dictator Franco dies

1976
- Grunwick strike in London

1978
- King Daoud overthrown in Afghanistan
- FSLN begin guerrilla war against Somoza in Nicaragua

1979
- Shah of Iran overthrown
- Soviet troooops go into Afghanistan
- Gen. Romero dictatorship overthrown in El Salvador
- Revolution in Grenada
- Somoza dictatorship overthrown in Nicaraguan victory of Sandinistas

1980
- Archbishop Romero assasinated in El Salvador
- First free elections in Zimbabwe after liberation

1981
- Ronald Reagan elected president of USA

1982
- Britain goes to war with Argentina over Malvinas Islands
- US steps up aid to Contras fighting Sandinista government
- Israeli invasion of Lebanon

1983
- USA invades Grenada

1984
- Uruguay military dictatorship collapses – return to democracy

1985
- Gorbachov elected to position of Gen. Sec. of CP in USSR
- Civilian government returns to Brazil

1986
- USA bombs Libya

1988
- Hungary and Poland end one-party rule
- First free elections in Chile after dictatorship collapses

1989
- GDR and CSSR end communist party rule
- Paraguay – Stroessner dictatorship overthrown
- Namibia free – first free elections, which SWAPO wins

1990
- Nelson Mandela released
- German unity – GDR ceases to exist
- Gulf conflict begins after Iraq's invasion of Kuwait.